# Education Studies:

## An issues-based approach

### Second edition

Editors

John Sharp

Stephen Ward

Les Hankin

# Education Studies:

## An issues-based approach

## Second edition

LearningMatters

First published in 2006 by Learning Matters Ltd.
Reprinted with amendments in 2007.
Second edition published in 2009.
Reprinted in 2010.

*British Library Cataloguing in Publication Data*
A CIP record for this book is available from the British Library

ISBN: 978 1 84445 273 6

Cover design by Topics – The Creative Partnership
Project management by Deer Park Productions, Tavistock
Typeset by Pantek Arts Ltd, Maidstone
Printed and bound in Great Britain by Bell & Bain Ltd, Glasgow

Learning Matters Ltd
33 Southernhay East
Exeter EX1 1NX
Tel: 01392 215560
info@learningmatters.co.uk
www.learningmatters.co.uk

**Mixed Sources**
Product group from well-managed
forests and other controlled sources
www.fsc.org   Cert no. TT-COC-002769
© 1996 Forest Stewardship Council

FSC

# Contents

# Part 2: Themes in education 105

# Editors

**John Sharp** is Professor of Education and Head of the Department of Education Studies at Bishop Grosseteste University College Lincoln.

**Stephen Ward** is Professor of Education and Dean of the School of Education at Bath Spa University.

**Les Hankin** led the development of the Education Studies degree pathway at Liverpool Hope University. His research interests include global citizenship education and the engagement of non-traditional students in schools' Workforce Career programmes.

# Contributors

**Kate Adams** is Senior Lecturer in Education Studies at Bishop Grosseteste University College Lincoln. Her research interest lies in children's dreams and spirituality.

**Steve Bartlett** is Professor of Education Studies at the University of Wolverhampton. He has written a range of books and articles in the field.

**Jane Bates** is Principal Subject Leader for Education Studies at Manchester Metropolitan University (in Cheshire). Her research interests include ways of facilitating graduate employablity within Education Studies programmes.

**Wendy Bignold** is Vice Dean of Education at Liverpool Hope University. Her main research interest focuses on diversity and inclusion.

**Diana Burton** is Professor of Education and Dean of the Faculty of Education, Community and Leisure at Liverpool John Moores University. She has written a number of papers and books covering a range of issues within Education Studies.

**Mark Chater** was until very recently Reader in Education at Bishop Grosseteste University College Lincoln. He now directs Religious Studies and Theology on behalf of the QCA.

**Howard Gibson** lectures at Bath Spa University and enjoys thinking about the areas where political philosophy, language and educational issues meet.

**Nasima Hassan** is Senior Lecturer in Education at Liverpool Hope University. She has worked in India and South Africa with disadvantaged communities in developing inclusive education and she researches Muslim faith schools.

**Denis Hayes** was formerly Professor of Primary Education and is now a freelance education writer with a special interest in initial teacher training, the teacher's role and the emotions associated with teaching.

**Ruth Hewitt** is Senior Lecturer in Education and Subject Studies at Bishop Grosseteste University College Lincoln where she specialises in the teaching and learning of English.

**Elizabeth Hopkins** is Senior Lecturer at Bishop Grosseteste University College Lincoln. She is interested in dynamic English teaching and work-related learning as a means of engaging disaffected pupils.

**Pat Hughes** is Senior Lecturer at Liverpool Hope University and a non-executive Director of a Primary Care Trust (NHS) heavily involved in the integration of Children's Services.

**Viv Kerridge** is Senior Lecturer at Bishop Grosseteste University College Lincoln. She specialises in applied drama.

**Sue Lewis** is Principal Subject Leader for Education Studies at Manchester Metropolitan University (in Cheshire). Her research interests include ways of facilitating graduate employability within Education Studies programmes.

**Sacha Mason** is Senior Lecturer in Children's Services at Bishop Grosseteste University College Lincoln. Her research interests include Sex and Relationships Education in primary schools.

**Graham Meeson** is Senior Lecturer in Education Studies at Bishop Grosseteste University College Lincoln. He is particularly interested in leadership and management in educational settings.

**Barbara Murphy** is Senior Lecturer in Education Studies at Bishop Grosseteste University College Lincoln. Her interests include unpicking the multifaceted dimensions of learning, understanding and memory.

**Stephen Newman** is Senior Lecturer in Education at Bradford College. His research interests include philosophy, philosophy of education and educational policies and politics.

**Mark Patmore** is Senior Lecturer in Mathematics Education at Nottingham Trent University. He is currently working with intending and practising secondary maths teachers.

**Ruth Sayers** is Principal Lecturer at Bishop Grosseteste University College Lincoln where she specialises in drama in the community.

**Keira Sewell** is Lecturer in Primary Education at the University of Southampton. She is particularly interested in education beyond the classroom and how this enhances provision.

**Carol Smith** is Senior Lecturer in Education Studies at Bishop Grosseteste University College Lincoln. Her main interest is SEN and children with Specific Learning Difficulties.

**Richard Walton** is Reader in Education at the Centre for Science Education at Sheffield Hallam University. He, is particularly interested in the relationships between learning in formal and informal settings.

**Richard Woolley** is Senior Lecturer in Primary Education at Bishop Grosseteste University College Lincoln. His research interests include citizenship, social justice and controversial issues in primary education.

# Acknowledgements

John Sharp and Barbara Murphy wish to thank Donald Clark for his kind permission to reproduce the Learning Styles questionnaire which appears in Chapter 2.

Every effort has been made to trace the copyright holders and to obtain their permission for the use of copyright material. The publisher and authors will gladly receive any information enabling them to rectify any error omission in subsequent editions.

# Introduction

What is education and why is it so important? Where does education take place and when? How is education studied? These are fairly obvious questions to ask, you'd think, but questions which are actually quite difficult to answer. Just go right ahead and try for yourself or, better, try with a group of friends. It's not so easy, is it? Behind the many stumbling blocks we hope you encounter lies the great scope, diversity and complexity not only of the content of education as a subject discipline itself but of the processes by which education takes place and the social, cultural, political and historical contexts in which it occurs. But it is this very scope, diversity and complexity that makes Education Studies so exciting and attractive.

## About this book

This book is intended to inform and support your own learning and personal and professional development as you go about studying education, whether you are in the first or final year of a formal course of Education Studies, training to be a teacher at university or college, or even undertaking research at a higher level for a masters degree or doctorate. We hope that you will be introduced to this book as a 'core text' by your own tutors, who might use it in an intellectually rigorous and systematic manner in lectures, seminars and tutorials. You might also find it essential as a background reader for self-study.

Features of the book include:

- 20 chapters written and presented in an authoritative and informative yet readable and accessible way by contributors from a great many institutions around the country, each bringing their own interest and expertise to bear on the issues raised and considered;
- research boxes and pause-for-thought boxes to help promote critical reflection and analysis and a deep exploration of ideas;
- fully referenced text to provide further reading for those who wish to pursue issues under consideration further.

The chapters presented here are arranged into two logically consistent groupings, though in reality the nature of the subject matter in each overlaps considerably:

- learning, teaching and the nature of education;
- themes in education.

### Learning, teaching and the nature of education

Education is something that we tend to take for granted as what happened to us in schools. But when we come to study education we find that there are many different ideas about what education and schooling should be. The chapters in this section begin by getting to grips with what education is about and what it means to study education as a university subject. They then go on to look at the nature of learning, education in the community and the implications for schools of the government's Every Child Matters agenda. Education Studies and teacher training are very definitely not one and the same but they are joined at the hip to a greater or lesser degree. It all depends on who you ask. Whether as a reader of this book you go on to teach or to make a career in one of the newer education professions, you will certainly find the curriculum chapters interesting and informative and free of the shackles and narrow confines of the compliance-driven culture typical of most courses leading to Qualified Teacher Status. This is important in an increasingly vocationalised world driven by measurable outcomes and generic transferable skills. Questioning the very basis upon which any curriculum is established, that is, understanding a curriculum's theoretical, philosophical and ideological underpinning, is as important as getting trained to deliver one. Some might say more so.

## Themes in education

The second section of the book looks carefully at those all-encompassing themes that shape the educational landscape and influence our increasingly uncertain lives. Globalisation, with its opportunites and threats, is explored in terms of market forces, cultural and ethnic dominance and the responses society must make as it changes and adapts to meet new challenges. The motifs of lifelong learning, citizenship, faith and inclusive regard for all members of society are interwoven here. All entail the mantle of responsibility as citizens and, for some of us, as leaders. Coursing through all the universal themes set out in these chapters is a concern for identity and the fulfilment of the individual.

# Part *1*

# Learning, teaching and the nature of education

# Chapter 1

# What is education?

## Keira Sewell and Stephen Newman

### Introduction

Ask anyone what education means and the answers are likely to be varied. Many primary-aged children might suggest that it helps them to learn, whereas secondary-aged children often think that education helps to get a job. Adults have different views, often based on their own experiences of the education system. Thus the term education is not an easy one to define, often being wrapped up with the ideas of schooling, earning and training. This chapter examines the debates about the nature of education and the possible definitions or meanings of education. It looks at the different ways philosophers have analysed education and it asks you to do some philosophical analysis of your own in thinking about the different language-games played by educational thinkers and policy-makers.

## Defining education

The notion of education has taxed the minds of philosophers since the times of Plato and Socrates. Despite the multitude of definitions put forward, Matheson and Wells (1999) have argued that we are still no nearer reaching one that is wholly satisfactory. Gregory (2002) has suggested education is concerned with equipping minds to make sense of the physical, social and cultural world, while Peters (1966) has proposed that when we use the term 'education' it brings with it the implication that there is an 'intention to transmit', in a 'morally acceptable' way, something considered worthwhile. Yet, can we really equip young minds with the ability to make sense of a world which will look very different in ten or twenty years from now? Who determines what is, and what is not, worthwhile and on what do they base such decisions? What is meant by Peters's phrases 'intention to transmit' and 'morally acceptable'? It is no easier to answer these questions if we take Hirst's (1965) view that liberal education has value for an individual because it fulfils the mind rather than fulfilling vocational or utilitarian needs.

One of the difficulties in defining education lies in the interchangeability of those terms associated with it. Where some may see the term 'schooling' as synonymous with the term 'education', or suggest that the relationship between learning and teaching is causal (e.g. Carr, 2003), Gregory (2002) has indicated that the terms are distinct and that the relationship between the two cannot be assumed. Indeed it is this distinctiveness that enables individuals to determine their own education on leaving a schooling system that they may believe has failed them.

# Schooling, education, learning, training

The argument that the notions of schooling and education are distinct raises the question of whether education can simply be assigned to *product*, or whether it is the *process* of education that is of paramount importance. However, if education is regarded as a process, a further question arises: what should this process entail? There may initially appear to be a strong argument in support of learning playing a fundamental role, particularly if learning is taken to mean the acquisition of knowledge, understanding or skills that were not previously held. Perhaps the starting point for this debate should therefore be learning rather than education; that is, that the type of learning taking place may determine whether we refer to education as training or even schooling.

This regress of questions continues in the notion of training. Becker (1964) described training as focusing on the development of technical abilities that are linked to specific vocations or are generic across the field of employment. Cohen (1982) described it as applying to a specific and limited learning goal. Thus attention turns to the nature of technical abilities, what defines limited learning goals, and whether training promotes a different kind of learning than education.

Papadopoulous (1998) acknowledged the many possible interpretations of the term 'education', arguing that it can be regarded as an all-embracing term, serving a number of different purposes in ways that recognise both product and process. He has suggested that education is variously seen as promoting:

- economic prosperity;
- employment;
- scientific and technological progress;
- cultural vitality in a society increasingly dominated by leisure activities;
- social progress and equality;
- democratic principles;
- individual success.

# A philosophical approach

The remarks thus far have illustrated that there is little, if any, consensus about any one precise meaning of the term 'education'. Not only does the term seem to have many meanings but the search for criteria for the term that are relevant for all the meanings it has also seems fraught with difficulty. It seems far from easy to identify any core attribute that each and every use of the term 'education' must share.

An alternative approach that may be helpful in considering what education is takes as its starting point the reminders provided by Wittgenstein, particularly those provided in his *Philosophical investigations* (Wittgenstein, 1953). Wittgenstein suggested that most terms get their meanings from the contexts – the 'language-games' – in which they are used. He proposed that most words do not have fixed meanings and hence uses; rather, they are like tools in a toolbox and can be used for varied purposes. If someone makes a mistake in their use of a term, then the relevant criteria from the appropriate 'language-game' can be made explicit in an attempt to provide clarification. Thus the judgement of whether a use is appropriate comes from the context in which the word is used.

Instead of considering the term 'education', let us consider the term 'chair' as an apparently more straightforward example. Is there a core or central meaning of that term? Perhaps your instinctive first thoughts lead you to think that there is. But a chair may differ in size, shape or colour; it may have legs, it may have none. A chair may seat one person, or maybe more than one. A Chair might be used to mean a professorial post in a university, or a person convening a meeting. Interestingly, however, in spite of this diversity of meanings, there is no apparent confusion when this term is used in our everyday language. This is, in everyday life, far from being a puzzling or surprising fact. This example suggests that the criteria for deciding whether the use of the term 'chair' is appropriate come from the context, rather than from the term 'chair' itself.

The notion that words do not have fixed meanings is closely allied to that which suggests that words can have more than one meaning. Take as a further example the term 'games'. Wittgenstein suggested that the uses of this term form a network where there may be overlaps of meaning between some of the uses, but that there is nothing in common to all of the uses. Wittgenstein also suggested that this network of similarities can be characterised by the phrase 'family resemblances'. The same notion can be taken to represent a series of related 'language-games', each 'consisting of language and the actions into which it is woven'; as before, some of these 'language-games' are closely related, others are not.

---

*Pause for thought* | meanings and contexts

The word 'red' (like other ordinary words) takes its meaning from the way in which it is actually used. The use of the word depends not just on an object being described, but also on context. Think, for example, of the differences between the uses of 'red' in the phrases 'red paint', a 'red pillar box', someone with 'red hair' or 'being in the red'. Consider the uses of the term 'white' in 'white coffee', 'white wine', 'white skin' and 'white paint'. Try to make up some phrases of your own using the word 'deep', but where 'deep' has different meanings.

# The meanings of education

Having considered some of the examples with which Wittgenstein highlighted the issues of meanings, let us return to consider the implications for attempting to define education. With these ideas in mind, we can see that if the social context provides the structure for understanding the use of language and meanings then, in asking the question *What is education?*, we may expect a range of diverse answers, depending on the other contexts in which the question is asked. We should not expect education to have one fixed meaning; rather we may expect the term to have many meanings, meanings that may change.

Does this mean that we can never answer the question *Why do you call this education?*. Not at all. But according to Wittgenstein such a definition would be context-specific and probably given for a special purpose. Thus, one interpretation of the term 'education' in *this* context may be to conceptualise education as involving developing expertise in various 'language-games'. At a general level this may be all that can be said; such an interpretation being descriptive rather than prescriptive and explicitly context-specific. In this sense, to engage in education is indeed to be involved in a social process of meaning making.

Consider, for example, trainee teachers. The purpose of their training is to prepare them to meet the professional competences expected from someone entering the teaching profession. However, Lang (1995) has argued that we cannot assume a commonality in the individual belief systems of trainees and that teacher education must be reflective, providing opportunities for trainees to examine and explore the values, beliefs and attitudes that underpin their approach to education and identify those factors that may determine how they resolve conflict. Such an approach, it is argued, enables them to move beyond mute acceptance of policy and procedure to a deeper understanding of the philosophies and principles that underpin these and an appreciation of the extent to which their own values and beliefs support or inhibit putting them into practice. Newman (1999) supported this distinction, characterising teacher *training* as a means of developing a beginning teacher's ability merely to follow the rules of a 'language-game', and teacher education as a way of developing:

*a critical practitioner: someone who is capable of thinking about what they do, justifying and explaining it where appropriate, and adapting their playing and their understandings [of language-games] to varying circumstances.*

*(p159)*

As a further example, consider the teacher who needs to manage a bully/victim problem. Training might equip them with the skills to follow school policy and procedure but not to address some of the deep-rooted, values and beliefs that affect the way they feel. Education, it is suggested, can explore these feelings and, while not always promoting change, at the very least can raise awareness of the presence of these feelings, of the ways in which they may determine responses, and help to develop the ability to articulate and justify particular actions in a way appropriate to the context (that is, the 'language-game' being played).

# Education for differences

If education has many meanings which vary according to context, then it would be appropriate to consider the notion that education should not be limited to any one definition. Such a decision thus frees us to consider the range of educational opportunities available to us throughout our lives.

On one level it is likely that all of us will have experienced the traditional contexts of formal education. These contexts are normally long-term, extending from primary through to higher education, and include institutions such as schools, colleges and universities. They frequently involve a government-set or institutionally devised curriculum, and assessments that lead to nationally or internationally accepted awards or qualifications. Such outcomes appear to be valued by all generations, even though younger generations no longer see qualifications as a passport to high level or even stable employment (Aro et al., 2005).

Despite the high esteem in which the outcomes of formal contexts are held, however, for some, these traditional contexts of formal education, far from being neutral in their approach, seek to impose a particular view of knowledge, of language, of relationships and of reasoning on those who attend them (Giroux, 1985). Schools are thus regarded as instruments of social control (Freire, 1972), serving to reinforce the interests of a particular dominant group and to work against the interests of those who are less influential. This perception of traditional contexts of education as authoritarian (Meighan, 2005) perhaps helps to explain the increasing interest in alternative forms of education, such as home tuition, spearheaded by such groups as Education Otherwise. Just how alternative these approaches are is often determined by the curriculum offered and the methods and contexts of delivery. As Webb (1990) has noted, provision at home may vary considerably in terms of motive, method and aims, ranging from delivery of the statutory curriculum through to a much more individually determined learning programme available in a variety of environments including museums, galleries, science centres, field study centres, or even on extended trips around the world. While the first type of provision might appropriately be described as home schooling, the latter types are more likely to be identified as non-formal or informal education.

Even within the traditional contexts of so-called formal education there are examples of different forms of education. Thus, for example, some schools (such as Summerhill) may not subscribe to all that others may consider to be the characteristics of formal education. Similarly, activities such as yoga classes, cookery classes, music lessons and evening classes may take place within the physical confines of a school but may sometimes be characterised as non-formal in their purpose. Other examples could include driving lessons, youth clubs, guide and scout groups, play schemes and holiday camps.

Informal education might be characterised as describing contexts that are neither formal nor non-formal. Examples might include museums, galleries and science centres, which see their function as public education rather than education limited to a specific client group. Both non-formal and informal education can perhaps often be characterised by an emphasis on choice in that they provide opportunities into which learners can opt, and which may sometimes include opportunities for learners to set their own learning outcomes.

Perhaps some contexts that deliver or support the delivery of statutory curricula are best described as 'alternative' forms of formal education. These include Playing for Success, Learning by Achievement, field study centres and themed museum visits. Such contexts often support learning in a way that could not be achieved within the classroom and often rely heavily on the theory that learners learn best when immersed *in situ* where they have access to specific artefacts, experiences and approaches. However, the description of a year-long trip by a family across Europe, designed to provide access to such experiences as learning a new language, exploring a different culture, trying new foods, and so on, as an 'alternative form of formal education' would not seem appropriate. While possibly contributing to the statutory curriculum, such experiences go far beyond it, often resulting in outcomes that are difficult to quantify. Yet it could be argued that the development of additional skills, knowledge and understandings of the whole family could not be achieved in any other way. To also describe such learning as informal seems unsatisfactory as the objectives of such a trip may be clearly defined and the route planned to specifically achieve these.

Other approaches, such as e-learning, provide opportunities to access information in a place other than the classroom, thus providing access to the curriculum for a range of learners at different times. Technologies, such as the internet, may also enable learners to access learning contexts that may otherwise be impossible; for example, viewing the Antarctic via a webcam at Davis Station. Access to the world wide web also opens up a wealth of opportunities for individualised informal learning that allows learners to determine their own interests and outcomes. Some uses of such resources, we may wish to argue, are educational; others not. Such arguments may depend on our view of education and the purpose it serves. Playing on a computer game, for example, may develop children's ICT skills but not all may wish to describe such an activity as educational.

The past two decades have seen the rapid growth of a new generation of enterprises such as the Eden Project (in Cornwall), the Jorvik Viking Centre (in York), Dynamic Earth (in Edinburgh), Eureka! (in Halifax) and Odyssey (in Belfast). These can be characterised by their clear objectives (often related to collective citizenship and the promotion of change), the utilisation of a resource base (physically impressive, exciting and incapable of being replicated in schools), the adoption of an interactive approach, and an ability to respond to a wide range of clients. In exploring the distinct nature of these enterprises, Peacock (2005) suggests the term 'peri-formal' as a means of identifying their unique contribution to education which neither formal nor informal contexts can achieve.

## Research box

### how do different users use interactive resources?

Much has been made of the interactive, hands-on nature of activities in constructivist, child-centred learning within schools and this debate has informed the ongoing development of museum education. However, the extent to which such an approach can develop conceptual knowledge and understanding is a matter for debate; museums and other 'peri-formal' providers recognise that different users engage with resources in different ways. One example of this was demonstrated by research carried out by Fernández and Benlloch (2000) in Spain, who looked at participant use of the travelling interactive display 'Ver para no creer' ('seeing, not believing'). The focus of their research was the collection of quantitative behavioural data relating to the duration of visit, duration of group conversations and reading behaviour. Their results indicated that different users interact with the exhibit in markedly different ways. Lone users approach the exhibit calmly, reading the information at appropriate points to enable them to make sense of their interactions. Groups of adults have a much more light-hearted approach, with one of the group members usually dominating the interaction while others in the group read the display panel and observe their actions. Children in groups normally commence interaction without reading the display panels while the adults in their group attempt to guide their actions in order to help them manipulate the exhibit rather than explaining the concepts underpinning it. Conversations are brief and limited to 'doing' rather than 'understanding'. Once the exhibit has been experienced they move on. Learners therefore appear to take what they want at that moment from the activity offered, suggesting that less formal contexts for education not only have to address the needs of a broader range of learners, but that they also may have difficulties in ensuring learning is both 'hands-on' and 'brains-on

Meighan and Siraj-Blatchford (2003) discussed the notion of flexitime education that allows learners to spend part of their time in a formal education context, such as a school, and part elsewhere. Such an initiative enables learners to take advantage of the range of learning contexts available, including e-learning. In the United States, there is increasing interest in the development of independent study programmes, designed to meet the needs of individual learners, and in the development of learning systems that have as a central premise the notion that learning can take place anywhere and can be directed by the learners themselves. Meighan and Siraj-Blatchford have recognised the benefits of these approaches. They also pointed out that the notion of flexitime is not readily accepted. While current legislation allows a child to be educated at home or at school, permission for each flexitime arrangement requires separate negotiation. It could be argued that legislation in the UK inhibits the development of flexible approaches such as these. Perhaps some of the responsibility lies with the legislation laid down in the Education Reform Act 1988, which devolves funding to schools based on numbers of pupils in school; the 'bums on seats' approach. As a consequence, schools may be unwilling to formalise a flexitime arrangement or maintain places for pupils on extended trips, no matter how educational such arrangements may be. The extent to which schools may use visits to other educational environments to support curriculum delivery is also influenced by the need to fund such visits, either through the limited budget available or by relying on voluntary contributions from parents or carers. While many museums (e.g. the Natural History Museum in London) have removed or reduced entry prices for educational parties, the cost of transport to and from such venues may preclude schools from making full use of the opportunities they offer.

It seems probable that developments in the use of information and communication technology will facilitate online and virtual access to many such resources, thus helping to widen participation and extend access to these facilities. Good use is already being made of this in education programmes for children in the Australian outback, and Meighan (2000) reported on the success of 'cyber schools' in Canada. If Gregory's (2002) view of education is accepted, an education that hopes to enable learners to make sense of the physical, social and cultural world must at least keep pace with the changes in that world, and many would see change as both necessary and inevitable. However, while it would seem obvious that educational institutions will need to make full use of funding strategies, educational policies and technological initiatives in order to initiate change, it is important to remember that education is deeply embedded in national culture (Wood, 2004). Attempts at educational change will need to reflect this and, as a consequence, approaches used in one country may not necessarily be transferable to another. Despite the increase in home education in countries such as the United States, the UK, Australia and Canada, for example, this approach is still rare in the Netherlands (Bluk, 2004), perhaps because parental expectations demand that education takes place in schools.

## Summary and conclusions

It is evident that strategic thinking that goes well beyond current educational policy will be required to make best use of the educational opportunities available to us in the UK. At present, government funding is used mainly to support formal educational environments, such as schools, leaving other providers, such as the 'peri-formal', to rely on grants, funding by industry, or the National Lottery.

Given that the term 'education' has a variety of meanings and that education can take place in many contexts, those who seek to open up the opportunities afforded by adopting more flexible and context-specific descriptions of education will need to be able to argue their case, to be able to play the various 'language-games' of policy-makers, funding agencies, opinion-shapers, educators and others. Traditional views of education may then be replaced by a recognition that a diversity of approaches is possible, where the criteria of education will vary depending on the context, and where explanation, persuasion and justification have an accepted and expected place.

# References

Aro, M, Rinne, R, Lahti, K and Olkinuora, E (2005) Education or learning on the job? Generational differences of opinions in Finland. *International Journal of Lifelong Education*, 24(6): 459–74.

Becker, GS (1964) *Human capital: a theoretical and empirical analysis, with special reference to education*. New York: National Bureau of Economic Research.

Bluk, H (2004) Performance in home schooling: an argument against compulsory schooling in the Netherlands. *International Review of Education*, 50(1): 39–52.

Carr, D (2003) *Making sense of education*. London: RoutledgeFalmer.

Cohen, B (1982) *Means and ends in education*. London: George Allen and Unwin.

Fernández, G and Benlloch, M (2000) Interactive exhibits: how visitors respond. *Museum International*, 52(4): 53–9.

Freire, P (1972) Education: domestication or liberation?, reprinted in Lister, I (1974) *Deschooling*. Cambridge: Cambridge University Press.

Giroux, HA (1985) Introduction, in Freire, P *The politics of education: culture, power and liberation*. London: Bergin and Garvey.

Gregory, I (2002) The aims of education, in Davies, I, Gregory, I and McGuinn, N (eds) *Key debates in education*. London: Continuum.

Hirst, PH (1965) Liberal education and the nature of knowledge, in Archambault, RD (ed) *Philosophical analysis and education*. London: Routledge and Kegan Paul.

Lang, P (1995) Preparing teachers for pastoral care and personal and social education: to train or educate? *Pastoral Care*, 13(4): 18–23.

Matheson, D and Wells, P (1999) What is education?, in Matheson, D and Grosvenor, I (eds) *An introduction to the study of education*. London: David Fulton.

Meighan, R (2000) *Natural learning and the natural curriculum*. Nottingham: Educational Heretics Press.

Meighan, R (2005) *Comparing learning systems: the good, the bad, the ugly, and the counter-productive*. Nottingham: Educational Heretics Press.

Meighan, R and Siraj-Blatchford, I (2003) *A sociology of educating*. London: Continuum.

Newman, S (1999) *Philosophy and teacher education: a reinterpretation of Donald A. Schön's epistemology of reflective practice*. Aldershot: Ashgate.

Papadopoulous, G (1998) Learning for the twenty-first century: issues, in Delors, J (Chair) *Education for the twenty-first century: issues and prospects. Contributions to the work of the International Commission on Education for the Twenty-first Century*. Paris: United Nations Educational, Scientific and Cultural Organisation.

Peacock, A (2005) The emergence and characteristics of peri-formal education, Paper presented at the seminar on non-formal education, King's College, London, June 2005.

Peters, RS (1966) *Ethics and education*. London: George Allen and Unwin.

Webb, J (1990) *Children learning at home*. Lewes: Falmer Press.

Wittgenstein, L (1953) *Philosophical investigations*. Oxford: Blackwell.

Wood, K (2004) International perspectives: the USA and the Pacific Rim, in Ward, S (ed) *Education studies: a student's guide*. London: RoutledgeFalmer.

# Chapter 2

# The mystery of learning

## John Sharp and Barbara Murphy

### Introduction

Learning is widely regarded as a lifelong activity which may occur intentionally or otherwise in a range of different learning environments, including schools, colleges, universities and the workplace. At times, of course, learning takes place with remarkable ease. Committing a simple fact to memory and being able to recall it on demand, or completing a relatively simple practical task successfully having been shown how to do it only once or twice, rarely presents much of a challenge. More often than not, however, what we are expected to learn, or indeed have to learn, is considerably difficult and requires effort. But can we be said to have learnt something if, for example, we take copious notes during a lecture and then repeat them back in an examination? Have we learnt something better if we get good grades in assessed coursework? Have we learnt anything at all if we cannot transfer our knowledge from one context to another? This chapter examines how we come to know what we know by reviewing evidence from within the fields of neuroscience, cognitive psychology and education itself. It also looks critically at learning styles and the growing use of learning style questionnaires as a practitioner-based activity in schools.

## What do we mean by learning?

According to Driscoll (2000), most authors share a common view of learning which can be defined as a *persistent change in human performance or performance potential* that cannot be ascribed to growth or maturation. Fortunately, the results of learning are often observable in the outcomes of human behaviour and taxonomies of learning outcomes are well known. Bloom's taxonomy of learning outcomes, for example, consists of six levels of activity which start with a demonstration of knowledge before working their way through comprehension, application, analysis and synthesis to evaluation (Bloom et al., 1956). The higher the taxonomic level, the more advanced the learning and intellectual challenge involved. By way of contrast, Gagné's taxonomy of learning outcomes is broader and considers learning in terms of a variety of cognitive, social, affective and psychomotor factors (Gagné, 1985). While Driscoll's definition of learning is valuable in helping to identify learning in terms of human performance and potential, it does not help to understand how knowledge is acquired in the first instance.

# Learning and the brain

The origin and acquisition of knowledge in humans has been a matter of intense philosophical debate which can be traced back at least to Plato. Historically, views have tended to fall within one of three main camps: nativists considered all individuals to be born with the knowledge they needed and that anything else was acquired by some innate or inherited characteristic; empiricists considered all individuals to acquire knowledge out of experience; and rationalists considered all individuals to acquire knowledge by engaging in reasoning. Today, individuals are considered to be born at least partly 'hard-wired' with an architecture of the mind which facilitates cognition, rather than with a mind full of knowledge *per se*. Understanding that architecture is fundamental to understanding how we learn.

Summarising from the work of Greenfield (1997), the human brain is a creamy-brown coloured organ which reaches full development in late adolescence or early adulthood. Visual inspection of the brain reveals three immediately obvious components, each of which can be identified just prior to birth:

- the cerebrum;
- the cerebellum;
- the brain stem (which runs into the vertebrae or bones of the neck and spine as the spinal cord).

The cerebrum, the outermost layer of which is referred to as the cerebral cortex, is particularly striking and consists of two almost symmetrical and highly convoluted cerebral hemispheres (Fig. 2.1). These hemispheres, together with their frontal, temporal, parietal and occipital lobes, are connected by a number of inter-cortical nerve fibres including the corpus callosum. Different regions of the brain, including the sub-cortical structures hidden from

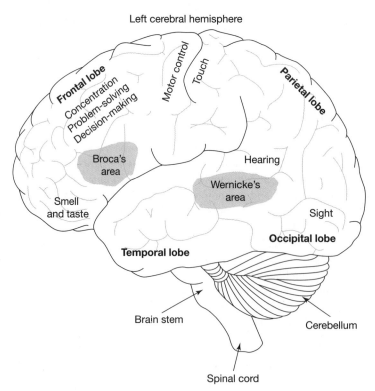

**Figure 2.1** The human brain showing main structural components and functional areas

view by the cerebral cortex itself, are responsible for the bewildering array of different brain functions, from the receipt and processing of information from receptors located all over the body (the sensory areas) to the co-ordination of almost every action that the body performs, voluntarily or involuntarily (the motor areas). Some regions carry out combined functions that link sensory and motor information and are active when interpreting experiences, concentrating, problem-solving, decision-making and reasoning (the association areas). Brain function also determines just 'who we are'.

While the techniques available to study learning and the human brain are wide and varied, non-invasive neuro-imaging has proved particularly productive. Positron emission tomography or PET scans, for example, have revealed that different regions of the brain are active when carrying out related but subtly different language tasks, including hearing words (Wernicke's area and the auditory cortex), speaking words (the motor cortex), seeing words (the visual cortex) and generating words (Broca's area). PET scans have also revealed that language development and comprehension are sometimes lateralised and gender-specific. That is, they involve both hemispheres of the brain in subtly different ways and to subtly different degrees in men and women, statistically at least. But knowing about which areas of the brain are active as we perform very specific tasks is one thing. Determining the exact nature of that activity and how it results in learning is something else.

According to O'Shea (2005), the adult brain as a whole, but particularly the cerebral cortex, is densely packed with cells of different types, including an estimated 100 billion neurons. Neurons come in different shapes and sizes and do different jobs. A 'typical' brain cell, however, measures less than about one tenth of a millimetre across and consists of:

- a squat cell body or soma which contains the nucleus;
- a number of dendrites which branch out from the cell body and taper;
- a single axon which extends outwards from the cell body and ends in an array of synaptic terminals or synapses.

What appears to distinguish neurons from other cells in the human body is their ability to network with each other and communicate. This is made possible by a whole series of signals that begin with action potentials or electrical currents generated in the bodies of neurons themselves, which are then transmitted along their axons. These action potentials arrive at synaptic terminals where they stimulate the release of chemicals called neurotransmitters. As neurotransmitters cross the gap or synaptic cleft between the axon of one neuron and the dendrite of another, synapses are said to 'fire'. This electrochemical means of communication between neurons is the neuroscientific basis of learning. Even learning a simple fact, however, is a process thought to involve not two but entire populations of neurons distributed around the brain and networked in ways that we cannot even begin to imagine. But there is little point in learning something if you simply forget it. The constant firing of synapses and the connections they make allow certain synapses to become temporarily strengthened, forming short-term memories which may last only a few seconds. Further firing, however, results in a remodelling of synapses themselves which become strengthened on a more permanent basis. The adaptability of neurons and the brain to learn and remodel itself in this way is referred to as 'plasticity'. The effects of plasticity are particularly evident in neuro-imaging studies of the brains of musicians which reveal enhanced development in areas that correspond to how particular instruments are played (Weinberger, 2005).

Compelling as it may seem, and despite all of the advances made within the field of neuroscience in recent years, the working of the human brain is simply far too complex to formulate any sensible, practical, everyday educational application even in its broadest sense. Indeed, the range of 'neuro-myths' surrounding the brain and education remain an endless source of entertainment to neuroscientists themselves (Blakemore and Frith, 2002; Geake and Cooper, 2003; Goswami, 2004).

> ### *Pause for thought* | fact or fiction?
>
> In his book *The brain's behind it*, Smith (2002) has pointed out that it is incumbent upon educators to show responsibility to ask more precise questions of neuroscientists and their findings and vice versa if only to question and eradicate the great variety of neuroscientific and educational fallacies that have arisen over the years. Together with a friend or a group of colleagues, consider what you believe to be the truth or otherwise in some of Smith's examples:
>
> - the brain cells you get at birth are those you have for life;
> - there are critical periods within which specific brain development occurs;
> - you use only 10 per cent or less of your brain;
> - your brain is like a sponge;
> - stress stops you learning;
> - your memory is perfect;
> - your left brain is logical, your right brain creative;
> - listening to Mozart makes you intelligent;
> - children can concentrate for only two minutes more than their chronological age;
> - male and female brains are so different we ought to teach boys and girls in different ways.
>
> Now consider the personal and educational implications of your beliefs. Of course, not all of these statements are true ... but which ones? Would you be surprised to find out that most are actually half-truths, distortions or just plain wrong? Take a look at Smith's commentary on the matter and reflect upon the significance of his findings. For more information on this topic consult Geake (2008).

# Modelling memory

While the complexities of learning and memory formation at the level of the neuron are considerable, learning and memory are widely regarded as emergent properties of the human brain which can be investigated in other more readily observable ways. From a series of highly controlled laboratory-based experiments and recourse to how computers work as a suitable metaphor, the limitations of which are well understood if often overlooked, psychologists have modelled the human cognitive system in terms of at least three inter-connected storage areas. These include:

- sensory memory;
- short-term or working memory;
- long-term memory.

Summarising from the work of Eysenck and Keane (2005), learning and memory formation not only involve the processing and storage of information but other features, including attention, perception, encoding and retrieval (Fig. 2.2).

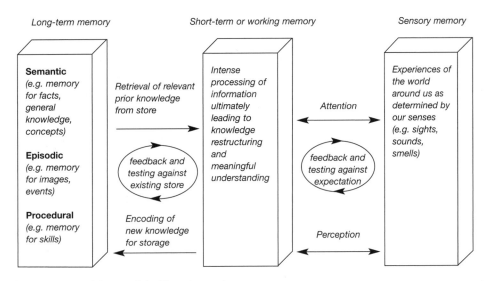

**Figure 2.2** Cognitive model of learning and memory

In their studies of learning and memory, cognitive psychologists often explore declarative or 'knowing that' knowledge, the main focus of our attention here, using the schema construct (the cognitive psychologist's equivalent of a neuronal network). A schema of an object such as a book, for example, is an idealised knowledge package that contains all of the information elements associated by an individual with that object. Because a schema is regarded as an organising structure for knowledge, it is convenient to consider a schema's information elements to be represented in memory in terms of concepts. In classical theories of concept formation, concepts have attributes. Attributes define what it is to be a member of a concept and concept learning takes place by association (similarity, contiguity and contrast). Explanation-based views of concepts and concept formation, however, are more useful when dealing with the complexities of attributes and the relations that exist between them which together give rise to higher levels of cognitive functioning. Theories of knowledge acquisition based upon the schema construct and the semantic networks they form assume that schema are not static and that their content, the arrangement of that content and the relations between information elements change as knowledge acquisition and concept learning take place (the cognitive psychologist's equivalent of plasticity). Of course, human learning involves more than information processing. People also deal with meaning and making sense of the world and the events going on around them. Interestingly, the most influential factor affecting the rate, accuracy and effectiveness of knowledge acquisition and concept learning, including what we forget, is what a learner already knows.

Cognitive psychologists have long used information processing as a means to explore potential instructional sequences and events for teaching. According to Gagné and Driscoll (1988), as one of many possible examples, these include:

- gaining attention (alertness);
- activating motivation by introducing objectives (expectancy);
- stimulating the recall of prior knowledge (retrieval to short-term or working memory);
- presenting stimulus materials (selective perception);
- providing learning guidance (encoding and entry to long-term memory storage);
- eliciting performance (responding);
- assessing performance and providing feedback (reinforcement);
- enhancing retention and transfer (cueing retrieval).

***Pause for thought*** | the condition of learning

Think of a lecture or tutorial you have attended recently, a seminar you have led, or a class you have taught. On reflection, can you identify any of the instructional events outlined by Gagné and Driscoll (1988)? Did they occur in any particular order? Consider the learning environment you found yourself in or created for others, the tasks you were asked to complete or gave others to do, and the social organisation and interactions of the people present. Can you define any effective teacher characteristics involved? What about the learners? What does all of this tell you about cognition and the condition of learning?

# Learning in an educational context

If the picture of learning painted in earlier sections seems somewhat clinical, we only have to look towards schools, classrooms and a curriculum area like science to add a little 'mess'. Science is a particularly valuable curriculum area to consider, as learning theory in science education has advanced far beyond the global theorists such as Piaget and Vygotsky into constructivism in a domain-specific way (Driver et al., 1994). Research into children's ideas in science education seeks to consider how children conceptualise the objects, events and phenomena of science by eliciting their knowledge and understanding of them. Much work in this area, and across the primary and secondary age phases in particular, has demonstrated repeatedly that scientific knowledge cannot be transmitted easily from one individual to another (e.g. didactically from teacher to child) but must be constructed through acts of personal and social cognition by learners themselves (Duit and Treagust, 2003). The emergent properties of knowledge acquisition and concept learning in science education are now well established.

- Children form their own ideas about the world in which they live long before any formal teaching takes place in school.
- Children's ideas frequently differ from the science taught at school and the ideas of scientists themselves.
- Children's ideas can be strongly held and resistant to change even in the most supportive, caring and stimulating of teaching and learning environments.
- Children's ideas can and do change as a result of learning science at school but often in unanticipated ways.
- Children often share similar ideas as a result of shared experiences, the use of language and interpersonal relationships.

More importantly, perhaps, the emergent properties of knowledge acquisition and concept learning in science resonate well with the features of learning and memory presented earlier from within the fields of neurosciences and cognitive psychology and established links have already been made, if only in the broadest and most qualitative way (Anderson, 1997; Mayer, 2002).

Research box

### the chaos in learning science

Basing their work on constructivist premises, and extrapolating from the non-linear principles of dynamical systems theory and chaos, Luffiego et al. (1994) have presented an advanced schema-based model of learning science involving the evolution of a conceptual schema in order to describe the state of a learner's cognitive system before, during and after teaching or instruction. While the application of dynamical systems theory and chaos to matters of an educational nature might at first seem unusual, their extension from the realms of mathematics and computing into many other disciplines has met with some success, particularly in terms of explaining the sometimes odd behaviour and predisposition of evolving systems that tend towards disorder and unpredictability, however brief that tendency might be (i.e. learning is limited, selective and incomplete). According to Luffiego et al., the human cognitive system is an open, dynamic and non-linear system capable of selecting, storing and processing information, and this system exhibits extreme variability between individuals as a result of the sensitivity of initial cognitive states (the 'butterfly effect'). Luffiego et al. have suggested that the conceptual schema within most cognitive systems are in fact powerful information 'attractors' for they exhibit general stability and resistance to change and give rise ultimately to 'final-states' of knowledge (which emerge as children's ideas). As a result, learning science may take place along similar or widely divergent and unpredictable pathways resulting in errors and misconceptions as well as scientific conceptualisation. At the very least, Luffiego et al. have provided a new language of learning, at best a whole new paradigm within which to explore science education and other curriculum areas in new and exciting ways.

However, learning science as a process of conceptual change (or learning in any other cognate discipline for that matter) may be overly simplistic. Science at school is an intellectual, practical, creative and social endeavour which seeks to help children and older students better understand and make sense of the world in which they live. Science education involves them in thinking and working in particular ways in the pursuit of reliable scientific knowledge. If, as Driver et al. (1994) have suggested, children are to be enculturated into science, then intervention and negotiation of meaning with a teacher are essential if the tools and conventions of the scientific community are to be made fully available. As Driver *et al.* have also noted, *the challenge is one of how to achieve such a process of enculturation successfully in the round of normal classroom life,* particularly when *the science view that the teacher is presenting is in conflict with the learners' prior knowledge schemes.* This, of course, places considerable demands on the curricular expertise of teachers. Linder (1993) has also argued from both cognitive and phenomenographic perspectives that individuals could construct a repertoire of conceptions of objects, events and phenomena ('domains of knowledge'), the one eventually chosen and used depending on the context, social, scientific or otherwise, for which it is required ('mode of perception'). Linder has proposed that learning by 'conceptual appreciation' might be more appropriate than learning by conceptual change.

But teaching, like curriculum development, is also strongly influenced by culture and ideology, not just how children learn (Millar and Osborne, 1998; Sharp and Grace, 2004). Hodson (1998), for example, has suggested that with child-centred, process-driven or discovery-led pedagogies it is often commonplace to find, say, children at school in Key Stage 1 constructing a knowledge of the world around them which is far from scientific, but that anything is allowed to count as science provided the children are working co-operatively and in a warm and friendly learning environment. As Hodson correctly noted, however, not all investigations and enquiries are scientific and not all forms of knowledge and understanding arising from them are equally valid from a scientific point of view. In secondary schools too, while it is accepted that practical work undoubtedly contributes towards securing interest, curiosity and progress in science, scientific knowledge and understanding cannot always be developed through practical work alone.

# VAK or VAK-uous?

In much the same way as metacognition, or learning how to learn, has grown in prominence as an effective learning strategy in educational circles over the years, the whole concept of learning styles has made an equally impressive recent appearance. Despite a long history and solid research pedigree from within the field of cognitive psychology, the apparent trivialisation of learning styles and their determination in schools throughout the UK is perhaps something of a concern (Sharp *et al.*, 2008). Much of this trivialisation revolves around the notion that an individual's preferred learning style can somehow be reduced to only one of three independently assessed modalities – visual, auditory or kinaesthetic – and that this can be identified using a simple instrument in the form of a self-assessment questionnaire. More worrying is the notion that the outcome from such a simple questionnaire could then be used to inform teaching or curriculum development to better match an individual's learning needs. Often implicit within this position is a view that working within a learner's preferred learning style will ultimately lead to improvements in various cognitive and intellectual abilities. Some sources go further, suggesting that there is a clear link between learning styles and 'multiple intelligences theory', when actually neither rests on firm foundations (Franklin , 2006), or that justification for learning styles can be found in how the brain works (Perks, 2004). In a special issue of the journal of *Educational Psychology* devoted to learning style issues, Cassidy (2004) has already pointed out that *whilst educators in all fields are becoming increasingly aware of the critical importance of understanding how individuals learn, it is equally important that any attempts to integrate learning style into educational programmes are made from an informed position*. With background provided by Cassidy and the extensive review provided by Coffield *et al.* (2004), we aim the following criticisms at VAK as it appears in schools to stimulate discussion and debate.

## Origin and terminology

Despite the history of learning styles research, which can be traced back through the psychology literature for some 40 years or more, the exact origin or source of derivation of VAK and VAK instrumentation used in schools remains uncertain. Indeed the range of instruments to be found and the variation between them can be quite startling. Few have found their way into schools with any indication of provenance and few come with any literature explaining how they should be used and interpreted. Even those that do, including the commercially available VAK questionnaires found on the internet, need to be interrogated critically. While the closest learning styles questionnaire with a school-centred focus is thought to be the Learning Style Inventory, or LSI, provided by Dunn *et al.* (1989), this bears no resemblance to the VAK-type found in schools. Indeed, the LSI actually attempts to match an individual's preferred learning style to the emotional, sociological, physical and psychological elements of the learning environment. Not only might those setting out to investigate using learning styles be daunted at the range of models, instruments and theoretical perspectives actually available, they might be equally daunted at the confusing terminology and definitions that also exist. Of course, there are mixed views about the nature of learning styles and there is no general agreement on a definition. Dunn and co-workers, for example, define learning styles as the ways students begin to concentrate on and process, internalise and remember new and difficult academic information. Riding and Rayner (1998) have added that a learning style might equally be defined as the process used by an individual to respond to the demands of a learning activity. The VAK instruments found in schools measure none of these things rigorously.

## Validity, reliability and dimensionality

The development, design and range of applicability of all sophisticated learning styles instruments from within psychology like LSI have been rigorously used and tested. Even then, the validity and reliability of some instruments remain the subject of controversy, the seriousness of which is closely related to the importance of the claims they make. From the most cursory glance at the VAK instrumentation used in schools, some questions asked of individuals would appear to probe attitudes towards learning, learning habits, learning preferences, personality traits and sociability. These are very different things. Some questions also appear to be so generally expressed as to be of little relevance to education or learning style at all. In addition to undermining validity, these features also raise doubts over dimensionality and whether or not VAK instrumentation measures one or a number of different learning attributes. The difficulty of establishing whether an individual's preferred learning style affects performance or an individual's performance affects learning style should not be overlooked.

## Universality

VAK instrumentation in schools adopts a 'one size fits all' stance. Schools and classrooms are, however, diverse learning environments filled with individuals with diverse learning needs taught by teachers with their own ideologies and philosophies of education. The demands imposed by each curriculum area are also diverse. Children in schools rarely work in isolation but in groups, and develop rapidly throughout the primary and secondary years. Most teachers and other educators agree that the choice an individual makes regarding how they approach a task is largely automatic and derived from prior experience and may vary according to each and every learning situation or context. What is less clear is whether or not such a preferred learning style remains constant over time. It would seem unreasonable, therefore, to claim that any preferred learning style made available by a single VAK questionnaire would provide any meaningful insight into any individual's needs on a day-to-day or even longer-term basis.

---

***Pause for thought*** | determine your own preferred learning style

The following questionnaire in three parts has been adapted from the work of Clark (1998). Its inclusion here is for illustration and discussion only. It should not be taken and used out of context.

Read each statement carefully and use the following Likert-type scale to score your response. Add all of the scores in each part together and record them as indicated (each part has a minimum score of 6 and a maximum score of 30). Are you a visual, auditory or kinaesthetic learner?

Score 1 – almost never applies
Score 2 – applies once in a while
Score 3 – sometimes applies
Score 4 – often applies
Score 5 – almost always applies

▶

## Part 1: visual

(a) I take lots of notes and like to doodle.

(b) When talking to someone else I have the hardest time handling those who do not make good eye contact with me.

(c) I make lists and notes because I remember things better if I write them down.

(d) I need to write down directions so that I may remember them.

(e) When recalling information I can see it in my mind and remember where I saw it.

(f) If I had to explain a new procedure or technique I would prefer to write it out.

Total score:

## Part 2: auditory

(a) When I read I read out loud or move my lips to hear the words in my head.

(b) When talking to someone else I have the hardest time handling those who do not talk back with me.

(c) I do not take lots of notes but I still remember what was said – taking notes distracts me from the speaker.

(d) I like to talk to myself when solving a problem or writing.

(e) I remember things more easily by repeating them again and again.

(f) If I had to explain a new procedure or technique I would prefer telling about it.

Total score:

## Part 3: kinaesthetic

(a) I prefer to start working on tasks without listening to instructions first.

(b) I take notes and doodle but rarely go back and look at them.

(c) My working space appears disorganised to others.

(d) I like to move around – I feel uncomfortable sitting for too long.

(e) If I had to explain a new procedure or technique I would prefer to demonstrate it.

(f) With free time I am most likely to exercise.

Total score:

Look at the statements again carefully. Do you think they measure learning styles or something else? Do you really think your preferred learning style can be determined so easily? Even if it could, what does your profile mean? What if it's mixed? At what point does an apparent preference actually become significant?

In learning styles research, most authors, recognising the significance of their work, do advocate a balanced and sensible approach that involves using a carefully chosen variety of teaching strategies which consider a variety of styles with the aim of providing all individuals with the opportunity to learn in different ways. But is this not just good practice? Even the most 'traditional' primary classroom provides an active learning environment with children's senses stimulated in all kinds of different ways and even the most 'traditional' lecture is more likely to be a multimedia event than a recital. At best, and within certain academic journals, some published studies involving rigorously tested psychological learning styles instruments do report improved understanding and self-reflection of individuals as learners themselves.

But the majority of such studies involve adults not children. Cassidy (2004) reminds us, *for those working within an educational setting wishing to utilise learning style to promote more effective learning, whether through individual or group profiling, design of instructional methods, or identifying learner preferences, operationalising learning style is a necessary but highly problematic endeavour.* VAK in schools, if it is ever to be taken seriously and beyond generalisation at an intuitive level, has a long way to go.

## Summary and conclusions

Learning is hard work and far from straightforward. Developments from within the fields of neuroscience, cognitive psychology and education have shed a great deal of light on how we learn and how we come to know what we know, yet at the same time confirming that learning is a profoundly complex process. While tempting, making close links between all three fields is a hazardous activity. Even when neuroscientists, cognitive psychologists and educators appear to explore similar things, they usually do so in very different ways and at very different levels of abstraction. The harsh truth is that even relevant findings from within each field are all too often ambiguous and hotly debated. Occasionally, and in our search to unlock the mysteries of learning and how best to maximise our own learning potential and that of others, we all have to be reminded at times not to simply believe, rely upon or readily accept without question what we are told. This in itself is a part of learning. Of course, what we learn and learn to do throughout a lifetime is vast, extending well beyond the simple acquisition of knowledge. Some of the many factors that contribute to this can be identified but a great many others elude us still. Even in formal learning environments such as schools, colleges, universities and the workplace, the extent to which we reach our full potential as learners is often about opportunity rather than ability, and knowing when and how to seize it. To achieve our full potential we also have to learn how to learn, to acquire good learning habits and to take or share responsibility for our own learning as well as the learning of others. There are no short cuts, no quick fixes and no magic bullets.

## References

Anderson, OR (1997) A neurocognitive perspective on current learning theory and science instructional strategies. *Science Education*, 81: 67–89.

Blakemore, SJ and Frith, U (2002) The implications of recent developments in neuroscience for research on teaching and learning. Available at **www.icn.ucl.ac.uk/sblakemore/SJ_papers/ESRCmainreport.pdf** (accessed 12 May 2006).

Bloom, BS, Englehart, MD, Furst, EJ, Hill, WH and Krathwohl, DR (1956) *Taxonomy of educational objectives. Handbook I: Cognitive domain.* New York: McKay.

Cassidy, S (2004) Learning styles: an overview of theories, models and measures. *Educational Psychology*, 24(4): 419–44.

Clark, D (1998) Visual, auditory and kinaesthetic survey. Available at **www.nwlink.com/~donclark/ hrd/vak.html** (accessed 1 December, 2005).

Coffield, F, Moseley, D, Hall, E and Ecclestone, K (2004) *Should we be using learning styles? What research has to say to practice.* London: Learning and Skills Research Centre.

Driscoll, MP (2000) *Psychology of learning for instruction.* Boston, MA: Allyn and Bacon.

Driver, R, Asoko, H, Leach, J, Mortimer, E and Scott, P (1994) Constructing scientific knowledge in the classroom. *Educational Researcher*, 23(7): 5–12.

Duit, R and Treagust, DF (2003). Conceptual change: a powerful framework for improving science teaching and learning. *International Journal of Science Education*, 25(6): 671–88.

Dunn, R, Dunn, K and Price, GE (1989) *Learning styles inventory*. Lawrence, KS: Price Systems.

Eysenck, MW and Keane, MT (2005) *Cognitive psychology*. Hove: Psychology Press.

Franklin, S (2006) VAKing out learning styles – why the notion of 'Learning styles' is unhelpful to teachers. *Education 3–13*, 34(1): 81–7.

Gagné, RM (1985) *The conditions of learning*. New York: Holt, Rinehart and Winston.

Gagné, RM and Driscoll, MP (1988) *Essentials of learning for instruction*. Englewood Cliffs, NJ: Prentice Hall.

Geake, J (2008) Neuromythologies in education. *Educational Research*, 50(2): 123–133.

Geake, J and Cooper, P (2003) Cognitive neuroscience: implications for education. *Westminster Studies in Education*, 26(1): 7–20.

Goswami, U (2004) Neuroscience and education. *British Journal of Educational Psychology*, 74: 1–14.

Greenfield, S (1997) *The human brain*. London: Phoenix.

Hines, M (2004) *Brain gender*. Oxford: Oxford University Press.

Hodson, D (1998) *Teaching and learning science: towards a personalized approach*. Milton Keynes: Open University Press.

Linder, CJ (1993) A challenge to conceptual change. *Science Education*, 77(3): 293–300.

Luffiego, M, Bastida, MF, Ramos, F and Soto, J (1994) Systemic model of conceptual evolution. *International Journal of Science Education*, 16(3): 305–13.

Mayer, RE (2002) Understanding conceptual change: a commentary, in Limón, M and Mason, L (eds) *Reconsidering conceptual change: issues in theory and practice*. Dordrecht: Kluwer.

Millar, R and Osborne, J (1998) *Beyond 2000: science education for the future – a report with ten recommendations*. London: King's College.

O'Shea, M (2005) *The brain: a very short introduction*. Oxford: Oxford University Press.

Perks, D (2004) The shattered mirror: a critique of multiple intelligences theory, in Hayes, D (ed) *The RoutledgeFalmer guide to key debates in education*. London: RoutledgeFalmer.

Riding, RJ and Rayner, S (eds) (1998) *Cognitive styles and learning strategies*. London: Fulton.

Sharp, JG and Grace, M (2004) Anecdote, opinion and whim: lessons in curriculum development from primary science education in England and Wales. *Research Papers in Education*, 19(3): 293–321.

Sharp, JG, Bowker, R and Byrne, J (2008) VAK or VAK-ous? Towards the trivialisation of learning and the death of scholarship. *Research Papers in Education*, 23(3): 293–314.

Smith, A (2002) *The brain's behind it: new knowledge about the brain and learning*. Stafford: Network Educational Press.

Weinberger, NM (2005) Music and the brain. *Scientific American*, 291(5): 66–73.

# Chapter 3

# Community education: innovation and active intervention

## Viv Kerridge and Ruth Sayers

### Introduction

This chapter is concerned with education that occurs in the broader community rather than in a formal educational institution. It highlights the theoretical aspects of community education and consider its roots, function and importance. Set alongside the philosophical exposition will be a number of illustrations to place community education within a drama and theatre context as we perceive a constructive and vibrant connection between the two. There is a strong tradition of using drama and theatre in active community projects and a coherent theoretical basis which explains its usefulness and illustrates its effectiveness. The chapter introduces interventionist techniques designed to enable communities to recognise and negotiate external restrictions. Distinctions are drawn between theatre-in-education, community theatre and educational drama. The political perspective offered includes a consideration of the financial, social and political pressure placed upon the development of community education and the level of attention and funding given to mainstream theatre as opposed to 'people's theatre', including street arts. The professional perspective offers a practical guide to establishing community projects with regard to ethical, philosophical and logistical frameworks.

## Background

Formal education is a relatively new construct whereas some sense of community has always been fundamental to human development. Many of our life skills are absorbed *in situ* by informal means; that is by the family or the workplace. Humans learn many things effectively, if sometimes painfully, from observation and trial and error. Traditionally, crafts and trades worked on an apprenticeship basis through active learning, and formal theoretical assessment was not part of the process. There was of course nothing idyllic about this arrangement; it too was subject to economic restrictions and dictated to by the basic need to survive. Community cooperation and education are difficult to untangle. Even formal education generally takes place in the local community, and educational institutions form communities of their own in which personal relationships and individual identity play a significant part in the learning process. To this extent it is misleading to suggest that education, in its broadest sense, can be anything but a community issue. So what is it that differentiates 'education in the community' from formal education?

Formal education is taken here to mean that which takes place in schools and other educational institutions. It undergoes constant development, or at least change, according to such criteria as pressures of finance, local and global pressures, government priorities and pedagogical fashion. Formal education can be flexible and fluid or very closely prescribed. Education in the community is also an umbrella term for a wide variety of activities which vary in terms of formality from drop-in play sessions for mothers and toddlers to fully accredited lifelong learning courses. It is also closely connected with community development and the connection between social welfare, community and education.

A trawl of the internet uncovers a wealth of community education centres throughout the UK which offer a vast array of services such as:

- education–business partnerships (which put schools in touch with potential business sponsors);
- links with local services (police, social services, health services);
- learning resource services (facilities such as desktop publishing, video editing, internet access);
- community cafes (or other relaxation areas where people can socialise and pick up information leaflets on local facilities);
- activities for the elderly;
- parents' groups (often with speakers and facilitators of parenting skills);
- basic skills sessions;
- youth organisations;
- professional advice (grant aid and advice on funding and training for community initiatives);
- citizens' advice sessions;
- free legal advice sessions;
- a range of classes at a variety of levels.

Some of these centres are based in community schools, libraries or other public buildings, while some have their own separate premises such as welfare halls and local institutes. These are open to all local residents. Some of the facilities are free and others are subsidised. Many of these facilities may seem more 'community' orientated than 'educational'.

---

**Pause for thought** | community education

Look through the list of services provided by community education centres. How many of them seem to you to be educational? Which do you consider to be community based? Are any of them difficult to differentiate? Do you think that any of the functions on the list help to 'create' a sense of community or do they 'service' a local area?

---

# The history of community education

This level of provision is not a new phenomenon. During the second part of the nineteenth and the whole of the twentieth centuries, there was a strong tradition of working people's clubs and institutes throughout the country. In his fascinating history of British working class intellectual life, Rose (2002) referred to the miners' institutes of South Wales as *one of the greatest networks of cultural institutions created by working people anywhere in the world.* He mentions that, by the time of the Second World War, the Tredegar Institute Library, for example, circulated 100,000 books per year, and many similar institutes had cinemas and film societies and had staged numerous concerts and cultural performances. There is evidence that institute libraries stocked a vast range of books on a variety of subjects and that people's reading habits included the classics and social and political texts. While some of the people who benefited had aspirations beyond their cultural background, the majority used them as a form of personal enrichment and empowerment.

In addition to the wide range of cultural pursuits there was a strong tradition of political debate which often manifested itself through drama. Throughout the 1930s, radical theatre groups such as the Red Megaphones in Salford (MacColl, 1973) were producing agit-prop theatre performances for the working classes in order to raise awareness of political, social and ideological issues. They used street theatre as a way of delivering their message. Their work was inspired by similar experiments in the United States led by the 'Living Newspaper' units that had been established as part of the Federal Theatre Project during the 1930s (Witham, 2003).

Susan Mansfield (cited in Allen and Martin, 1992) traced both the lesser-known contribution that women made to the development of community education and the patriarchal values which manifested themselves as powerfully in community education as they did in the school system. The Suffrage Movement and the socialist Sunday Schools raised the political awareness and confidence of women; the Women's Cooperative Guild moved from an association concerned with women's traditional roles to a campaigning body which championed women's education. Later, movements such as the Townswomen's Guild and the Women's Institute included education programmes and campaigned for women's issues. The Suffragette Movement used drama in the form of propaganda sketches and full-length plays to further their political aims.

These movements and institutions and others like them across the country were largely self-generating and run by those they served. Rose (2002) noted that while the miners' libraries and other facilities were fed by the Miners' Welfare Fund set up by parliament to tax coal production and direct the revenue to the institutions, the miners themselves controlled the budget. They enjoyed a high level of cultural and intellectual freedom and were instrumental in the development of a culturally and politically aware populace beyond the jurisdiction of formal educational institutions. This is in contrast to many current community education centres which offer similar facilities but are often run *for* the community rather than *by* them and rely on local authorities for subsidy. The system of applying to a variety of bodies for funding ensures certain standards but places a variety of obligations on the centres which may be counter-productive or restrictive. Such restrictions have been placed on theatre programmes that have been specifically designed to address community needs.

Theatre-in-education, often referred to as TIE, began in the UK in the 1960s. The history of TIE has been influenced by the political and economic context of each decade. Prior to the Education Reform Act of 1988, local education authorities were major funders. During the late 1970s and early 1980s there was little accountability and considerable freedom in designing programmes of work. A company was able to work for several days, or even weeks, with one class of students. With the implementation of Local Management of Schools as part of the 1988 Education Reform Act and its resulting restrictions, companies began to search for alternative sources of funding, often resorting to short-term projects designed to address a single issue quickly.

# Emerging pressures

Michele Erma Doyle (cited in Richardson and Wolfe, 2001), referring to youth and community workers, remarked on the pressure of external expectations on the field of informal education. She noted that both adult education and youth work are under increasing pressure to focus on formal accreditation of learning. She recognised that community workers needed to be aware of the underlying educational theory to their work and lamented the 'how-to' nature of the current literature which detracted from their professionalism. This, she suggested, was a direct result of the impact of the National Curriculum and its concentration on what is learned and how it is learned:

*This 'product' approach to learning [is] in contrast to the traditional focus of informal education which ... has focused on relationships and thus on the process by which learning happens, rather than on what is learnt.*

(p6)

These observations are reminiscent of the philosophy of Paulo Freire (1970) and his reference to formal education as 'the banking concept of education'; a storing process where students build up deposits of knowledge supplied by the teacher. The 'banking concept' can be perceived as a restriction on the educator who is required to teach a highly prescribed curriculum. Freire called for educators to abandon the deposit system of education and to replace it with 'the posing of the problems of human beings in their relations with the world'. This approach is seen, at least in part, in a number of community initiatives. The national strategy plan for neighbourhood renewal launched in 2001 as a government initiative recognises that:

*neighbourhood renewal starts from a proper understanding of the needs of communities, and that the most effective interventions are often those where communities are actively involved in their design and development. This includes community of interest, such as people who are black or from minority groups, as well as geographically defined communities.*

(White, 2002, p1)

Theoretically at least, the sense of grassroots participation in community planning and development is seen as a positive and necessary step. Lawton (2001) referred to 'The Third Way', a political philosophy adopted by the Labour government at the turn of this century which recognised the impossibility of sustaining the welfare state as chief provider, and sought to combine the complexities of capitalist globalisation and free markets with a social obligation on behalf of the state to support individuals and communities to help themselves:

*The basic ideas entailed in the Third Way focus is on empowering individuals, families and communities to lift themselves out of poverty, unemployment and social exclusion by a combination of individual responsibility, education, social support and welfare to work initiatives.*

(p95)

This recognises that, if people are to play an active part in local democracy, new skills and attitudes need to be developed. Government initiatives such as the citizenship curriculum in schools brings a new focus on community and active citizenship into the twenty-first century. A report of a Liverpool City Council initiative on a neighbourhood renewal skills and knowledge programme, for example, offered the following insight:

*Most people associate learning with formal education, in schools, universities or a training course. But neighbourhood renewal is a new challenge, and everyone involved will need to develop new skills. For some this may involve individual training. But it also means learning from experience, learning jointly with other partners, and talking to people facing similar challenges.*

(White, 2002, p23)

This advocates discussion, involvement and personal and group commitment. While obviously challenging, the approach to learning is empowering and life-enhancing on both an individual and community level. Freire (1970) referred to *problem-posing education* and contended that people, when challenged with problems that relate in a direct way to their own or their community's well-being, will feel obliged to respond to the challenge. By presenting challenges as personal and yet universal, the individual is encouraged to develop a sense of connection and personal involvement with the community. If this connection becomes proactive, it can in turn lead to the decentralisation of power and closer, interactive communities of responsible citizens who are involved and confident enough to make a difference. This approach has been developed in the work of Brazilian theatre practitioner Augusto Boal (1998, 1999). Boal's Marxist interventionist theories, influenced by Freire, were used frequently by TIE practitioners during the latter part of the twentieth century. One example is the work of Kaos Theatre Company, whose 1993 TIE programme was designed to address issues central to a growing understanding of AIDS and was constructed to encourage young people to recognise the epidemic and to change their views before they entered adulthood. Phil Morle (1993), artistic director of the project, worked alongside the company to create a series of workshops that began with an exploration of Boal's 'Image Theatre'.

---

### *Pause for thought* | proactivity

It is interesting to note that, for very different reasons, many western governments in pursuit of Lawton's 'The Third Way' should mirror a number of the pedagogical recommendations of a revolutionary such as Freire. Consider for a moment what the advantages and disadvantages of proactive communities might be for:

- a community?
- a government?

---

# What is a community?

The concept of community is multifaceted and fluid. The term is often used to describe:

- physical proximity, as in neighbourhood;
- civic identity, as in a populace;
- collective identity, as in unity, co-operation and shared interest.

A sense of locality may well be fundamental to an individual's sense of identity, but this can be negative as easily as it can be positive. A sense of belonging, being recognised and accepted is psychologically healthy, but many people at some point in their lives feel marginalised or stifled by a community that is based purely on proximity. However, locality can provide a network of support. In addition to locality, there is a broader sense of community which operates on a less personal level. This includes such things as a wider regional or national identity or a shared language with loose classifications such as the 'black', 'gay', or 'asylum seeker' community. In normal, unstressed situations these broad classifications tend to remain on a level of recognition rather than meaningful engagement. Nicholson (2005) pointed out that these broader identities can obscure enormous differences and frequently ignore multiple identities. Each individual belongs to a number of communities some of which satisfy a transitory need, others which are more lasting. Sometimes people from different locations and from different backgrounds find a common cause which initiates a sense of community, if only for a short time.

An increasing form of community identification, described by Nicholson as *the paradigm shift from communities of locality to communities of identity*, involves a sense of community dictated less by geography and more by interest and common experience, beliefs or values. This concept is made easier by effective communication services. To some extent this is an 'imagined' community of shared identity with no material existence.

> ### *Pause for thought* | overlapping community
>
> The concept of community is not singular. Consider for a moment how many 'communities' you belong to and write them down. How far do they overlap? If you have left a community, how much of it have you absorbed and taken with you? Have you ever felt on the margins of a community? Have you ever felt restricted by a community you belonged to? Does community imply exclusiveness? Compare your ideas of community with someone else's.

# Community intervention

Asking communities to become more active and to take more responsibility socially, educationally and politically is a form of intervention. Its success depends on how far individuals are able to identify with community issues, which will depend to some extent on how clearly they understand them and on how much influence they believe they can have. People's apparent indifference to global, national and local issues often stems from a sense of powerlessness and a lack of confidence that they can have any influence whatsoever. Offering practical information or education about how society functions and how individuals and communities can access legal, financial and social services is helpful, but there are more empowering ways of educating people which enhance confidence, offer insight and actually build a sense of community identity.

Neelands (2004) has developed the notion of social justice within the 'people's theatre', which he sees as participatory and active, belonging to all people within a community. Instead of defining form or genre, he refers to a living partnership between and within theatres, linking cultures together. He believes that stories are the building blocks of theatre and asserts that all communities share the common belief in the power of stories to help their youth make sense of the world. Neelands's vision included artistic transformations at the heart of theatre, with actors transformed through roles and the spaces they inhabit transformed into imaginary worlds. Even time is transformed and made symbolic through theatrical events, an aspect expanded by Schechner (2003). As well as being a stimulus for artistic action, Neelands has a vision of the 'people's theatre' within the social dimension, stating that this goes:

*beyond the recognition of cultural differences in our artistic work to include the opportunity for our social and economic differences to be publicly and socially negotiated in the interests of social justice.*

(p33)

Any kind of interventionist strategy can potentially damage as well as liberate. Practitioners are accountable for the effect that their work has on the communities they service as these examples demonstrate.

## Research box

### monitoring the challenge

To what extent should participants be 'projected into' or 'protected from' controversial material and methodologies? The balance between challenge and support is the key to this issue. An exposition of the HIV/AIDS workshops developed through the perspective of the director Phil Morle (1993) provides a good example. In an 'anti-intellectual' approach to learning, the Kaos Theatre Company used theatre games, contact improvisation and sculpting and physical manipulation of participants. Morle encouraged participants to use their hands and eyes instinctively, without taking time to plan and think ahead. Although Boal's theories were evident in this process, the deliberate avoidance of intellectual engagement with the form does not appear to have adhered to his practice in all respects:

*If individuals think in their heads first and then attempt to translate this into physical imagery, the result is compromised by limitations of translation, causing a constraint of the potential image and ultimately the debate.*

(Morle, 1993, p3)

Trusting in the language of imagery was central to the process in order to allow unconscious feelings to surface. The validity of such devices could be questioned since they do not offer protection to participants and encourage potentially embarrassing unguarded responses. Tensions could arise between the company delivering the workshop and the group leader entrusted with care of the group.

There are many examples of interventionist theatre programmes using Boal's Forum Theatre to address issues allied to the citizenship agenda (Dwyer, 2004). One such programme was the Brisbane Dracon project (O'Toole and Burton, 2005), which focused on the role of acting in helping young people towards a cognitive understanding of the nature, causes and dynamics of conflict and bullying. Students were given the skills to take control of their own conflicts and conflict agenda, with an assumption that educational drama techniques have *considerable potential to motivate and assist students to understand the causes of conflict.*

Community drama programmes claim to have had a positive impact in the area of social inclusion and social regeneration. Increasingly, such programmes have been expected to produce evidence of social outcomes as well as artistic realisation, taking theatre into new socio-cultural territory. Typically a company might be expected to produce statistical evidence about the participants and audiences serviced. London Bubble Theatre Company has placed these issues at the centre of its community programmes with the belief that the arts have the capacity to break down barriers of class, culture, age and gender. *The making of George* (Owen, 2004) was a collaborative project which sought to meet the objectives of the Southwark Community Cohesion Pathfinder Programme, a regeneration initiative. There was a meeting of social aims between funders and artists, but a tension emerged between a non-arts funding source and an arts programme. This community play could not rely simply on the benefits of bringing together people aged 15–75 from the area in a vibrant and innovative arts event. It also needed to produce evidence of social outcomes.

The community play is a medium for communities to take ownership of their own regeneration and is also an interventionist theatre form. The term defines a collection of voluntary, non-professional actors working together to create a performance, usually based on a local issue or story. It clearly falls under the mantle of educational theatre within the community and allows groups who inhabit the same cultural context to share their stories and learn to understand each other's problems, breaking down the barriers between groups and opening a dialogue with excluded groups in society. Van Erven (2001) wrote of a series of community plays throughout the world and suggested that the artistic processes involved in community theatre evolve under particular socio-cultural conditions. Whilst scripts are often used in community theatre, there is an emphasis on oral stories and personal recollection. Spare Tyre Theatre Company, a community group formed to develop performance with people aged 65 to over 80 years old, offers an example of the function of the community play in social inclusion, empowering and valuing the experiences of a social group who might otherwise feel socially excluded (Irving, 2003).

The status of the community play and street arts when set against mainstream theatre belies its significance in the lives of individuals. Gardner (2003) commented that street arts events are virtually ignored. Yet the Streets of Brighton Festival draws in an audience of more than 100,000 people. In France, the Cinescenie at Puy de Fou is performed on the largest outdoor stage in the world, with 1,000 actors aged from 5 upwards, a team of 300 staff and 100 animals in each show. Almost 7 million spectators have seen the event since its inception in 1978. The pastoral setting is combined with cutting-edge technology to exciting effect, with surround-sound, lasers, pyrotechnics, water screens and projections. Despite its scale, reporting of such an event is minimal beyond the region in which it is performed. Kershaw (1999, 2003) advocated greater radicalism in street performance, wanting to move away from spectacle and towards dialogue which might result in greater critical attention.

# Setting up a community project

'Education in the community' offers an exciting opportunity to make a difference to the lives of others, especially when using vibrant interactive methodologies such as drama and theatre. It also places a number of practical and professional demands on those charged with establishing such projects. Effective protocols are required to ensure that etiquette, ethical concerns and equal opportunities are in place that will provide respect for participants. When education students work in the community, additional issues affect the project such as health and safety, assessment and support. The complexities involved in setting up an educational community project are outlined below.

If a facilitator undertakes a project with an established group, he or she suspends the relationship between the group and their usual leader. Initiating a positive relationship between the 'normal' group leader and the facilitator of the project is vitally important.

If a facilitator hopes to establish a freestanding community group, he or she must decide whether or not to approach an umbrella organisation in order to recruit volunteers. Gaining access to a target group within a church or prison, for example, could be achieved through access to regular meetings, enhanced through an advertising campaign. Both the emerging group and the facilitator in this situation have the security of working within clearly established rules and codes of practice. The facilitator will be required to observe the policies and procedures of the host organisation and will have the responsibility of ensuring that participants in the project do the same. A positive aspect of this situation is that individual rights and responsibilities are assured, with behaviour contracts in place and minority interests preserved. Individual needs are addressed through existing legislation and the whole group, including the facilitator, is protected by the organisation's public liability insurance, health and safety legislation and risk assessments.

It is possible, however, that the umbrella organisation may inhibit the behaviour of the participants and promote an atmosphere that the facilitator finds inappropriate. For example, there may be codes relating to appearance and use of language that meet the needs of the organisation in its day-to-day operation but prevent the facilitator from achieving the atmosphere required for learning outcomes to be realised. If interventionist drama theories are to be employed in the liberation of individuals from aspects of their lives that cause oppression, it is inappropriate to work within oppressive regimes. Yet if the organisation is sponsoring the work, its aims and values cannot be ignored even when they contradict those of the facilitator.

Given these negative possibilities, the facilitator may elect to establish a 'freestanding' community group, perhaps to celebrate a single event such as a community festival or national celebration. Arts events in this category could include a community play, torch-lit procession, street party, exhibition or entertainment for a village fete. Such events would be more likely to emerge from within a locational or geographical community group than an interest group. If the facilitator is an insider, then local loyalties, friendships and shared understanding will provide the pressure and motivation for the formation of the group. A disadvantage of the local leadership arrangement is that the group may fall victim to historical rivalries and disputes and may find it hard to attract funding.

Further observations, following logically from comments above about the establishment of a freestanding community group, relate to the increased risk accepted by the facilitator. Without the cushion of respectability and legislative support offered by an institutional framework, the lone facilitator may lack even basic facilities such as meeting or rehearsal space.

Having identified a community group, the facilitator must produce a detailed project outline. This might include:

- targets;
- earning outcomes;
- identified target-group needs;
- timelines;
- budget;
- outcomes;
- legislative issues;
- research;
- risk management;
- workshop plans and content;
- resource needs;
- partners' interests;
- review processes.

A professional contract is needed in order to clarify roles, responsibilities and liability. It is essential that all partners are aware of the function, scope and expected outcome of the community project and that an appropriate balance is struck with participants between ownership and accountability.

## Summary and conclusions

There is a rich history of education within communities in non-formal settings. This goes beyond the accumulation of facts and information and deals with ideas, aspiration and personal and community identity. While it is vulnerable to outside manipulation, it is also responsive to positive intervention.

Intervention can be political, social or educational. Communities may be empowered to accept or reject intervention and can develop their own strategies for change from within. Theatre and drama structures are ideal for active intervention as they offer physical examples which can be viewed, deconstructed and re-negotiated. They also allow effective and cognitive responses to occur simultaneously, encouraging rounded engagement. Intervention is always value-laden and so any attempt to work within communities using active learning methods demands a level of self-awareness on the part of the facilitator in order to avoid imposing attitudes and assumptions.

It has been suggested that communities work most effectively when they form self-supporting units and also that theatre can be a powerful medium for initiating responses. Since theatre programmes can sometimes seem transitory and imposed, and also risk unearthing sensitive issues for vulnerable members of society, there is perhaps greater benefit in using sustained, active drama methodology to empower communities to solve problems. A well-prepared drama project in which a single facilitator moves into the community and works within it is an effective vehicle for building a confident, proactive community.

## References and further reading

Allen, G and Martin, I (1992) Histories of community education: a feminist critique, in *Education and community*. New York: Cassell.

Boal, A (1998) *Theatre of the oppressed*. London: Routledge.

Boal, A (1999) *The rainbow of desire*. London: Routledge.

Dwyer, P (2004) Making bodies talk in Forum Theatre. *Research in Drama in Education*, 9: 9–23.

Freire, P (1970) *Pedagogy of the oppressed*. London: Penguin.

Gardner, L (2003) Out of the ashes. *Street Arts: A User's Guide*, 1: 8–10.

Irving, E (2003) Old age ain't no place for sissies. *Mail Out: National Magazine for Developing Participation in the Arts*, 3: 9.

Kershaw, B (1999) *The politics of performance*. London: Routledge.

Kershaw, B (2003) Seeing through the spectacle. *Street Arts: A User's Guide*, 1: 10–13.

Lawton, D (2001) *Education for citizenship*. London: Continuum.

MacColl (1973) Grass roots of theatre workshop. *Theatre Quarterly*, 9: 58–68.

Morle, P (1993) Art can save lives: drama and AIDS. *Journal of National Drama*,12(1): 2–4.

Neelands, J (2004) The opening address to the 5th World Congress of IDEA. *Drama Journal*, 12(1): 31–8.

Nicholson, H (2005) *Applied drama*. Hampshire: Palgrave Macmillan.

O'Toole, J and Burton, B (2005) Education acting against conflict and bullying: the Brisbane Dracon Project 1996–2004. *Research in Drama Education*, 10(3): 269–84.

Owen, L (2004) The Making of George. *Drama Journal: One Forum, Many Voices*, 12(1): 5–7.

Richardson, LD and Wolfe, M (2001) *Principles and practice of informal education*. London: RoutledgeFalmer.

Rose, J (2002) *The intellectual life of the British working classes*. New Haven, CT: Yale University Press.

Schechner, R (2003) *Performance theory*. London: Routledge.

Van Erven, E (2001) *Community theatre: global perspectives*. London: Routledge.

White, L (2002) *Neighbourhood renewal, case studies and conversations*. London: NIACE.

Witham, B (2003) *The Federal Theatre Project: a case study*. Cambridge: Cambridge University Press.

# Chapter 4

## Schools and classrooms

## Denis Hayes

### Introduction

When most people think of schools and classrooms they have a mental image of places where pupils sit around tables in light and airy spaces with teachers supervising proceedings, and one or more assistants helping out with specific learning needs. In the mind's eye, schools are orderly, well-equipped and designed. The curriculum is planned. Older pupils might be taking tests and grappling with the question papers; knitted brows and thoughtful looks, pens clicking across the page, eyes glancing anxiously at the clock. Younger children might be working, playing, dancing, singing and chattering excitedly. Computers and printers hum and emit their odour of technology. Teachers might be marking books, discussing pupil progress, drinking coffee, moaning about the government and swapping ideas. Indeed, most schools are happy, industrious places and an integral part of the community. But it has not always been this way. This chapter briefly chronicles the long and turbulent history of schools and classrooms within the UK, including the role of the church, the growth of state involvement, and the influences that have helped to shape educational provision today. The lessons of history are important. If they are ignored, we will learn very little and simply repeat the same mistakes over and over again.

## The growth of formal education

The formal education of pupils in Britain has its roots deep in history and is inextricably linked to the growth and mission of the Christian church. For a long time national education was unknown. There were no colleges, universities or centres for academic learning available for the general public, or 'the masses' as they were described. There were no schools and no paid teachers of the kind we are familiar with today. For the small number of children from wealthy backgrounds who had access to schooling, some received an education rooted in literature and Latin. This was known as 'grammar' education, from which the term 'grammar school' would emerge. Over time, the grammar schools insisted that pupils were literate at the point of entry, so elementary education in which reading and writing were key components became essential for the privileged few.

Unfortunately, political turbulence during the sixteenth and seventeenth centuries meant that systematic education almost ceased to exist for the vast majority of the population. Most people were too concerned with eking out a living to worry about such niceties as being able to read and write, even if they could afford the time to master the skills. As the industrial revolution swept through the country in the eighteenth century, the plight of children working in factories and mines became a serious political and social issue. Pioneers such as Robert

Raikes, who founded the Sunday School movement in 1780, Charles Gordon, who built 'ragged schools' to educate and provide sustenance for the destitute, and Charles of Bala, in Wales, were determined to provide an education for these child labourers. The Quaker Joseph Lancaster and, a little later, the priest Andrew Bell promoted a system of elementary schooling in which more experienced and capable pupils ('monitors') would help to teach the younger and less able scholars. This 'monitorial' system required a very small number of teachers, thus reducing the cost of schooling considerably, and became the means of providing mass education for working class children.

The first publicly funded schools that we would recognise as such were only established as recently as the mid-nineteenth century to give a basic education to children from poor families. Throughout this time, control of education gradually switched from the church to the state, though provision was uneven and there was intensive and sometimes acrimonious debate about whether church or state should have the greater influence over the way that education was organised and managed, and the content of the curriculum (Chadwick, 1997). One of the key political figures determined to extend state provision of education in the first half of the nineteenth century was James Kay-Shuttleworth. He not only founded training colleges for teachers but also encouraged newly founded Board Schools (funded from taxation) and voluntary schools to widen the curriculum beyond reading, writing and arithmetic (the so-called three Rs). As the nineteenth century progressed it became increasingly clear that government intervention would be needed if education were to become universally available. However, there was genuine anxiety expressed by many sections of society about the adverse impact on the economy of removing children from the workplace and sending them to school each day. Employers were concerned about labour shortage, and poor parents, often with large families to feed, were worried about the loss of earnings, a situation reflected in impoverished nations today.

A feature of schooling during the mid- to late-nineteenth century was the 'payment by results' system that was introduced in 1861 and persisted until its abolition in1895. With 'payment by results', the government gave a grant to a school based on the assessment of each child's academic ability and their attendance. Teachers felt obliged to introduce rote learning and to drill the pupils to absorb factual knowledge, though the process did not, of course, guarantee understanding. After the abolition of 'payment by results', the curriculum was extended in many schools to include a wider range of subjects and teaching approaches. It is interesting to note the similarity with schools today, where teachers are expected to ensure that pupils meet the necessary 'standards', the same term that was used in the 1800s, as assessed through tests and examinations.

Similar advances in educational provision were being made in other areas of the UK during the nineteenth and early twentieth centuries. Thus, between 1846 and 1848, the Welsh Education Committee and the Cambrian Society were formed, which evolved into national schools in Wales. The 1867 report of the Royal Commission on Education led to the Education Act of 1872 that resulted in improvements in education for every child in Scotland. In the period running up to the setting up of the state of Northern Ireland in 1920, education became one of the areas of tension between Ulster unionism and Irish nationalism. Before partition, the overwhelming majority of Irish schools were under denominational control even though they were financed chiefly from public funds (Harris, 1993).

Meanwhile, in the face of considerable opposition, and as a means of guaranteeing education free of charge for all pupils, W.E. Forster introduced the important 1870 Elementary Education Act in England. At that time, the government's obligation was principally to 'fill the gaps' where voluntary provision did not exist. Reforms were slow in being implemented and even at the commencement of the twentieth century schooling was inconsistent and attendance spasmodic. Paradoxically, however, there were more 3- and 4-year-old children attending school at the end of the 1800s than there were almost one hundred years later. With singing, handwork, games and dancing, the infant curriculum at the turn of the new century was surprisingly innovative.

---

***Pause for thought*** | gender issues in schooling

Miller and Davey (2005) have argued that too little emphasis was placed on the role of women and girls in nineteenth century society. They have claimed that debates about citizenship and liberal democracies which underpinned much theory about schools were too patriarchal. To what extent is the modern day secondary school operated from what may be broadly described as a male perspective? Is the situation different in primary schools where the vast majority of staff are female? What, if any, are the implications for pupils and their learning?

---

Secondary and further education also has its roots in the mid-1800s. Increasing concern that Britain's lack of competitiveness in the world was widely perceived as a skills shortage, with the result that there was increasing emphasis placed on vocational education and training. At the same time, the much-debated Education Act of 1902 ushered in three key changes which were that:

- education came under county council control;
- money from local rates was made available to voluntary schools;
- councils were empowered to fund secondary education.

These changes were revolutionary for two main reasons. Public funds were made available for education for the first time and secondary education was formally established. Indeed, the year 1902 can rightly be described as the birthday of secondary education. Important, too, was the fact that voluntary schooling that had dominated the nineteenth century was struggling to cope with the increasing demands for education. Without state financial intervention the school system would have collapsed.

In 1918 the school leaving age was raised to 14 years. A few years later the influential Hadow Report published in 1926 gave official sanction to the principle that the elementary phase of education in England should formally conclude for all children at age 11 (to be known as the 'primary' phase) followed by separate provision of secondary schooling. There were many important Education Acts over the following years, most notably the highly influential Butler Act of 1944 which introduced the following statutory requirements that have, with minor changes, remained in force to the present day:

- the appointment of a Minister for Education in England and Wales;
- local authority funding for secondary as well as primary schools;
- raising the school leaving age in stages from 14 years to 15 years to 16 years;
- the requirement for schools to hold an act of worship;
- free medical (including dental) care for all pupils;
- education provision for pupils with special learning needs;
- payment for all teachers according to a nationally agreed scale;
- the prevention of schools from debarring or dismissing a female teacher when she gets married.

**Pause for thought** | contrasting 'then' and 'now'

Look again at the summary of reforms drawn from the Education Act of 1944. Consider the similarities and differences between the conditions for teachers in 1944 and today. Are there any surprises? Note that female teachers did not receive equal pay until 1955 and, until the 1970s, teachers' pay was similar to that received by manual workers. Was the post-war period the 'golden age' that it is sometimes described as?

In the years between 1944 and the early 1980s there was a series of curriculum developments, including a major extension of so-called 'sandwich' courses (periods of study in the middle of regular employment), and the establishment of a Schools Council. A major school rebuilding programme was undertaken and the comprehensive (all-ability, non-selective) secondary schools made their appearance. A limited number of more academic pupils was able to gain free places in a grammar school if they passed an examination at the age of 11 years (the so-called 'eleven-plus'). This policy led to divisions of pupils across the country and was the subject of intense political debate that has continued to the present time. Pupils who did not sit or failed the examination could only gain access to a secondary modern school, and later on, to the newly-founded technical schools for children of average ability who were considered more suited to practical rather than academic work. In 1965, an additional external examination (the Certificate of Secondary Education or CSE) was introduced for pupils in the middle ability range for whom the traditional Ordinary level examination (O level, introduced in 1953) was too demanding. After fierce debate throughout the 1970s and 1980s, the O level and CSE examinations were combined in 1986 to create a new national secondary examination known as the General Certificate of Secondary Education (GCSE) in England (equivalent to the TGAU or Tystysgrif Gyffredin Addysg Uwchradd in Wales and the Standard Grade in Scotland). The GCSE is usually taken by secondary school pupils at age 16, though more able children may sit the examination earlier.

# Introduction of a National Curriculum

Only a generation ago, primary teachers had great liberty in making decisions about what to teach and how to teach it. Secondary teachers were governed more strictly by syllabuses and national examinations but were not normally under pressure to adopt specific teaching approaches. In fact, the freedom that teachers enjoyed to organise learning in a way that suited classroom circumstances was considered to be an essential element of their professional autonomy (Silcock, 2002; Hurst and Reding, 2006).

By the mid-1970s there had been very few studies about the aims of education from the teacher perspective (see Ashton et al., 1975). There was also a dearth of research about 'school effectiveness', which in more recent times has been separated from the concept of 'school improvement' (Kelly, 2003; MacGilchrist and Buttress, 2004; Harris and Bennett, 2005). The famous (some would say, infamous) Ruskin College speech by the then Prime Minister, James Callaghan, in 1976 was yet to unleash what was grandly titled 'The Great Debate' about the future of education. There was an increasing political awareness, however, about the large amount of public money that was being spent on education and the need for rigorous accountability. The mood of the education world was conducive to a close scrutiny of the purpose of education and a move towards radical change.

One of the most significant events that resulted from this wide-ranging review of educational provision was the 1988 Education Reform Act (ERA) from which emerged a National Curriculum (NC) that would operate in all state-maintained schools and many private ones in England, Wales and Northern Ireland (through the Department of Education in Northern Ireland or DENI). The NC was designed to provide a minimum educational entitlement for pupils of compulsory school age, to ensure that the curriculum of each school was balanced and broadly based, and to promote the spiritual, moral, cultural, mental and physical opportunities, responsibilities and experiences of adult life. Prior to 1988, schools had been able to make their own decisions about curriculum provision at a local rather than a national level but the NC curtailed this freedom. Educational provision was divided into four key stages:

- Key Stage 1 (KS1) for pupils aged 5 to 7 years;
- Key Stage 2 (KS2) for pupils aged 7 to 11 years;
- Key Stage 3 (KS3) for pupils aged 11 to 14 years;
- Key Stage 4 (KS4) for pupils aged 14 to 16 years.

Since its introduction in 1989 there has been a number of versions of the NC. Additionally, there has been considerable emphasis placed on the teaching of English (focus on literacy) and mathematics (focus on numeracy). In 1999, a Foundation Stage curriculum was published for children aged 4 and 5 in Nursery and Reception classes. After the turn of the new century, the lower end of secondary education (KS3) became the focus of attention, as it was perceived that standards of attainment levelled out once pupils left primary school. Consequently, a national strategy was introduced to raise standards of teaching and learning across the curriculum for all 11- to 14-year-olds.

Another significant dimension of the NC was the introduction of pupil assessments by means of national tests at the end of each key stage. KS1 pupils take the 'end of key stage' tests at age 7, KS2 pupils at age 11, and KS3 pupils at age 14. There are other optional tests available to primary pupils at the end of other school years but, unlike the end of key stage tests, the results of the optional tests are not published. KS4 is assessed by levels of pupil achievement at GCSE. Having completed GCSEs, pupils have a choice of whether to continue with further education at school or college or to seek a job, though the government tries to encourage students to remain in full-time education after the age of 16.

# Political intervention

One of the particular characteristics of the English education system in recent years has been what is seen by some educationalists as an over-simplification of complex educational issues in political debate (e.g. Carr and Hartnett, 1996; Richards, 2001; Alexander, 2004). The UK government has opened national policy decisions to critical scrutiny through extensive forms of consultation, though there is widespread scepticism about the usefulness of the process. Education priorities have moved a considerable way from the time of the Taylor Report in the mid-1970s when a key characteristic of teachers' professionalism was deemed to be their freedom to design and teach unhindered by external pressures (Taylor et al., 1974). Astonishingly, at the time, surveys of teachers concluded that they believed that politicians were the least influential people in school life. Today, the situation is almost the exact opposite, as political priorities are imposed, promoted, scrutinised and complied with.

The government's insistence that schools and teacher training institutions follow its educational agenda (DfES/TTA, 2002) has resulted in a situation where failure to comply with its demands invites sanctions for the schools and colleges concerned. Every institution, from those providing childcare for the under-fives to the largest higher education establishment, has its education provision closely monitored by the Office for Standards in Education (OFSTED). A poor inspection outcome results in the worst cases in school or college closure. Success in reaching the required targets for examination success, on the other hand, results in increased resources, public accolades and the possibility of salary enhancements for staff. A system has gradually emerged in which the government, rather than the school staff, has most influence over the curriculum to be taught, the teaching methods to be employed and the assessment criteria to measure success.

---

### Research box

### curriculum provision in state-controlled education

Halpin et al. (2004) have researched educational standards in schools designated within Education Action Zones (EAZ) to which additional government resources have been allocated together with finance from private investment and links with the voluntary sector. EAZs were charged with raising educational standards and combating social exclusion and economic disadvantage by introducing innovative approaches to education, including new forms of curriculum provision. The research team found that innovations ranged from additional use of learning support assistants and volunteer reading mentors, to one-to-one counselling, activities to combat truancy and variations in staff deployment. Some schools innovated by increasing the resources spent on support for the basic skills; other schools did precisely the opposite, including *a few teachers who explicitly justified their involvement in these schemes in terms that stressed the need to ameliorate what they saw as shortcomings in the prescribed curriculum*. The research illustrated the difficulties of developing an innovative, responsive and inclusive curriculum within a highly regulated state system with high stakes testing.

---

The government's desire to exercise tight control, not only over *what* is taught but *how* it is taught, has created a situation in which teacher professionalism is being transformed from one of autonomy to one of compliance (Hayes, 2001). It is difficult for schools today to avoid being sucked into an attitude of deference that threatens to stifle initiative and restrict professional autonomy by refusing to trust teachers to act in pupils' best interest. Frowe (2005) reasoned that while the amount of money invested in education necessitates accountability and monitoring of practice, *the over-regulation of the profession is corrosive of many of its most valuable elements*. The attempt to telescope all teaching and learning situations into a single model flies in the face of reason. Circumstances from school to school and class to class are so diverse that it is difficult to justify a policy that is so utilitarian that it takes little account of the immediate choices and decisions that all teachers have to make every working day. As Wrigley (2003) noted: *Improvement by command from above results in the problematic implementation of macro initiatives by teachers who feel unable to question or even fine-tune them*.

# Education provision today

There are four types of mainstream school operating within the education system in England and Wales today.

- *Community schools* (formerly known as county schools). The vast majority of schools fall into this category. The local authority (LA) employs staff, owns the school land and buildings, and determines the arrangements for admitting pupils.

- *Foundation schools* (formerly grant-aided schools). The governing body employs staff and has primary responsibility for admissions. The school land and buildings are owned by the governing body or a charitable foundation.
- *Voluntary aided schools*. Most of these schools are church schools. In similar fashion to foundation schools, the governing body employs staff and has responsibility for admissions. The school land and buildings are owned by a charitable foundation.
- *Voluntary controlled schools*. These schools are almost always church schools and the same conditions apply as pertain in aided schools, except for the important provisos that the LA employs the staff and has responsibility for admissions.

Statutory schooling lasts for 11 years between the ages of 5 and 16. Children are legally required to start attending school at the start of the term after their fifth birthday, on 31 August, 31 December or 31 March, though in practice children often start earlier than this owing to the widespread provision of nursery education. Pupils are required to stay in school until the last Friday in June of the school year in which they reach the age of 16. During this time children must receive an appropriate full-time education suited to their age, ability, aptitude and special educational needs. Most pupils transfer from primary to secondary school at the age of 11. Students who remain in education after the age of 16 are described as being in the post-compulsory stage of education.

The late twentieth and early twenty-first centuries have seen great changes take place in the way that education is organised and monitored. The KS2 primary curriculum has become more subject-focused with the introduction of lessons of fixed duration located within a predetermined timetable. Secondary education has also undergone a transformation, including the founding of specialist and 'beacon' schools (those with proven academic excellence – primary schools are also able to claim 'beacon' status) and of more private involvement in the state sector.

The KS3 curriculum now consists of English, mathematics, design and technology, ICT, history, geography, modern foreign language, art and design, music, PE and citizenship. Other areas of the curriculum that must be taught are religious education (RE), sex and relationships, and careers' education (from Year 9). All schools must teach RE according to the locally agreed syllabus, unless they are designated as voluntary-aided or faith schools. However, a detailed critique of KS3 in the 14–19 White Paper (DfES, 2005) noted that the design of the curriculum had encountered significant problems. Some programmes of study were considered incoherent and some material was repeated in different subjects. The heavily prescribed curriculum left schools with little space to assist struggling pupils or to extend gifted students. Consequently, science, history, geography and design and technology are now receiving extra attention, with an emphasis on real-life issues. The KS3 strategy is properly referred to as the Secondary National Strategy as some of its work extends to KS4.

A vocational GCSE was introduced in 2000 to encourage students to take a work-related route at school and includes courses such as engineering, applied business, and leisure and tourism. From September 2004, however, the word 'vocational' was dropped to show that the vocational side of learning was equivalent in status to the traditional academic side. Some private schools have encouraged their pupils to progress straight to A level (disregarding GCSE) or to take the international baccalaureate diploma.

The appropriateness and relevance of testing and examinations continues to be actively debated among educationalists, in particular the suitability of formal tests for young children and the need for a public (national) examination for all pupils at the age of 16. In the primary sector, there has been a rediscovery of the significance of play in the education of younger children (Broadhead, 2004; Moyles, 2005) and creativity in learning (Fisher and Williams, 2004; Jeffrey and Craft, 2004). A decision about using so-called 'synthetic phonics' (a system based on teaching children letter sounds so that they recognise the different components within a word) as the core strategy in teaching reading to be employed in schools was made by the government early in 2006.

The present education system obliges schools to ensure that pupils and students attain the highest possible scores on national tests and have introduced the concept of 'individualised learning' to provide a bespoke curriculum for pupils. In late 2005, the Department for Education and Skills (DfES) introduced a new system called the 'pupil achievement tracker' (PAT) that allows schools and LAs to import and analyse their own pupil performance data against national performance data. There are four areas of analysis available: school level analysis; pupil level value added; target setting; and question level analysis.

Meanwhile, scrutiny of existing learning provision continues apace. For instance, in 2009 both the *Primary Review* – an independent study led by Robin Alexander – and the *Primary Curriculum Review* – a government-sponsored report led by Jim Rose – reported their findings. The *Primary Review* (PR) indentified the purpose the primary phase of education should serve; the values it should espouse; the curriculum and learning environment it should provide; and the conditions necessary to ensure the highest quality and address the future needs of children and society. The *Primary Curriculum Review* (PCR) advised on how the primary curriculum should change to ensure all children gain a good grounding in reading, writing, speaking, literacy and numeracy; offer schools greater flexibility of choice about content and delivery; allow time for a foreign language; place greater emphasis on personal development; support a smoother transition from play-based learning to formal learning; and encourage creativity. However, whereas the PR commented on the damaging effects of national testing on children and recommended a substantial rethink, the PCR did not take account of assessment issues in its report. The Secondary National Strategy (SNS) for school improvement forms part of the government's major reform programme for transforming secondary education to enable young people to attend and enjoy school, achieve personal and social development and raise educational standards in line with the Every Child Matters agenda. The aim is to create a dynamic and diverse education system built on high expectations and a commitment to the needs of every learner, where schools maintain a focus on their priorities through sharper self-evaluation, simplified data and information systems and a new inspection regime. The key strategic aim of the SNS is to raise standards of achievement for children and young people in all phases and settings. There has also been a move towards the creation of 'federations', a term used to describe different types of collaborative school groups, partnerships and clusters, including mergers and the creation of new schools. Clusters involve groups of schools with a formal agreement to work together to raise standards, promote inclusion, find new ways of approaching teaching and learning and build capacity. These aims are brought about through structure changes in leadership and management, in many instances through making use of the joint governance arrangements.

## Research box

### vocational learning for 14- to 16-year-olds

In their study of the effectiveness of the Increased Flexibility for 14- to 16-year-olds Programme (IFP) to provide vocational learning opportunities at Key Stage 4 for those young people who would benefit from them, Golden et al. (2005) found that around 90 per cent of young people who had been involved in the first cohort of IFP had continued into further education or training post-16. Some 42 per cent of young people said that their participation in vocational learning had influenced their decision about their post-16 education futures. It is clear that motivation for learning was a key factor affecting the young people's view of education and its significance in their lives.

## Summary and conclusions

For the past hundred years or so governments of every persuasion have taken a deep interest in educational provision, not least because of the considerable national expenditure involved. This close attention on the best way to educate pupils reflects the fact that it has invested increasingly large political as well as financial capital in the process, with two broad consequences, one positive, the other less so. The positive consequence has been an improvement in the continuity and coherence of educational provision across England and Wales. The adverse consequence has been constraints on teachers' ability to exercise professional judgement about what is appropriate for their pupils. In particular, there is anxiety among many teachers about the way in which the climate of testing and inspecting has developed at the expense of attending to the social needs of children and young people. School leaders and practitioners at every phase of education constantly grapple with implementing the latest government initiative while ensuring that educational standards are maintained.

In reality, there is a difference between the 'specified' curriculum (the formal programme of work) and the 'operational' curriculum (the classroom practice) found in schools. The hiatus between 'specified' and 'operational' largely depends on the experience and confidence of the teachers concerned, though the support of school leaders (head teachers, heads of departments, curriculum leaders) is crucial for staff that wish to employ more imaginative and creative teaching approaches. Regardless of government edicts or externally imposed requirements, each educator's personal framework of values is of crucial significance in determining the choices and decisions about the curriculum and its implementation. Learning is not only about delivering subject knowledge, it is about the attitudes and behaviours fostered by teachers. Winning hearts and minds has been the challenge and inspiration for every teacher since schooling began and will, hopefully, always remain at the core of education.

## *References*

Alexander, R (2004) Still no pedagogy? Principle, pragmatism and compliance in primary education. *Cambridge Journal of Education*, 34(1): 7–33.

Alexander, R (2009) *The Primary Review*. Cambridge: University of Cambridge/Esmee Fairburn Trust.

Ashton, P, Davies, F and Kneen, P (1975) *Aims into practice in the primary school: a guide for teachers*. London: University of London Press.

Broadhead, P (2004) *Early years play and learning*. London: Routledge.

Carr, W and Hartnett, A (1996) *Education and the struggle for democracy*. Maidenhead: Open University Press.

Chadwick, P (1997) *Shifting alliances: church and state in English education*. London: Cassell.

DfES (2005) *14–19 Education and Skills*. London: Department for Education and Skills.

DfES/TTA (2002) *Qualifying to teach*. London: Teacher Training Agency.

Fisher, R and Williams, M (eds) (2004) *Unlocking creativity: teaching across the curriculum*. London: David Fulton.

Frowe, I (2005) Professional trust. *British Journal of Educational Studies*, 53(1): 34–53.

Golden, S, O'Donnell, L, Benton, T and Rudd, P (2005) *Evaluation of increased flexibility for 14- to 16-year-olds programme: outcomes for the first cohort* (DfES Research Report 668). London: Department for Education and Skills.

Halpin, D, Dickson, M, Power, S, Whitty, G and Gewirtz, S (2004) Curriculum innovation within an evaluative state: issues of risk and regulation. *The Curriculum Journal*, 15(3): 197–206.

Harris, A and Bennett, N (eds) (2005) *School effectiveness and school improvement: alternative perspectives*. London: Continuum.

Harris, M (1993) *The Catholic Church and the foundation of the Northern Irish State*. Cork: Cork University Press.

Hayes, D (2001) Professional status and an emerging culture of conformity amongst teachers in England. *Education 3–13*, 29(1): 43–9.

Hurst, B and Reding, G (2006) *Professionalism in teaching*. Upper Saddle River, NJ: Pearson.

Jeffrey, B and Craft, A (2004) Teaching creatively and teaching for creativity: distinctions and relationships. *Educational Studies*, 30(1): 77–87.

Kelly, T (2003) *Benchmarking for school improvement: a practical guide for comparing and achieving effectiveness*. London: Routledge.

MacGilchrist, B and Buttress, M (2004) *Transforming learning and teaching*. London: Paul Chapman.

Miller, P and Davey, I (2005) Family formation, schooling and the patriarchal state, in McCulloch, G (ed) *The RoutledgeFalmer reader in history of education*. London: RoutledgeFalmer.

Moyles, J (ed) (2005) *The excellence of play*. Maidenhead: Open University Press.

Richards, C (ed) (2001) *Changing English primary education*. Stoke on Trent: Trentham.

Rose, J (2009) *Primary Curriculum Review*. London: HMSO.

Silcock, P (2002) Under construction or facing demolition? Contrasting views on English teacher professionalism from across a professional association. *Teacher Development*, 6(2): 137–55.

Taylor, PH, Reid, WA, Holley, BJ and Exon, G (1974) *Purpose, power and constraint in the primary school curriculum*. Basingstoke: Macmillan Education/Schools Council.

Wrigley, T (2003) Is school effectiveness anti-democratic? *British Journal of Educational Studies*, 51(2): 89–112.

# Chapter 5

## The child, family and society:
## Early Years in context

## Wendy Bignold

### Introduction

Early Years education is considered here in the broadest sense and from birth to age five. This chapter looks at how education, or learning, takes place before formal schooling even begins and it examines the ways in which young children develop a sense of themselves and of those around them and the role that the family, gender and society have in this process. It concludes by considering the role and demands made of Early Years practitioners operating in an increasingly complex world.

## Developing a sense of self

From the moment they are born, young children begin to learn about themselves, the people around them and the world in which they live. While the statutory age for starting school is fixed at five, formal education in nursery or reception classes can begin as young as three or four. A young child's sense of self has a significant impact on his or her relationship with other people and with all subsequent learning (Dowling, 2000). The importance of a strong self-identity or self-image cannot be underestimated. This is recognised in the Early Years curriculum in England:

*Gaining knowledge and understanding of their own culture and community helps children develop a sense of belonging and strong self-image. Each child has a culture defined by their community and more uniquely by their family… A positive self-image and high self-esteem gives children the conveyance and security to make the most of opportunities, to communicate effectively and to explore the world around them.*

(QCA, 2000, p29)

If young children are to explore the world around them, making sense of it and engaging with it, then a secure knowledge of who they are and a sense of their own worth will give them the confidence to do this. There are essentially two elements to self-image, namely:

- self-concept or becoming aware of who you are;
- self-knowledge or recognising your own strengths and weaknesses.

From birth onwards, young children build a picture of themselves based on other people's responses to them and particularly on the responses of significant adults around them (e.g. mother, father, siblings, carer). Babies recognise that they matter when they smile at a face that smiles back. Having one or more stable relationships with an adult provides a sense of continuity for a young child to develop a concept of himself or herself within. The development of self-concept has been written about at length. Bee and Boyd (2004) have identified the two main stages:

- a subjective stage, which takes place during a child's first year when a baby is learning that he or she matters and can make things happen (e.g. can move an object);
- an objective stage, when, as a toddler, a child learns that he or she has a name, is a boy or girl, is big or small, and so on.

As children get older they also become more knowledgeable of what they can and cannot do and how this relates to other children and adults. They begin to recognise what they need help and support with. When they are acknowledged, praised, respected or rejected, this contributes to the regard they have for themselves. The two components of self-image (concept and knowledge) become more complex as children grow older and have a wider range of experiences to draw upon.

# The family

Young children are heavily reliant on adults or older children to help them make sense of their world. Because of a lack of experience and understanding, they are easily influenced by others. For the majority of babies, the immediate environment includes their families. Parents have now been acknowledged as children's first educators (e.g. Barber, 1996; Glauert *et al.*, 2003). Children look to those people who are familiar to them and who they feel an attachment to for information and security. The views of family members, or other key adults, are hugely influential. The different ways in which family members behave towards a child will help that child to develop an understating of who he or she is and how he or she relates to others. This informal education, which takes place within the family or care unit, is called primary socialisation. With primary socialisation, values, morals, prejudices, stereotypes and attitudes are all passed from one generation to the next.

Siblings, particularly older siblings, are hugely influential in primary socialisation. It is well known that a younger sibling will copy an older sibling's behaviour thereby adopting the values and attitudes of older children. A young child learns that not everything he or she does will be approved of and that certain types of behaviour are not acceptable and will have to be modified. It is only as children grow older and start to become independent of their families that they may adopt values and attitudes of their own.

---

### *Pause for thought* | primary socialisation

*...the significance of family relationships for their [children's] well-being and sense of identity is now increasingly being taken into account by researchers and professionals working with children.*

(Gabriel, 2004, p71)

Reflect upon your own childhood. Consider the many things that you were socialised into by your family such as mealtime conventions or religious worship. To what extent has this early education influenced you in your life so far and impacted on your sense of identity? Reflect upon the different roles played by families in educating young children. Are there other institutions which could do these roles more effectively?

The process of gender socialisation begins at birth. The first words which announce a baby's arrival are usually *It's a girl!* or *It's a boy!* This is generally reinforced by family and friends in the toys and clothes which are given as presents. By the age of two, children can usually identify themselves as girls or boys (Dowling, 2005). They have a working, if not yet fully formed, definition of their own gender identities and the gender identities of others. A child of this age may think that anyone with short hair is a boy, for example. It takes a little longer to learn that gender is a constant. That is, that people stay the same even when they change their appearance, when they wear different clothes, or change the length of their hair. By the age of four, most children are developing a stronger gender identity based on their personal name and how they belong to a wider community of family and friends (Linden, 1993). This is the process of socialisation where attitudes and reactions of those around them help children recognise and understand accepted values and behaviour of the group to which they belong. This can be both positive and negative depending on the stereotypes held by key family members and strongly held beliefs may lead to the imposition of restrictions. Comments such as *You're only a girl, so you can't* or *Big boys don't cry* influence behaviour in young children. It is suggested by Gelder (2004) that young children are praised by close adults when they display gender-appropriate behaviour. The importance of the family to primary socialisation is paramount.

# The role of society

Secondary socialisation involves the development of a child's understanding of social expectations, rules, and so on. This occurs outside of the family in the community and wider society through key groups such as:

- the media;
- the government;
- the influence of peers;
- Early Years practitioners.

Values held by certain groups in society and social conventions are learned by young children through the process of secondary socialisation.

## The media

Boys and girls are expected to play in very different ways. This can be seen in the gender-biased adverts for toys on television. Manufacturers now target very young children before they can even speak and so the media impacts on children's play from an early age (Burke, 2005). In socio-dramatic play, pretend activities are often based on domestic scenarios such as putting baby to bed, shopping or cooking. Thematic fantasy play is based on fictional narrative and imaginary events such as acting out the plots of television programmes. Stone (1981) has suggested that dramatic play functions as an 'anticipating socialisation' device. In other words, as a way of children preparing themselves for the roles they may adopt as adults. Stone claimed that in western societies socio-dramatic play involving domestic themes is more characteristic of girls than it is of boys and that boys are more likely than girls to act out thematic fantasies with the result that *the dramatic play of children in our society may function more to prepare little girls for adulthood than little boys.*

*Pause for thought* | the media

The media play an increasingly important part in secondary socialisation as children are bombarded with images, both visual and verbal, through television, radio, books, newspapers and now computers (Marsh, 2005). Watch a set of adverts in between children's TV programmes. What do they promote? Consider what messages they are giving children about:

- personality traits and characteristics of boys and girls;
- gender roles within the family;
- gender professions.

Think how these images might influence young children as they develop a sense of themselves and of others around them. Are stereotypes evident? Do you agree or disagree with the stereotypes they generally promote? Do you think current social trends linked to gender or other influences are damaging the individual or the family?

Young children's early sense of others can be positive or negative and may develop into prejudices or stereotypes. What is important is where these categories are used and to what purpose they are put. Stereotypes are dangerous when they provide a false and misleading picture of what people are actually like. Continuing with the example of gender, the Sex Discrimination Act (1975) introduced legalisation which made it unlawful to discriminate against someone on grounds of gender. It was recognised as a significant issue in society which required government legislation in order to combat it. However, over 30 years on, it remains an issue in society and one which Early Years practitioners need to be aware of so that they may combat Early Years prejudices.

## The government

With a government committed to offering good quality and affordable childcare for every parent who wants it, Early Years provision for the under fives has developed rapidly in the past 10 years (HMT, 2004). In the late 1990s, the government recommended that there should be a fully integrated approach to Early Years education and care or 'educare' which resulted in the publication of the National Childcare Strategy (DfES, 1998). Subsequent public initiatives have seen an increase in multi-agency provision for young children (Whalley, 2001). These have come under various headings including Centres of Excellence and SureStart. All have offered services to children under the age of 5 and to their families. The emphasis is on 'one-stop provision' offering a variety of education, health and welfare services on one site. The government has also committed itself to providing 3500 Children's Centres by 2010 (Ball and Vincent, 2005). Such government initiatives now recognise the key role that parents and families have in young children's early learning. These have been set out in the Early Years Framework (DfES, 2002), which has indicated that:

- parents and families are central to the well-being of young children;
- relationships with other people (both adults and children) are of crucial importance in the lives of young children;
- a relationship with a key person in an Early Years setting other than a home is essential to young children's development;
- babies and young children are social beings and competent learners from birth.

If there is such a comprehensive provision of 'educare' underpinned by the principles from the Early Years Framework, this must surely have a positive influence on young children's socialisation. However, there have remained many barriers to access of provision for different groups of families. This lack of access has reduced the impact of publicly funded Early Years services in secondary socialisation.

## Research box

### issues of access

Government childcare funding is targeted mainly at the most economically disadvantaged areas in the country. The Daycare Trust (2004) investigated the impact of this policy on those families living outside these areas and highlighted childcare gaps for other disadvantaged parents and children. Although cost was a huge barrier to parents accessing childcare for under fives there were other key barriers too. These included:

- inflexibility of provision in terms of 'opening hours';
- information on childcare generally being inaccessible or not coming in minority languages (many parents from ethnically diverse groups were not aware of what provision was available);
- a lack of childcare workers from black and other minority ethnic groups (diverse communities were not reflected in the staff of the settings);
- a monocultural curriculum or the lack of a truly multicultural curriculum over and above tokenism;
- poor transport facilities to get children and families to the settings;
- a lack of trust of childcare workers.
- a monocultural curriculum or the lack of a truly multicultural curriculum over and above tokenism;
- poor transport facilities to get children and families to the settings;
- a lack of trust of childcare workers.

## Peer influence

Relationships with other children outside the family often begin with children of a similar age (e.g. through parent and toddler groups). These relationships can develop through different stages of play, such as:

- parallel play or playing alongside another child independently;
- co-coordinated play or play involving interaction with another child;
- co-operative play or play positively engaging with another child.

As children are developing a sense of self and a recognition of their gender identity, they may start selecting toys to play with that they see same-sex peers playing with. Young children are particularly influenced by older peers around them too and so may be influenced in their choice of toys by those who are already aware of stereotyped gender-specific behaviour. In this way young children may also be influenced by peers in their early attitudes towards individuals and groups as well as to themselves.

*Pause for thought* | peer pressure

Ramsey (1991) has identified four categories which encompass children's social status and behaviour. These are described as follows:

- popular children – have lots of 'friends' who often want to play with them or be near them;
- rejected children – want to play with peers or be near them but are often refused this, have backs turned on them or may even be pushed away;
- neglected children – do not try to interact with others and their company is not sought by peers;
- controversial children – may be popular with peers but are often in trouble for aggressive behaviour or breaking rules.

Consider how the social skills of children in each category might influence their sense of self. While practitioners cannot make friendships happen or make a child popular with peers (Peters, 2003), how might they help a child to develop positive social skills and so a more positive self-identity?

## Early Years practitioners

Early Years practitioners play two key roles in secondary socialisation:

- to pass on their own values and attitudes;
- to provide a curriculum for young children to learn from.

Being in a position to pass their own values and attitudes on to the children they work with, it is crucial that practitioners can identify their own prejudices and stereotypes so that they are aware of them. They need to learn to deal with them in positive ways (Siraj-Blatchford, 2001). This is important to ensure that they do not adversely influence young children or their families. Only once Early Years practitioners have acknowledged their own prejudices can they help young children to overcome theirs through planned and unplanned experiences (Bignold, 2005). Early Years practitioners are also responsible for the curriculum or experiences that children will have while in their setting. The experiences and opportunities available to children and the images they see, or don't see, through resources, influence them in the way in which they view themselves and relate to others. Learning social conventions through planned routines is one example of this. This is a key element to the Early Years provision in other countries such as the Reggio Emilia centres in Italy, acclaimed as one of the best Early Years education systems in the world. In Reggio Emilia centres, mealtimes play a key part in every child's day. Mealtime conventions, such as eating manners, are 'taught' to children through the act of socialising around the dinner table. Children are encouraged to engage in this social experience as soon as they are able to sit up. The practitioners encourage the children to become independent as this has a positive impact on their self-worth and self-esteem. They are 'helped to value their own competencies', whatever these might be (Rinaldi, 2005).

---

**Pause for thought** | recognising your own attitudes and prejudices

We all hold stereotypes and prejudices about groups and individuals whether we would like to admit it or not. This is because we have all been through the process of socialisation. For some of us, our attitudes and prejudices will be very similar to those of our parents or 'carers', for others, they will have changed and been influenced strongly by peers and partners or by experiences as we have grown up. The important thing is to recognise them so that we may combat them and not influence others with them. Consider your own attitudes, stereotypes and prejudices. What are they? Can you recognise where they have come from? How might you combat them or overcome them?

---

# Nature *vs* nurture

A child's identity and sense of self is not just a product of primary and secondary socialisation or nurture. Nature, involving genetically inherent characteristics, also plays its part. While there has been much debate over the differing effects and contributions of nature versus nurture and which is most influential on a child's development, it is now generally accepted that both are influential (Griffiths, 2004). Two key theories of why boys and girls and men and women are different, for example, included:

- biological determination;
- feminisation.

Biological determinism argues that boys and girls are predisposed towards acquiring certain knowledge and skills and to presenting certain behaviours because of inherent genetic biological differences (nature). One complication for Early Years practitioners is that these inherent sex differences create differences in learning between boys and girls. This requires a variety of learning styles to be catered for in order to provide equality of opportunity. Feminisation presents a different perspective on gender difference. It argues that boys and girls are naturally the same but that they are conditioned by parents, peers and society (nurture). Girls are conditioned to be submissive and to be dominated by boys. This conditioning is *institutional in the way that racism is institutional* (Epstein, 1998). This clearly has implications for Early Years practitioners too.

# The impact of socialisation and other influences on young children

In recent times, gender has been identified as an issue for Early Years practitioners in three different arenas (Gaine, 1999):

- in equal opportunities concerns;
- in the interplay between class and ethnicity;
- in levels of achievement.

The 1970s saw concern emerge over equal opportunities in relation to gender and about girls' experiences within male-dominated structures in particular. This supported the idea that girls' choices in relation to activities and the Early Years curriculum were a result of opting for choices less popular with boys and so not dominated by them. It was argued that this prohibited girls from having equal access to provision. In the 1980s there was renewed interest in issues of gender, class and ethnicity and how these related to each other and to children's identities. This began to recognise the complexity of these issues. There was concern that equity and social justice should be facilitated. From the 1990s to the present day there has been an emphasis on gender and achievement. Education has been dominated by analysis of performance data in relation to gender. Boys' underachievement in literacy has been of particular concern and has regularly been picked up by the media as newsworthy. According to Siraj-Blatchford (2001):

*Recently we have heard a good deal in educational debates about (working class) boys' underachievement. The results from the school league-tables suggest some boys do underachieve in basic literacy.*

(p100)

Siraj-Blatchford does warn Early Years practitioners of not making general assumptions about all boys underachieving. These assumptions would be stereotypes in themselves and children should always be treated as individuals. Indeed, as many gender studies have demonstrated, there can be as much variation within any one gender as there is between them.

The three broad areas of concern identified above highlight the general ways in which gender impacts on young children. These are:

- in access to provision;
- in self-identity and self-esteem based on stereotyped expectation behaviour;
- in achievement or underachievement in the Early Years or later in life possibly affected by prejudices held by others.

These are recognised in the Early Years curriculum where practitioners are required to meet the needs of both boys and girls equally. If equal opportunities to access the curriculum are to be provided then different activities or resources may be needed to meet the requirements and interests of both groups. There is a number of strategies which Early Years practitioners can implement in order to reduce negative effects on gender and to combat prejudices. These can be categorised into the broad areas:

- training;
- provision;
- resources;
- employment.

Practitioners should receive appropriate training to enable them to meet the needs of both boys and girls. This includes confronting stereotypes as part of basic childcare training (Penn, 1998). Provision in Early Years settings should be examined to ensure that a variety of learning styles is catered for. Girls are more likely to request help with an activity and to work cooperatively than boys. Girls often have longer concentration spans than boys who tend to become bored more quickly. Practitioners should be trained to cater for these differences in their provision. Boys are more likely to receive negative comments from an adult in a setting than girls and so, not surprisingly then, more adult talk is in communication with boys than with girls. This can give the message that boys are more important than girls even if they are 'seen' as more 'disruptive'. Resources can go some way to encouraging boys or girls to choose activities that they may not normally select. Boys and girls tend to adopt gender-stereotyped behaviour from an early age. Reading and writing activities may be seen by boys as female activities while maths, science, ICT and PE-related activities tend to be rated as 'masculine'. Exciting resources which engage and motivate both gender groups and individuals can have some impact on what children choose to do, as can practitioner expectations. The employment of male role models in the Early Years continues to be a key issue which needs both local and national commitment if progress is to be made. Various estimates put the number of men who work with young children between 1 and 3 per cent:

*Design of courses as well as the gendered nature of the profession (It's women's work) are to blame as well as low pay and lack of career opportunities.*

(Abbott and Pugh, 1998, p157)

Men working directly with young children provide a way of challenging gender-stereotyped roles as well as encouraging greater involvement of fathers in their children's Early Years education. This must be seen as a priority for all providers of Early Years services.

## Summary and conclusions

This chapter has considered how young children develop a sense of self and of others. It has identified the role of the family, peers, the media and the government in primary and secondary socialisation. It has taken gender as a particular illustration of the socialisation process. Issues relating to gender have been analysed in terms of how they impact on young children and how Early Years practitioners might overcome them. There are other significant influences on children's identity, and these include social class, ethnicity (including culture, language and religion), family income, and disability (of the child or family member).

Research has shown that even by the age of about 22 months, there are differences in children's learning as a result of family and other influences. These differences may impact on young children in ways which are based on stereotyped expectation, behaviour and achievement or underachievement in the Early Years or later in life, possibly affected by the prejudices held by others.

With common trends come common solutions. Having a diverse workforce in the Early Years, for example, can provide positive role models for the wide variety of children who see themselves reflected in the staff who care for them. It can also help other children to overcome their own stereotypes as they get to know individuals from backgrounds different from their own. In order to be successful it requires a whole-setting approach underpinned by government support and initiatives. However, it is the family and the Early Years practitioner who will have the greatest impact on a young child's sense of self and subsequently his or her relationship with society.

# References

Abbott, L and Pugh, G (eds) (1998) *Training to work in the Early Years*. Buckingham: Open University Press.

Ball, S and Vincent, C (2005) The childcare champion? *British Educational Research Journal*, 31(5): 557–70.

Barber, M (1996) *The learning game*. London: Victor Gallancz.

Bee, H and Boyd, D (2004) *The developing child*. Boston, MA: Pearson Press.

Bignold, W (2005) Valuing diversity: the role of support workers in the Early Years, in Campbell, A and Fairburn, G (eds) *Working with support in the classroom*. London: Paul Chapman.

Burke, D (2005) Two year olds branded by advertising. *Ecologist*, 35(7): 17.

Daycare Trust (2004) *Talking about childcare*. London: Daycare Trust.

DfES (1998) *National Childcare Strategy.* London: Department for Education and Skills.

DfES (2002) *Birth to Three Matters: An Introduction to the Framework.* London: Department for Education and Skills.

Dowling, M (2005) *Young children's personal, social and emotional development.* London: Paul Chapman.

Epstein, D (ed) (1998) *Failing boys? Issues in gender and achievement.* Buckingham: Open University Press.

Gabriel, N (2004) Being a child today, in Willan, J, Parker-Rees, R and Savage, J (eds) *Early Childhood Studies.* Exeter: Learning Matters.

Gaine, C (1999) *Gender, race and class in schooling: a new introduction.* London: Falmer.

Gelder, U (2004) The importance of equal opportunities in the early years, in Willan, J, Parker-Rees, R and Savage, J (eds) *Early childhood studies.* Exeter: Learning Matters.

Glauert, E, Heal, C and Cook, J (2003) Knowledge and understanding of the world, in Riley, J (ed) *Learning in the early years: a guide to teachers of children 3–7.* London: Paul Chapman.

Griffiths, L (2004) Becoming a person, in Willan, J, Parker-Rees, R and Savage, J (eds) *Early Childhood Studies.* Exeter: Learning Matters.

Her Majesty's Treasury (2004) *Choice for parents, the best start for children: a ten year strategy for children.* London: Her Majesty's Treasury. Available at **www.hm-treasury. gov.uk/prebnd_pbr04_adchildcare.htm** (accessed 23 April 2009).

Linden, J (1993) *Child development from birth to eight.* London: National Children's Bureau.

Marsh, J (2005) Digikids: young children, popular culture and media, in Yelland, N (ed) *Critical issues in early childhood education.* Maidenhead: Open University Press.

Penn, H (1998) Facing some difficulties, in Abbott, L and Pugh, G (eds) *Training to work in the Early Years.* Buckingham: Open University Press.

Peters, S (2003) Children's experiences of friendship during the transition to school. *Early Years,* 23(1): 45–53.

QCA (2000) *Curriculum Guidance for the Foundation Stage.* London: Qualifications and Curriculum Authority.

Ramsey, P (1991) *Making friends in school.* London: Teachers College Press.

Rinaldi, C (2005) *In dialogue with Reggio Emilia.* Abingdon: Routledge.

Sex Discrimination Act 1975. London: HMSO. Available at **www.pfc.org.uk/legal/sda.htm** (accessed 7 April 2006).

Siraj-Blatchford, I (2001) Diversity and learning in the Early Years, in Pugh, G (ed) *Contemporary issues in the Early Years – working collaboratively for children.* London: Paul Chapman.

Stone, J (1981) *International Year of the Child: the continuing challenge.* (Report of the UK Association for the International Year of the Child.) London: International Year of the Child Trust.

Whalley, M (2001) *Involving parents in their children's learning.* London: Paul Chapman.

# Chapter 6

## Education and the integrated Children's Services

### Pat Hughes

**Introduction**

In 1973, a primary school pupil named Maria Colwell was murdered by her stepfather. In the subsequent inquiry it was shown that a significant number of public services, including education, were involved with the family and that many of them were unaware of each other's work. As a direct result, area child protection committees (ACPCs) were set up to ensure that the same thing never happened again. Operational structures were put in place and designed to promote communication between different aspects of service provision. Twenty-seven years later, in 2000, Victoria Climbié, another primary school pupil known to at least 12 agencies, was also murdered by her carers. The resulting inquiry again demonstrated that the services worked in an unco-ordinated way. During the 27-year interim between the deaths of Maria and Victoria, many other children identified formally as being 'at risk' were failed by the very services set up to prevent the occurrence of such neglect and abuse. This chapter explores the implications of the most recent attempt to 'join together' different areas of Children's Services to provide a more effective service for children and young people. It has direct implications for anyone studying education, as it includes educational professionals with a particular interest in children's well-being other than teachers.

## Teachers

Compulsory education has always played an important role in providing formal educational and pastoral services for children and young people. Teachers have often been the only individuals who maintained substantial contact with individual children, apart from their parents and carers. Teachers have always felt this duty of care, as school log books from the nineteenth and early twentieth centuries document (Purkis, 1993). This care might have been demonstrated in different ways from that of today, but it was nevertheless an integral part of the teacher's role.

The role of the teacher has changed considerably since those first years of compulsory schooling. Schools are now charged with becoming learning communities (Pariser, 2000) and teachers encouraged to see themselves as lead learners (Greenhalgh, 2002). The increase in the number of allied educational professionals working in classrooms has meant that many class teachers, particularly in primary schools, are now leaders of small teaching teams within their own classroom. The great majority have had no training in such a role and, if the integration of Children's Services is to be truly effective, teachers as key classroom practitioners will need to have support in working in a teaching team and being able to liaise with other agencies involved with children. Once teachers become confident about their changing role in children's learning it should provide greater opportunities for interaction with individuals and small groups of children and greater opportunities for developing trusting relationships thereby creating a sense of belonging and creating an understanding of responsibility in 'the real world'.

---

**Pause for thought** | the implications of social change

Society is constantly changing and with this comes a need for schools and teachers to respond. It is important not to have a false nostalgia about the past. Schools must prepare children for an unpredictable future, as well as for living in sometimes difficult conditions right now.

Dryden and Vos (2002) in *The learning revolution* have identified the major trends that they think will shape the coming years:

- continued change in family units – both nuclear and extended;
- a greater awareness of how learning develops;
- the growth of the internet and its potential;
- the changing shape of work and leisure;
- a growing underclass often associated with ethnicity and underachievement.

How might each of these trends influence the teacher's role in relation to those they teach?

---

# Allied educational professionals

Today, there are far more people working in schools who are not teachers than who are. Some are employed directly by the school, others are employed by agencies. And there are those who work in schools in a voluntary capacity. A useful definition for allied educational professionals employed by schools is 'professionally trained staff who work usually with teachers to support learning'. These include learning mentors, bilingual support workers, higher-level teaching assistants (HLTAs), teaching assistants (TAs), classroom assistants (CAs), parent support workers, parent mentors, special needs assistants (SNAs), behaviour management workers, library staff, technicians and counsellors (Campbell and Fairbairn, 2005). The nomenclature varies from school to school and from one local authority to another. This certainly makes it more confusing when education students are on placement in school and may wonder about the varying titles, roles and responsibilities of those working with pupils. What joins all these allied educational professionals together is their general remit to break down children's and young people's barriers to learning. They must be seen, recognised and paid as an essential element in improving children's lives. They form some of the most poorly paid workers in the education sector.

# The expanding role of the allied educational professional in school

The image of the Victorian teacher is of someone often standing alone in a school hall, surrounded by large numbers of children sitting on chairs, supported only by pupil teachers and monitors. Today's schools are very different in the support provided for learning. It is this difference which will be a key element in the real success of integrating the Children's Services. The growth of the allied worker, sometimes known as 'the paraprofessional', was heralded by the 1994 Code of Practice for children with special educational needs (SEN). Among other things, this Act:

- standardised funding for the support of children with SEN;
- standardised the diagnosis and management of children with SEN in mainstream schools;
- resulted in SEN children having statements of need with money attached;
- introduced the SEN support worker.

This, and later legislation, increased the number of professionals working directly with children and other young people. The inclusion agenda rapidly increased the number of statemented children and  doubled the number of support assistants available (Goddard, 2005). This was largely a result of pupils coming into mainstream schools from special schools. These statemented pupils had individual support for all or part of the day (Hall, 2005).

The late 1990s saw a major increase in the numbers of allied professionals in primary schools with the introduction of the National Literacy Strategy (DfEE, 1988) and the National Numeracy Strategy (DfEE, 1999). These focused on small group teaching. Most schools responded to this challenge by employing classroom assistants to work with the small groups. Initially, these workers were mainly unskilled and teachers took on the role of training them to work with the strategies. This changed when the National Strategies themselves adapted to responses from schools by providing training centrally and for those working with booster groups and specific intervention strategies, such as the Additional Literacy Strategy (ALS), Further Literacy Strategy (FLS) and Springboard for Mathematics (Goddard, 2005). These initiatives were written to be 'delivered' specifically by support workers. This quickly increased the professionalism of classroom assistants as teachers recognised the significance of their increased involvement in pupil learning, rather than simply concentrating on the management of pupil behaviour. Many schools formally changed their job description from 'classroom assistant' to 'teaching assistant'. There is no doubt that these classroom-based, allied professionals working with groups of children have a unique and integral role to play in identifying potential issues related to pupils' basic needs. They are also probably the very people in whom vulnerable children and young people are most likely to confide.

The increased numbers of allied professionals involved directly in teaching pupils, often in smaller groups, resulted in the development of further training in the form of the specialist teaching assistant (STA) programme. This provided a paid day-release course for STAs who had to have English and mathematics at GCSE as a strict admission requirement. The training resulted in an A level equivalence qualification. Many of those who did the course successfully were encouraged to move on to degree courses, some of which were specially designed for them. From 2004, higher-level teaching assistants (HLTAs) made their appearance. Cynics might say that this was because the training was much cheaper for central government to run. Initially a 50-day training programme was planned, but this was replaced with a three-day assessment programme to ensure that specific educational standards had been met.

In secondary schools too, there was a recognised shortage of teachers in particular subject areas and specialist training was given in addition to the HLTA assessment. The HLTAs were initially seen by central government as the most highly qualified of the teaching assistants and able to cover classes by themselves. Central government's workforce remodelling agenda was intended to push this forward, although many schools proved reluctant to pay the true cost of employing an HLTA because, for slightly more outlay, they could employ a newly qualified teacher (Goddard, 2005). The unions representing teachers and the allied professionals have since been engaged in a long debate about the rapidly decreasing distinction between teachers and allied professionals. For most allied professionals, pay and conditions are not nearly as attractive as those for qualified teachers, and in many schools they are paid on a part-time pro-rata basis rather than full-time.

Other allied professionals, such as learning mentors and counsellors, have a wider whole-school brief. Learning mentors, for example, emerged in the Excellence in Cities (EiC) programme (EiC/DfES, 2003). The first learning mentors were trained and employed to tackle 'specific problems' facing children in cities. These were seen as key personnel in helping individual pupils to overcome barriers to learning and acting as an advocate for pupils (Hughes, 2005). The guidance and the National Training Programme for learning mentors recognised that many of these barriers to learning involved basic needs such as those identified by Maslow (1962).

## Research box

### identifying basic needs

Maslow (1962) suggested that needs vary in order of importance. Lower order needs, such as hunger and thirst, take precedence over higher order needs, such as realisation of personal potential. It is the failure of lower order needs that often forms the major barrier to learning for children and young people.

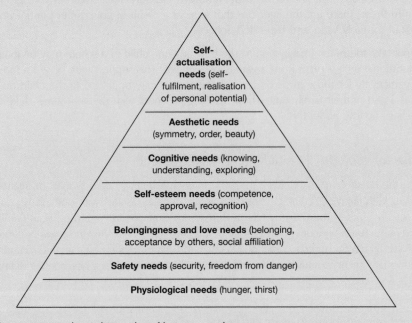

**Figure 6.1** Maslow's hierarchy of human needs areas

Each of these basic needs strands can be linked to different elements of the role of anyone working with children. Learning mentors, for example, are nearly always involved in monitoring attendance. After all, schools cannot make a difference to lives if pupils do not attend. They frequently run breakfast clubs to fulfil physiological needs, and work on anti-racist, anti-bullying and other safety strategies. They also work with individual and small groups of children and young people who have barriers to learning linked to needing to belong and having self-esteem. Increasingly, they are used by schools to make the formal and informal liaison between schools and other children's services (Hughes, 2005).

# Educational support workers and external providers

Schools are often involved in working with agencies and professionals that are able to give them extra support and advice. These include educational support workers and external providers. Educational support workers are those whose services are based within the sphere of education such as the Education Welfare Office (EWO), the educational psychologist and the Connexions Service for careers. Educational support agencies tend to focus their work around general welfare issues, attendance, behaviour, educational progress, social and emotional development, and ethnic minority issues. Then there are the external providers. These agencies may be involved in assessing the needs of children or young people and their families, offering them practical support. The key agencies vary from area to area and are frequently subject to name, personnel, funding and remit changes. They include health and social services, charities involved with children and/or their families, faith agencies, and community and housing agencies. More legalist services, such as the police and courts, are increasingly employing trained personnel to work with school pupils. This may be with whole-school groups, but is often as a preventative measure with small 'at risk' groups. In addition to these, there are the agencies that arise as a result of government initiatives such as SureStart for Early Years and Extended Schools.

It does not take too much imagination to see how any one child in a school may be in contact with educational professionals from a variety of agencies. This support may be at an individual level – particularly for those in secondary schools – or it may be linked to the child or young person as a part of their family unit. Those working in school with the very same child may in practice have no idea about this.

> **Pause for thought** | multi-agency involvement
>
> Since the death of Maria Colwell in 1973, there has been a rapid growth of agencies working with families, carers, children and young people. Contact with one agency, such as social services or the Citizens Advice Bureau, for example, will often result in families being put in touch with other forms of help. It is useful to unpick the challenges presented by this multi-agency approach and look at one particular example to gain an understanding of how many agencies could be involved. John could attend a primary or secondary school.
>
> John's attendance at school is inconsistent and he often appears tired. His class/form teacher has become concerned that he is mixing with a group of older boys (including his brother) who are known to truant and be involved with petty crime.
>
> - What support may John get in school, either formally (e.g. via a learning mentor) or informally (e.g. a welfare assistant who knows his family)?
> - What other educational support services may be involved?
> - What other agencies could be involved with John's family?

# Every Child Matters

After the death of Victoria Climbié in 2000, the government commissioned an inquiry which reported several years later (Laming, 2003). This was rapidly followed by a government response on how children should be kept safe and later by a Green Paper entitled *Every Child Matters* (DfES, 2003). This made a series of recommendations to improve multi-agency working, acknowledging that child protection could not be separated from policies to improve children's lives as a whole. This report recognised, really for the first time, the problem of children 'falling through the cracks' between different services. It went much further than the last-minute patching and bureaucracy that were identified within existing child protection procedures. It recorded that too often children experienced difficulties at home or at school but received 'too little help too late, once problems have reached crisis point'. Whether or not many of those working hard with individual children and their families would agree with this widespread condemnation of their efforts was not examined.

*Every Child Matters* covers children and young people from birth to age 19. In education terms, this encompasses several distinct sectors. These include:

- under-5s provision within schools and nurseries (both within the public and private sector) and under-5s within their own homes or in the homes of others paid to look after them;
- those in compulsory education between the ages of 5 and 16 (this also includes those who have been excluded from schools, those being educated at home and those for whom formal education is being provided in settings other than school such as behavioural units and 'Oasis' units for excluded children);
- those in post-compulsory education such as further education, higher education and other training settings.

It also covers all those outside these educational settings, in particular those whose basic skills are seen as an ongoing matter for concern.

The privilege and challenge for all of those working within the education sector is that they are in the forefront of working with children and young people. Indeed, teachers and other educational professionals may see more of children and young people than their parents do. From an estimated child population of 11 million, this will include the 50–100 children and young people who die from abuse or neglect every year, the 25,700 who are on the child protection register, the 59,700 looked after children, the 300,000 to 400,000 children in need, and the 300,000 to 400,000 vulnerable (DfES, 2003).

Translated into more concrete terms, one local authority with a population of about 150,000 audited its own child services from the data it had already collected. It was estimated that, in any one year, the local authority had approximately:

- 254 children in the care of the local authority;
- 145 children on the Child Protection Register;
- 156 children known as 'young carers' (youngest aged 3);
- 430 children with enduring mental health problems;
- 2,699 reported incidents of domestic violence where children were either involved or watching;
- 300–500 children under the age of 18 going into the local accident and emergency unit of the hospital;
- well over half of under 5s with dental decay;
- 20% of girls and 10% of boys aged 11 upwards who smoke;
- 90 babies born to teenage mothers, of whom 20–25 smoke.

***Pause for thought*** | collecting data

All local authorities gather data about the children within their jurisdiction and, with the development of more integrated Children's Services, these data are much easier to access. It may, for example, be produced as part of their Public Health Annual Report. Issues within local areas vary.

Education Studies has long been concerned with the politics of education (Bartlett and Burton, 2003; Matheson, 2004; Ward, 2004), and considering local figures provides an opportunity to look for statistics on national sites, such as the Deputy Prime Minister's Office, as well as regional sites, such as your own local authority's website. Identify those organisations which might collect such data and see if they have their public documents online. If not, it is possible to request the data by telephone. The relative ease of access to these statistics is important. After all, access to school league tables is simple and it should be as easy to access numbers of vulnerable children. Indeed, it is often possible to show direct relationships between the two when examining your own authority or one in which you have had a placement.

# The Every Child Matters agenda

*Every Child Matters: Change for Children* (DfES, 2004) covers all children from birth to age 19 and is given legal force in the Children Act 2004. It established an outcome framework underpinned by the principles:

- be healthy;
- stay safe;
- enjoy and achieve;
- make a positive contribution;
- achieve economic well-being.

Within this framework, each outcome was extended to include five specific aims. For achieving economic well-being, for example, the aims were identified as:

- engaging in further education, employment or training on leaving school;
- being ready for employment;
- living in decent homes and sustainable communities;
- having access to transport and material goods;
- living in households free from low income.

Support for each of these aims is targeted at parents, carers and families. There are national targets and other indicators to be judged through inspection.

For schools, the OFSTED inspection framework has changed to include all five of these outcomes (OFSTED, 2005). OFSTED reports are required to *evaluate the extent to which each area is meeting the ... five outcomes for children and young people.* The Every Child Matters agenda also permeates the Self Evaluation Form (SEF) which head teachers of schools are required to complete every year.

The Every Child Matters agenda recognises the need to have some practical (operational) guidelines. The Children Act 2004 gave a particular leadership role to local authorities in setting up the arrangements to secure cooperation among local partners. It appointed a Children's Commission for England and required every local authority to have a Director of Children's Services and a senior local councillor to be a lead member for Children's Services. It was believed that this would lead to a high profile administrative structure which would improve services for children and young people. The Act also provided guidelines for inter-agency arrangements. These had to involve, among other services, schools, GPs, health centres, local culture, sports and play organisations, and the voluntary and community sector.

# Some challenges for the integrated Children's Services

There is little about integrating Children's Services with which anyone could disagree. The framework for it gives a vision of what children's lives should be. It is possible to question it from a philosophical point of view and to be suspicious of the neatness of five outcomes each with five aims, all fitting neatly onto an A4 sheet. It has become strategic policy, but like many such political ideals the operational structures may take time to come into practice. Birth to age 19 is a long period of time and few governments, let alone policies, last so long.

There have been challenges in the past to multi-agency working (EiC/DfES, 2003). Problems include:

- a shortage of operational workers in many of the public services involving children – administrative workers as well as those 'in the field';
- time and resource pressures which affect communication – busy people are often unavailable and attempting to contact them can result in frustration;
- gender and status issues – for example female day care workers and support assistants not feeling that their views are being taken seriously;
- misunderstanding of professional roles – resulting in agencies having stereotypical and unrealistic views of others;
- fear of criticism by other agency workers – which can result in defensiveness and withdrawal;
- problems left to fester – with no one taking responsibility for their resolution.

## Research box

### Children's Workforce Strategy

The challenges of the Every Child Matters agenda were recognised to some extent in the many supplementary documents that followed the original Green Paper. One included key provision in the Children's Workforce Strategy (DfES, 2005). This looked at the whole issue of workforce remodelling and training. It aimed to build on good practice already taking place, recruiting high-quality staff into the children's workforce, retaining people by offering better development and career progression, strengthening inter-agency and multidisciplinary working, and promoting stronger leadership and management.

A key reform within workforce remodelling established a Common Assessment Framework (CAF) for assessing children with additional needs. Training for implementation was intended to cross agencies and services and involve a common core of skills and knowledge. This included:

- effective communication;
- knowledge of children's and young people's development;
- safeguarding and promoting the welfare of the child;

- supporting transitions;
- multi-agency working;
- sharing information.

Multi-agency and multidisciplinary professional development at this national level represented an important change. It was an attempt to move professionals working with children out of their 'own professional silos' (Coyne, 2005). In schools this has meant that all staff have had to be included in professional development. The Training and Development Agency (TDA) has increased its centralised power and training potential across the whole schools-based workforce.

There has always been concern that such centralised training can be over-prescriptive and involve briefing personnel with government directives rather than engaging them in fundamental issues of operational practice. In order for such training to be truly successful for those undertaking it, it needs to be dynamic and responsive to changing needs. Providers of continuing professional development need to listen and respond as well as to brief.

For those working either directly or indirectly in the education sector, workforce remodelling has provided a real opportunity to engage both with other professionals in the same sector and with other professionals working in related sectors. Whether this will achieve the very ambitious outcomes outlined in Every Child Matters remains to be seen.

---

### *Pause for thought* | looking at implications for educational professionals

Workforce remodelling initiatives have been triggered by the Every Child Matters agenda but a number of challenges have hindered similar initiatives in the past. Professional development in this area has been deeply involved with the theory of change and how it can be managed (e.g. NHS Institute, 2005). This has been linked with the belief in lifelong learning that is seen as essential and which has to be developed early in a child's life (Bartlett and Burton, 2003). Choose any educational setting with which you are familiar and identify some implications for professional development and lifelong learning that are involved with:

- an understanding of multi-agency working in relation to Children's Services;
- a common core of skills and knowledge;
- information sharing;
- creation of a multi-agency lead professional;
- workforce reform and professional development.

You then might like to look at what is happening in your own educational setting.

---

### Summary and conclusions

Child protection legislation in the past has seemed to be aimed at those working in social services and health with a nod towards education: attendance at a case conference or a request for a school report. The education service has often been seen as an 'add-on' in terms of integrated services. Yet looking at the increasing number of allied professionals working in schools, it is clear that many of them are involved directly in helping to reduce the need for legislation to aid the children in their care. Any vision for education involves 'making a difference' to children's and young people's lives. The rationale behind the Every Child Matters agenda was presented as a vision for the start of the twenty-first century. All those working in schools are part of this integration of children's services, a movement to improve children's life chances in the widest sense.

The practical outcomes of the Every Child Matters agenda in schools and for other agencies means policy-makers initially concentrating on the outcomes in relation to inspection. The permeation of the more fundamental aspects of the agenda will take longer. The formal, hidden, experienced and observed curriculum will need to incorporate health, safety, enjoyment and achievement if the final outcome for all school leavers is to be able to make a positive contribution to society and to achieve economic well-being. This is not just about sharing a vision for children and young people, but having the very practical and operational strategies to put the vision into action. All those reading this book have their own particular role to play.

# *References*

Bartlett, S and Burton, D (2003) *Education studies: essential issues*. London: Sage.

Campbell, A and Fairbairn, G (2005) *Working with support in the classroom*. London: Paul Chapman.

Children Act 2004. London: TSO. Available at **www.opsi.gov.uk/acts/acts2004/ukpga_20040031_en_l** (accessed 23 April 2009).

Coyne, A (2005) *Why workforce planning?*. Presentation from 'Growing the New Primary Care Workforce'. Liverpool: Liverpool University Press.

DfEE (1988) The National Literacy Strategy. London: Department for Education and Employment.

DfEE (1999) The National Numeracy Strategy. London: Department for Education and Employment.

DfES (2003) *Every Child Matters*. London: TSO/ Department for Education and Skills.

DfES (2004) *Every Child Matters: Change for Children*. London: HMSO/Department for Education and Skills

DfES (2005) Children's Workforce Strategy. London: Department for Education and Skills.

Dryden, G and Vos, J (2002) *The learning revolution*. Stafford: Network Educational Press.

EiC/DfES (2003) *Learning mentor training*. London: Excellence in Cities/Department for Education and Skills and Liverpool Excellence Partnership.

Goddard, G (2005) The changing role of the teaching assistant. Presentation at the TA Conference, Stafford, March 2005.

Greenhalgh, P (2002) *Reaching out to all learners*. Stafford: Network Educational Press.

Hall, W (2005) Making the most of the teaching assistant for special educational needs, in Campbell, A and Fairbairn, G (eds) *Working with support in the classroom*. London: Paul Chapman.

Hughes, P (2005) Learning mentors in primary classrooms and schools, in Campbell, A and Fairbairn, G (eds) *Working with support in the classroom*. London: Paul Chapman.

Laming, S (2003) *The Victoria Climbié Inquiry Report*. London: DfES.

Maslow, A (1962) *Towards a psychology of being*. New York: Nostrand.

Matheson, D (2004) *An Introduction to the study of education*. London: Fulton.

NHS Institute (2005) *Managing the human dimensions of change*. Warwick: National Health Service Institute for Innovation and Improvement.

OFSTED (2005) *Inspecting schools – inspection report template*. London: Office for Standards in Education.

Pariser, E (2000) The community school: developing the approach of 'relational education', in *A coalition for self-learning: creating learning communities*. Available at **www.creatinglearning communities.org/book/schools/pariser.htm** (accessed 17 April 2009).

Purkis, S (1993) *Using school buildings*. London: English Heritage.

Ward, S (ed) (2004) *Education studies: a student's guide*. London: RoutledgeFalmer.

# Chapter 7

# Polarisations in English

## Ruth Hewitt and Elizabeth Hopkins

### Introduction

Considering the fact that English is no real newcomer to the school curriculum, it is quite remarkable that it has been an almost constant subject of controversy and debate. Strong views and polarisations have characterised the history of English teaching that continue to the present day. It has been argued, for example, that even as recently as the 1980s, English teaching concentrated too much on personal responses and creativity to the detriment of other things more formal. The fact that English teaching experienced a massive shift back towards formality with the introduction of a National Literacy Strategy in the 1990s is typical of the pendulum-like nature of developments in English in schools. This chapter explores both the history of English as a curriculum subject and the dilemmas facing educationalists today. Teaching English is doubtlessly far too important a topic to be distracted by opposing factions or beliefs. However, a close look at some of the apparent dichotomies, both past and present, gives an insight into how English got to where it is now, as well as giving greater knowledge on which to base decisions about where English might go in the future.

## The concept of English as a subject

Do changes in English teaching priorities go round in cycles reflecting the prominent educational, cultural or political mood of the day? Or would it be more accurate to say that disparate aspects of the subject can be seen as belonging to a continuum over which the pendulum swings slowly backwards and forwards over time, with more emphasis being given at different points to some knowledge, understanding and skills rather than others? The very nature of English as a curriculum subject has always been complex and variable and this, in turn, has affected issues of how to teach it.

Before the eighteenth century, the teaching of oral expression, written expression, logic, grammar and literacy were well-established educational elements in English. However, by the nineteenth century, comprehension and interpretation had gained in prominence. The thinking skills needed for the comprehension and interpretation of texts, that would probably be the domain of English literature teaching today, had gained in importance at the expense of oral expression and logic, although grammar and literacy were still taught. By the early 1900s, the English curriculum was made up of standard English and grammatical correctness, emphasising an instrumental or utilitarian approach to what was needed for adults to play a useful role in society. As was indicated by the Board of Education (1910), *pure English is not merely an accomplishment, but an index to and a formative influence over character*. However, during the First World War the high level of illiteracy among conscripts caused concern to the government. As a result, the government set up an inquiry that led to the Newbolt Report (Board of Education, 1921) which emphasised literary values with the intention of making available the supposed civilising and humanising values of the public school to all people, whatever their class. A 'liberal education' emerged as a feature of all schools, at the heart of which lay the nation's greatest literature. In this move, the twentieth-century swing from language to literature had begun again. This trend continued with a *series of sustained attempts on the part of literature specialists to eradicate the study of language or grammar* completely (Mittins, 1964).

During the 1960s, attempts were made by Dixon (1967) to reconcile these two separate elements by proposing that the main purpose of English teaching was to help pupils build their own 'representational world' through the use of literature and language. Dixon also propounded the idea that a study *of* literature enabled an exploration of human nature and situations and therefore led people to look at themselves and possibly develop and grow through this self-awareness. As Dixon himself indicated, *in ordering and composing situations that in some way symbolise life as we know it, we bring order and composure to our inner selves*. This model of English teaching, therefore, included literature that was closer to children's interests and experiences. It also focused on the acquisition of language skills through the study of literature. This is in contrast to the position today in Key Stages 1, 2 and 3 in which the acquisition of literary understanding is achieved through the study of language. Being narrower in focus than the English National Curriculum, which remains the statutory instrument in England and Wales, the literacy in question in the National Literacy Strategy may initially have had a slightly larger frame of reference but hotly debated issues still remain as to how to reconcile a greater concentration on knowledge about language with the maintenance of a love of and creative engagement with texts (Willinsky, 1994). A concern that primary-aged pupils' work at Key Stages 1 and 2 has moved too far away from whole texts and personal responses to them has been partially responsible for the recent introduction of the Excellence and Enjoyment strand of the Primary National Strategy.

The nature of English taught in the school curriculum has obviously been an issue of ideological debate long before the present era and this has always been influenced by the political context in which English has found itself. There have clearly been different emphases and priorities in English at different times in its history. But has it really changed in its fundamentals?

## Research box

### multitextuality and multimodality

It could be argued that the nature of English really does need to change more drastically in the present day if it is to reflect the advances in the types of texts that people now encounter in their daily lives (see Foucault, 1988; Robinson, 2000). How far English as a curriculum subject should ever reflect contemporary culture is, however, debatable. If it is to do so at all, aspects of current ways of reading, writing and engaging with texts need to be considered (see Meek, 1991; Andrews, 2001). According to Sefton-Green and Nixon (2003), it has become a truism that *most texts enjoyed by children are screen-based*, which seems to imply that the concentration on print-based fiction and information texts in schools is increasingly out of touch with the experiences that modern children bring to the classroom. This also points to the growing role of visual and graphical forms of communication. Modern texts are also changing in a qualitative way in that they are often multimodal in nature, drawing on more than one medium at the same time and utilising several different text types at once (see Goodman and Graddol, 1996). For example, computer games tend to incorporate a cinematic point of view, written and spoken texts, and music (possibly even with lyrical content). Also, the distinctions between speech and writing are becoming ever more blurred with the increasing visual representation in SMS messaging in particular, of what would, before new computer technology, have been essentially oral acts – spontaneous conversations between two or more people. Should English as a subject, therefore, become 'Textual Studies' and concern itself with reflecting modern culture and modern texts, embracing new technologies and the resultant modern ways of reading those texts, rather than restricting itself predominantly to books in general and to the literary canon in particular?

# Rationales for the teaching of English

Having looked briefly at the history of English in schools, it would be appropriate to consider the five rationales or models for English outlined in the influential Cox Report, which considered the place of English in the curriculum in the late 1980s (DES, 1989) and to use these to consider whether an emphasis on different rationales or models of English teaching has prevailed at different times. Cox's five rationales or models are presented as follows.

- Adult needs – this focuses on communication outside the school and emphasises the responsibility of English teachers to prepare children and young adults for the language-demands of adult life, including the workplace, in a fast-changing world. Is this the view that prevailed in the early 1900s?
- Cross-curricular – this focuses on the school and emphasises the need for all teachers to have a responsibility to help children and young adults with the language demands of different subjects in the school curriculum. Is this the view that prevails in the Primary National Strategy today?
- Cultural analysis – this focuses on values and society and emphasises the role of English in helping children and young adults towards a critical understanding of the cultural environment and the world in which they live. Children and young adults should know about the processes by which meanings are conveyed and about the ways in which print and other media convey messages. This view may never have been prominent in the past but should it be in the future?
- Cultural heritage – this focuses on the identification of prominent and influential literature and emphasises the responsibility of schools to lead children and young adults to an appreciation of those works that have been widely regarded as among the finest in the language. Is this the view embodied in all versions of the National Curriculum, particularly the literary canon drawn on for the list of texts to be read and studied at Key Stages 3 and 4?
- Personal growth – this focuses on the child and young adult and emphasises the relationship between language and learning and the role of literature in developing imaginative and aesthetic lives. This view rose to prominence in the late 1960s and continued for the next twenty years or so. Is it still the most important rationale for English teachers trained during this period?

As can perhaps be seen, the past, present and future shifts in priorities in English seem to rest upon the relative balance of these rationales for the teaching of the subject and all are important. But when it comes to deciding what the bulk of English curriculum time should be spent on and what should be at the heart of the curriculum there might well be differences of emphasis between individuals, and this could potentially cause problems. Cox, for example, was quite clear that the cross-curricular needs of learners should be met by all teachers. If this were to really take place, then the case for English or literacy lessons to predominantly address these needs would become diminished. Goodwyn and Findlay (1997) found in repeated questionnaires that personal growth was overwhelmingly given as students' and teachers' most important rationale for the teaching of English. If literacy in a primary school context, however, focuses mainly on the basic skills needed by pupils to access the rest of their learning across the curriculum, then this has the effect of making English a service subject and not concerned to any great extent with the development of personal and social knowledge and understanding, nor with the 'love' of literature cited as being so dear to many English teachers' hearts (Goodwyn, 2003). This could be a case of teachers and policy-makers being poles apart in what they consider to be the most important aspects of the subject.

---

***Pause for thought*** | Cox's five rationales or models

Having considered the five rationales or models presented by Cox (DES, 1989), place these into:

- your rank order of their importance as rationales for the teaching of English;
- your rank order of the strength of their influence on current classroom practice as you understand or remember it.

Share your own views with friends, colleagues and lecturers and try to draw some conclusions.

---

The fact that 'literacy across the curriculum' is one of the strands of the National Literacy Strategy for Key Stage 3 confirms that finding a definitive role for the place of English teaching in schools has never been easy to resolve. Bullock suggested that *all teachers are teachers of English*, and in his lengthy report, *A Language for Life* (DES, 1975), went far beyond the scope of what could be covered in the curriculum slot designated as English. His comment that *explicit instruction out of context is of little value* could, surely, not be disagreed with by many educationalists and yet the challenge for schools is in how to avoid doing this. Hopefully, if a school gets it 'right', whatever that means, the result is a shared understanding between all staff of the role of language in pupils' learning and how work in different subjects can contribute to and benefit from the development of pupils' ability to communicate effectively. But, as English language is both a subject and a medium of learning for others, it is always going to be difficult to negotiate and enhance this relationship.

---

***Pause for thought*** | literacy across the curriculum

**literacy across the curriculum**

Educational institutions are charged with a responsibility to ensure that English is studied in its own right as well providing a medium of learning for other subjects and to manage this relationship so that the knowledge, understanding and literacy skills of children and young adults can be effectively developed.

- How does an educational institution go about achieving a holistic approach to the teaching of literacy?

---

- Where and when should specific speaking, listening, reading and writing skills, and English knowledge and understanding, be explicitly taught and, more importantly, assessed?
- How can an institution ensure all aspects of literacy are covered effectively?
- What problems, if any, could occur when trying to ensure that literacy is taught across the curriculum?
- What benefits, if any, accrue when a literacy policy works well?

# Language, literature, culture and the great naming debate

One of the longer-lasting causes of the polarisations in focus in English lies in the fact that the subject can include the study of language, literature or culture. One possible solution to this could be to create a separate subject in the secondary curriculum entitled 'Language'. This could concern itself with language study and appreciation and encompass links with other languages such as French, German or Spanish already being studied by pupils. Socio-linguistic, critical linguistic and discourse-oriented models of language could open up a world of exploration to pupils of all ages and abilities. Topics such as *Language and power, Language and identity, Language and gender* and the study of spoken texts, currently restricted to pupils studying AS and A2 English language could be incorporated as well as more obvious areas such as grammar, syntax and morphology. If pupils were encouraged to know more about other 'Englishes' and other languages, this would surely be beneficial as a way of gaining insights into their own version of English, and maybe a greater tolerance of different languages, cultures and societies would also result. It would undoubtedly be educationally detrimental, however, if connections between language understanding and language use – in other words the links between the ability to read, understand and talk about texts and the ability to write them – were broken. Language study should not just take place in a separate part of the curriculum to that in which the study of texts produced in that language is carried out. Study of a broader range of spoken and written texts could be included within a wider remit for English as a subject. In this way the highly popular 'newcomers' to the curriculum, such as media studies, film studies, communications or even ICT, might be encompassed within the umbrella of English, and parallels between texts and ways of analysing them might more easily be drawn. Knowledge, understanding and skills gained from the study of one type of text could surely then be made more easily transferable to another. But what would this do for the study of our literary culture? Could experience of the English literary heritage be better placed within a citizenship-type curricular area, alongside the study of our democratic background and values, our cultural heritage and our society in general? If several different curricular areas, such as those outlined earlier, covered various strands of what is currently taught in English, would this imply an acceptance of their equal value as aspects of English? And if so, would this be appropriate? Are they equally important?

Before we leave this topic of naming, there is also, of course, the issue of literacy itself. The fact that literacy has replaced English in most primary schools signifies to many educationalists the current emphasis of curricular content on language skills and technical accuracy in reading and writing as opposed to the engagement with literature and creativity implied in the broader term (or as Cox would put it, cross-curricular needs as opposed to personal growth). For these people, the naming of the subject has become politically and ideologically charged.

*Pause for thought* | what else could English be called?

What else could English be called? Consider the suggestions below in turn and think about their potential benefits and drawbacks:

- cultural studies;
- culture;
- English language;
- English literature;
- English studies;
- language;
- literacy;
- literary studies;
- literature;
- textual studies.

Is there another name that would more effectively encompass the scope of English as a subject or do you think the subject should be split into various parts? What is your preferred term or set of terms? Justify and explain your own choices.

# English in higher education

Changes in the nature of English degrees and the growth of new varieties have been significant indicators of the underlying currents within English teaching in general. During the 1970s and 1980s, the emergence of a whole plethora of critical and theoretical approaches to literature took place replacing the previously predominant literary criticism based on the methods established by F.R. Leavis, where the study of literature was *an exercise in value judgement* (Hardman, 2001). In addition, the study of language that had grown and found strong voices in figures such as Chomsky began to offer insights not only into language itself but also into the understanding of the human mind and human society. This impinged on the study of literature directly through the concept of stylistics and indirectly through the role of linguistics as a major source of the structuralist movement. The growth of socio-linguistics led to a focus on the development of children's knowledge about language through close study and critical analysis of language as it was actually used, as opposed to focusing on how it should be used. It embraced an understanding and critical awareness of all forms of language and media texts and aimed to contribute to young people's literacy demands by providing them with tools for understanding the world. Other innovations in the study of language also had their impact on English in higher education. The growth of cultural studies, communication and media departments in universities led to a significant reconsideration of what constituted a text and of what could or could not be counted as English. English became perceived as a cultural or social semiotic study (Peim, 2000). Today, the wide variety in what can be studied as part of an English degree has been noted by the Higher Education Funding Council for England among others. In their *Subject Overview Report*, HEFCE (1995) commented on the diversity of provision in that *different emphasis can be given to knowledge of literature, skills in the use of English and the exploration of the cultural contexts of English and its uses.* There is, clearly, an acceptance of diversity in English curricula at this level of education that, unfortunately, no longer seems to be matched in others.

# Cross-phase discontinuity

One of the consequences of the movements in higher education in the 1980s was a breakdown in the shared purpose that had long existed between universities and schools. There had been very little difference between English literature teaching at universities and by sixth-form teachers in terms of pedagogical practice and the same texts tended to be selected from a shared canon with similar terms and methods of textual analysis applied to them. For the reasons outlined earlier, this common culture does not exist as it did today.

A discontinuity in English teaching between various phases of education is present in other ways too. The National Literacy Strategy was first introduced to primary schools in the late 1990s but it did not appear in secondary schools until 2000. There is currently quite a substantial number of sixth-form students who choose to study English language, either in a joint AS and A2, format with English literature or as a subject on its own. An emphasis on knowledge about language is therefore increasingly embedded in English teaching at Key Stages 1, 2, 3 and 5 and in many university degree courses, as we have already seen. Yet this is not the case at Key Stage 4 where there is still a strong focus on, and time commitment to, analysis of figurative language and literary written texts in GCSE courses.

So, what of the future? Will Key Stage 4 syllabuses change in line with this general trend towards knowledge about language just in time to see a reverse swing of the pendulum in other key stages, with a return to the primacy of literature for its own sake and a fostering of creativity and personal growth? If there is one thing we may have learned from a look at the past, it is that we should not be surprised if this were to be the case.

---

*Pause for thought* | the future of English

The Qualifications and Curriculum Authority's *English 21* survey asked teachers, students, parents and employers, as well as writers, academics, librarians and publishers, about what English as a curriculum subject might look like by 2015 (QCA, 2005). The survey invited responses on a diverse range of topics related to how English lessons *might need to change to embrace new thinking, priorities and technologies*. Reflect on some of the questions drawn from *English 21* below in the light of your own experience and consider your views on the future literacy needs of the population.

- What place should there be for creativity and imagination in English?
- How much time should be spent on teaching knowledge about language or allowing pupils to explore the way in which our language works?
- How can English in the future reflect the types of texts pupils will be familiar with and come across in their daily lives?
- What acknowledgement should be made of American or Australian English or of the place of English in the world as a result of the dominance of American culture in particular?
- What elements of English are essential and which should be offered as optional GCSE, A level or degree subjects?
- What sort of testing or assessment arrangements would be most appropriate for the knowledge, understanding and skills being taught?

## Summary and conclusions

In looking at the history of English as a curriculum subject there have been cycles in the relative emphasis given to language or literature. These cycles can be traced from the early twentieth-century preoccupation with standards of technical accuracy and reading skills and the opinion that English literature was a second-class subject, to the mid-twentieth century prevalence of ideas about personal growth and the importance of personal responses to literature, to the late-twentieth century rebirth of a concentration on knowledge about language. On past experience this cyclical nature of change could continue well into the future. In more recent times, there have been additional elements in English to consider. New types of texts have sprung to life as a result of advances in ICT and there have been increased study and awareness of spoken texts. These could either be thrown into the English melting pot, which would involve yet more jostling for position and priority in an already crammed curriculum area, or left as the domain of other, newer, curriculum subjects, leading to the redundancy of English itself.

The rationales or models for English teaching, as expressed by Cox, seem just as relevant to the English debate today as they did in the 1980s, but policy-makers and practitioners do not seem to be any closer to reaching a consensus as to which should be considered most important, or on reconciling a position in which these various rationales or models can happily coexist. It would be an interesting exercise, for example, for English educators to actually pinpoint which aspects of work covered in their lessons directly address the enhancement of personal growth, as opposed to preparing pupils for their literacy needs as adults, or to consider how much time they give to the five different rationales or models in their schemes of work. It could well be that the way they feel about the subject is not matched by the realities of the lessons that they teach. It could also be the case that learning about language through literature and learning about literature through language are not really as far apart as they might seem to be. They are certainly not mutually exclusive, either in theory or in practice.

English teachers remain the constant in the sea of change caused by politicians and the new curricula and syllabuses they introduce. Whether through laziness (e.g. simply not wanting to change the lesson plans they devised 20 years ago), recalcitrance (e.g. disagreeing with the principles behind an initiative) or ignorance (e.g. too little knowledge of grammar or ICT), teachers rarely swing from one extreme to the other. It is to be hoped that, in the case of the many reflective practitioners, a reasoned central standpoint will be taken, making use of the best new changes, but not losing sight of the same old effective ones.

## References

Andrews, R (2001) *Teaching and learning English: a guide to recent research and its applications.* London: Continuum.

Board of Education (1910) *Circular 753.* London: HMSO.

Board of Education (1921) *The Teaching of English in England* (the Newbolt Report). London: HMSO.

DES (1975) *A Language for Life: Report of the Committee of Inquiry appointed by the Secretary of State for Education and Science* (the Bullock Report). London: Department for Education and Science/HMSO.

DES (1989) *English for Ages 5–16* (the Cox Report). London: Department for Education and Science/HMSO.

Dixon, J (1967) *Growth through English*. Oxford: Oxford University Press.

Foucault, M (1988) What is an author?, in Lodge, D (ed) *Modern criticism and theory*. London: Longman.

Goodman, S and Graddol, D (1996) *Redesigning English: new texts, new identities*. London: Routledge.

Goodwyn, A (2003) We teach English not literacy: 'growth' pedagogy under siege in England, in Doecke, B, Homer, D and Nixon, H (eds) *English teachers at work*. South Australia: Wakefield Press.

Goodwyn, A and Findlay, F (1997) *English teachers' theories of good English teaching and their theories in action*. Paper presented at the BERA conference York, 1998.

Hardman, F (2001) What do we mean by Secondary English teaching?, in Williamson, J, Fleming, M, Hardman, F and Stevens, D (eds) *Meeting the standards in Secondary English*. London: RoutledgeFalmer.

HEFCE (1995) *Subject Overview Report – English*. Bristol: Higher Education Funding Council for England.

Meek, M (1991) *On being literate*. London: Bodley Head.

Mittins, WH (1964) *The teaching of English in schools*, in Quirk, R and Smith, AH (eds) *The teaching of English*. Oxford: Oxford University Press.

Peim, N (2000) The cultural politics of English teaching, in Davison, J and Moss, J (eds) *Issues in English teaching*. London: Routledge.

Poulson, L (1995) *Research, policy and practice in literacy and language education*. Exeter: University of Exeter.

QCA (2005) *English 21*. London: Qualifications and Curriculum Authority.

Robinson, M (2000) What is(n't) this subject called English?, in Davison, J and Moss, J (eds) *Issues in English teaching*. London: Routledge.

Sefton-Green, J and Nixon, H (2003) The challenge of popular culture, digital technologies and curriculum change, in Doecke, B, Homer, D and Nixon, H (eds) *English teachers at work*. South Australia: Wakefield Press.

Willinsky, J (1994) Introducing the new literacy, in Stierer, B and Maybin, J (eds) *Language, literacy and learning in educational practice*. Clevedon: Open University Press.

# Chapter 8

# Mathematics for the future

## Mark Patmore

### Introduction

There is increasing concern about the state of mathematics education across the UK. It is generally recognised that mathematics is vital. It matters to individuals and to society as a whole, it underpins research and development in the sciences, technology and ICT, and it is essential for the future economic prosperity of the nation. Additionally, it provides a set of key skills to enable individuals to reach their full potential in terms of life and work. Getting the teaching and learning of mathematics right is therefore a major education priority, yet the country is struggling to recruit or retain the number of mathematics teachers required. A large number of pupils is being taught in classes by teachers with no mathematics qualification. It is clear that a vicious circle is being established – a poor supply of mathematics teachers now will result in an even greater shortage in the future. Additionally there is debate, but no agreement, about what mathematics should be taught. This chapter is intended to challenge you to think about the nature of the mathematics we need to study now and about mathematics teaching. Some of you may have negative feelings towards mathematics, others may be more positive. However, the issues arising in mathematics education have to be recognised and faced by all and not just by those who have a vested interest in the subject.

## Concerns for mathematics

The frequently raised question *Where will the next generation of mathematicians and mathematics teachers come from?* is a serious one indeed. It may seem alarmist but it illustrates that many people engaged in education, industry and commerce feel that there are serious problems and issues associated with the teaching and learning of mathematics and with the future supply of the mathematicians needed in the twenty-first century.

There is now some evidence of a small increase in the actual number of students taking A level and further mathematics in England and Wales although the actual percentage of total candidates taking mathematics has hardly changed. At GCSE, press comments focus on the steady rise in the number of students gaining grades A* to C on papers that are perceived to be both getting easier and on which the marks required for 'acceptable grades' are getting lower. The Confederation of British Industry (CBI) and other similar bodies have also expressed concern about the mathematical capabilities and competences of 16- to 18-year-olds who are starting employment, and university departments of mathematics, science and engineering have all expressed concern over the content and lack of rigour of the mathematics courses in schools. At university, these concerns are supported by the evidence of deteriorating performance on the same tests set year on year to each new group of first year undergraduates. Indeed, some university departments now require their undergraduates to attend additional classes in order to acquire the knowledge and skills deemed to be lacking, while others have extended their courses from three years' to four years' duration with consequent financial implications for their undergraduates. Importantly, press reports frequently refer to a decline in the number and quality of students entering highly numerate university courses to a lack of qualified mathematics teachers, to a shortage in the number of high-quality IT specialists, to a shortage of mathematicians in industry and commerce, and so on. Contrary to popular opinion, the mathematical demands of the workplace have not been reduced by the introduction of calculators and computers. Instead, these tools have enabled people to introduce new and more efficient techniques and working patterns which in turn call for new levels of mathematical and statistical understanding.

> *Pause for thought* | perceptions of mathematics
>
> Together with a group of friends or colleagues, think back to when you last studied mathematics. This might have been at secondary school or as part of some work-related experience. You might be studying mathematics right now as part of your degree programme! Should mathematics be part of the formal school curriculum at all? Why do you think mathematics appears to be in decline as a subject area? What do you think could be done to 'turn mathematics around' and make it more popular? Does mathematics matter?

Many would argue that there is too little attention paid to mathematics, that mathematics education is deeply inadequate and misconceived, and that current attitudes and current practices need to be changed, both within the compulsory school sector and beyond – improving, for example, the provision for older students and adult learners, and reducing the mismatch between school and the demands of university. Anderson (2002) wrote:

*The continuing health of mathematics as a subject depends not only on recruiting students for advanced study but also of creating a wider understanding of why mathematics should be financially supported.*

(p31)

It is of course only fair to point out that some writers, including both academics and journalists, would argue that mathematics is an over-admired and over-privileged subject. Perhaps such views are commonly held by those whose qualifications are within the field of the arts rather than in the sciences. It must be of concern that the subject has no or few friends at court – very few politicians have either a scientific or mathematical qualification. So while politicians proclaim the importance of the knowledge society and of a skilled workforce, it seems that the reality is different. There is a risk that the most privileged parents, aware of the demands of society and work, will ensure that their children are well equipped and prepared mathematically. The independent schools, whose share in A level mathematics is already at a higher proportion than their A level share overall, might increase this share still further, and the less privileged will be left with qualifications that place them at a disadvantage. This cannot be good for the country or for the individual.

Research box

## international comparisons

Comparisons in the mathematical performance of children and young adults between countries are often made, with the UK frequently depicted as performing less well than its 'competitor' nations (e.g. IEA, 1995; BSA, 1997; Kaiser et al., 1999; PISA, 2000). It is worth reflecting on the fact that in the Pacific-rim countries of Japan, Hong Kong, Korea and Taiwan, the time devoted to mathematics in the school curriculum is considerably more than in the UK and probably more than in many other western countries. The question *Should the school curriculum be adjusted to give mathematics more time?* is one that surely would not receive a favourable response from the teachers of many other subjects. That said, the *School matters* effectiveness study of Mortimore et al. (1988) showed that the school effect had a significantly greater influence on progress in mathematics over time than did the impact of family background. In comparison, the study showed that for reading the school effect was much less though still greater than that of home. According to Hanson (2004), reasons why children in other countries perform better at mathematics than children in the UK (at least as far as the tests employed demonstrated) include a healthier and more positive attitude towards mathematics at school, a recognition of the importance of a general education, which includes mathematics, and certain culture-specific organisational features (e.g. teaching and learning strategies, classroom layout, setting by ability, and so on).

# Mathematics under the microscope

In recent years, school mathematics has been affected by changes imposed by central government. While the introduction of the Mathematics National Curriculum in 1989 resulted in reforms to the teaching and assessment of the subject, changes had, of course, been taking place before then. In the 1970s, for example, published reports stated that there was an apparent lack of basic computational skills in many children, increasing mathematical demands made on adults, and a lack of qualified mathematics teachers. The government's response was to set up an inquiry chaired by Sir William Cockcroft into the teaching of mathematics. Many of the recommendations in what is commonly referred to as the Cockcroft Report (DES, 1982) were implemented in the Mathematics National Curriculum that followed and in the examinations taken at the end of formal schooling. The teaching and learning of mathematics in primary and secondary schools and their testing and examination systems have been under the microscope ever since. As recently as 2002, the government set up an independent inquiry chaired by Professor Adrian Smith into post-14 mathematics education. The Smith Report, *Making Mathematics Count* (DfES, 2004a), made recommendations to further amend the curriculum, qualifications and pedagogy for those aged 14 and over in schools, colleges and higher education institutions to enable those students to acquire the mathematical knowledge, understanding and skills necessary to meet the requirements of employers and further and higher education today. So 22 years after the Cockcroft Report, the issues and concerns surrounding mathematics education were still very much evident. So how can the issues and concerns be addressed, if at all? Clearly, what mathematics is taught, as well as how mathematics is taught, must be considered together.

# What mathematics?

The opening words of the government's response to the Smith Report (DfES, 2004b) appeared to acknowledge the nature of the problem facing the status and purpose of mathematics in today's fast-changing world:

*It is difficult to overstate the importance of mathematics in today's world, both for the individual and for the economy. The acquisition of mathematical skills is essential for progression in education and employment. At the same time a sufficient supply of mathematical skills is critical if we are to maintain our economic competitiveness.*

(p5)

However, further reading of the response shows that the need to ensure that a *sufficient supply of mathematical skills* (i.e. a highly qualified workforce) is ignored and that the focus should be concentrated instead on the *needs of all learners*. This is a familiar line taken by successive governments over the years, effectively thinking that a reduction in the level of intellectual challenge will result in more students being prepared to engage with the subject. The fallacy in this line of reasoning can be seen in the decline in the number of A level mathematics candidates following the revisions to A level mathematics courses made in an attempt to improve the subject's attractiveness and accessibility. In 2005, there were about 60,000 entries for A level mathematics, 11 per cent fewer than in 2001 and 21 per cent fewer than in 1991. The latest change to the Key Stage 4 mathematics curriculum, the introduction of a two-tier GCSE, has been subject to the same line of reasoning and will, in terms of producing a mathematically qualified section of the population, almost certainly fail and exacerbate the situation, focusing as it does on raising the number of grade C passes at the expense of providing challenge to the higher-achieving candidates. While this might be politically good for league tables, it is not good for the take-up of the subject at A level, with the consequent implications for universities and employers. One consequence of what is sometimes described as the 'dumbing down' of mathematics is illustrated by Tall (1995):

*Thus it is that fractions prove difficult for some and impossible for many and so have no place in a democratic curriculum on a ladder which all will climb. But the more successful students, who would find such things cognitively simpler, may be denied adequate exposure to the topic to give it meaning.*

(p29)

One solution put forward to the problem of addressing the lack of skills for most, while maintaining the possibility of challenge for some, is the introduction of functional mathematics, success at which will be required for the award of a grade C at GCSE, together with a new examination called 'further mathematics for the more able'.

---

*Pause for thought* | mathematics in school

Spend a few minutes reflecting on the following questions. Try to ignore any thoughts about the demands of the end of Key Stage tests (primary or secondary) or GCSE and A level requirements.

- What mathematics should be taught in schools and who should make the decisions?
- Who should teach mathematics in schools and how should they be trained?
- How should mathematics be assessed and for what purpose?
- Should what is taught focus on employment and the world of work and the mathematics needed in society, or focus on more theoretical aspects?

As you reflect upon the final question, perhaps you should also like to think about the mathematical demands of different subjects and occupations (e.g. teaching, nursing, the legal profession, plumbing, electrical work, and so on).

Any discussion about the nature of school mathematics up to GCSE can be held at a number of different levels. Clearly mathematics in school is concerned with number, shape, algebra, measurement, data handling, and so on, and while these give the subject its particular 'flavour', they have applications in other areas of study. While the subject content of school mathematics is identifiable and distinctive, what is much less clear is that it also requires specific forms of learning. Skemp (1971), for example, a mathematician and psychologist, investigated just how mathematical concepts are formed. Skemp distinguished between two forms of teaching and learning: that which results in instrumental understanding and that which results in relational understanding. Skemp described instrumental understanding as involving memorisation and the routine application of procedures and formulas (e.g. focusing on what to do and how to get answers). In contrast, Skemp described relational understanding as involving meaning (e.g. being able to explain, reason and use multiple representations to arrive at solutions). It is obvious that these approaches exist in other contexts and in other subjects. Indeed, one could suggest that instrumental understanding could lead to better examination and test results overall, while relational understanding offers better preparation for work and adult life.

# Mathematics for public understanding

Most people, if stopped in the street and asked to look back at their own mathematical experiences in school, would probably identify Skemp's notions of understanding, although in many cases instrumental understanding would probably be more familiar than relational. Many people, for example, may remember the rule for dividing fractions but have no idea why it works. If the same people were then asked what they thought mathematics is, it would be a 'safe bet' that the majority of the answers would include descriptions such as 'hard' or 'only for the bright' or 'boring' or would list actual topics that had been imprinted on their minds such as Pythagoras's theorem or quadratic equations. Probably very few would list the skills and qualities that are developed through the study of mathematics or how it benefited them in later life. It is also very likely that their responses would reflect the fact that school mathematics has the potential to engender unhelpful attitudes and feelings such as 'anxiety', 'helplessness' and 'apathy'. The development of positive attitudes and values are valid objectives for mathematics education in their own right, together with other desirable qualities such as confidence, independence, imagination, cooperation, while not forgetting that the recognition of the simple fact that knowing mathematics can be personally satisfying and empowering. One challenge clearly is to think how positives can be developed and experienced by all and the impact of negatives reduced.

The perception that mathematics is a difficult and minority subject needs to be changed into one in which the acquisition of mathematical knowledge, understanding and skills is valued and seen as necessary. For example, encouraging positive attitudes towards mathematics could include:

- seeing mathematics as an essential element of communication;
- recognising that mathematics is a powerful tool;
- developing an appreciation of relationships within mathematics;
- developing an awareness of the fascination of mathematics;
- recognising that mathematics can encourage and develop imagination, initiative and flexibility of mind;
- developing the skills of working in systematic, independent and cooperative ways;
- developing confidence in one's mathematical abilities;
- developing the skills of critical reasoning.

This list recognises that some social development – the ability to work cooperatively for example – can and should take place within mathematics lessons or in a separate mathematical context. The list also acknowledges that the development of critical reasoning is important, allowing children and young adults to enhance their ability to understand the world around them and build their confidence. Compare the list above with the implicit list provided within the following quotation:

*Thus the aim is primarily to ensure that children leave school literate, numerate and with a modicum of scientific knowledge, it should not extend beyond these three core subjects, nor attempt to do more than set minimum standards in basic knowledge and technique.*

(Lawlor, 1988, p5)

This quotation suggests that, for example, Skemp's instrumental understanding is all-important. It also implies that numeracy and not mathematics is the aim. Note that if the aims of mathematics teaching are to embrace both independent and cooperative working and communication, a change to the traditional role of the teacher may be required. A view from America is useful here. According to the National Research Council (1989):

*Teachers' roles should include those of consultant, moderator and interlocutor, not just presenter and authority. Classroom activities must encourage students to express their approaches, both orally and in writing. Students must engage in Mathematics as a human activity; they must learn to work cooperatively in small teams to solve problems as well as to argue convincingly for their approach amid conflicting ideas and strategies.*

(p61)

The challenge must be to ensure that a sufficient supply of mathematical skills is generated while the needs of the more able are met, at the same time allowing all to have an opportunity to develop the transferable skills necessary for future employment.

# Mathematics or numeracy?

The word 'numeracy' has appeared earlier in this chapter but is not, other than in educational circles, a commonly used term. Indeed, every time numeracy is typed into a document, computer spell checkers indicate that the word should be replaced by numeric or innumeracy. So what is numeracy and can it be defined?

In the Cockcroft Report (DES, 1982) it was suggested that being numerate implied the possession of two attributes: an 'at homeness' with number (the ability to make use of mathematical skills in order to cope with the practical mathematics of everyday life) and an ability to have some 'appreciation' of information presented in mathematical terms (such as in graphs, charts, tables or equations). The essential elements of being numerate, as set out by Cockcroft, are still considered important today. Tout (1997), for example, has suggested:

> *We believe that numeracy is about making meaning in mathematics and being critical about maths. ... it is about using mathematics in all its guises – space and shape, measurement, data and statistics, algebra and, of course, number – to make sense of the real world, and using mathematics critically and being critical of maths itself. It acknowledges that numeracy is a social activity. This is why we can say that numeracy is not less than maths but more.*
>
> (p13)

Tout's definition, through the phrases *to make sense of* and *using mathematics*, suggests the need to work within a mathematics curriculum and extend it through context and application rather than producing a curriculum for numeracy. However, the current plans for numeracy, in the guise of functional mathematics, exclude all but the simplest forms of algebra and geometry and a large part of statistics, especially those elements that allow for the critical interpretation of data even at a fairly simple level. In some official circles, numeracy is seen to be synonymous with mathematics. In particular, this extends to the National Numeracy Strategy, which provides a structure or guide for teachers and is subtitled 'The framework for teaching mathematics'. On the other hand, if numeracy is taken to mean arithmetic and number sense, and if the assumptions that numeracy and mathematics are the same and that this is all that is needed by all students, then we are in fact doing our students, and by implication our future society, a major disservice.

There is, of course, a paradox here, because if we look at the mathematical activities in adults' working lives, we may only find traces of school mathematics and so conclude that the mathematical demands of adult life are insignificant. If we accept that there is little mathematics used in the workplace, then the mathematical knowledge of the school curriculum becomes less relevant and important and so a downward and negative spiral ensues – what is taught becomes less important to working practices as working practices show less evidence of making use of what is taught in school. If mathematics is reduced to simple arithmetic then most children will be able to learn what they need by the time they begin secondary school, in which case mathematics can be dispensed with. If that happens, so we dispense with any serious appreciation of science, engineering, statistics, and so on.

A further paradox also arises. If we acknowledge that many pupils have a lack of mathematical confidence and experience feelings of alienation towards the subject of mathematics but we seek to alleviate the problem, we run the risk of divorcing the subject from its roots in science and technology, leading to mathematics being disconnected from what is genuinely useful.

An additional factor emerges from the nature of mathematics itself. Mathematics consists primarily of mathematical problem-posing and solving. It is part of human culture and the mathematics of each culture serves its own unique purpose. Consequently, school mathematics should acknowledge the diverse cultural and historical origins and purposes of mathematics and the contributions made to mathematics by all, including women and people from other countries. But does it? Additionally, if the focus moves towards numeracy and mathematics for the workplace, how can the acknowledgement of its universal origins be achieved?

# Numeracy and literacy: a winning combination

We would probably all agree that being literate at some level is a basic skill that no one can afford to be without. But the importance of being numerate, particularly towards employment, has, until recently, not been fully recognised. The Department for Education and Skills (DfES, 2003), in their *The Skills for Life Survey*, produced a national profile of adult literacy and numeracy and assessed the impact different levels of skill had on people's lives. The survey found that:

*Those with level 2 or above numeracy (i.e. GCSE grade C or above) earned an average of ... £8,200 more than those with entry level or lower numeracy and that lower levels of literacy and numeracy can lead to social exclusion, denying people the opportunity to get the most out of what is available to the rest of society.*

(p77)

Indeed, Bynner and Parsons (1997) have listed four interrelated numeracy and literacy categories, each of which has a profound bearing on an individual's employment and earning potential. These are:

- poor numeracy and poor literacy;
- poor numeracy and competent literacy;
- competent numeracy and poor literacy;
- competent numeracy and competent literacy.

Research has shown that men and women sharing the lowest levels of full-time labour market participation tend to be those with poor numeracy skills rather than poor literacy. Men with poor numeracy skills tend to be those most prone to unemployment. Women with competent numeracy and poor literacy skills tend to be almost twice as likely as those with poor numeracy and competent literacy to be in full time employment. These conclusions may come as something of a surprise, as literacy has always had a higher profile than numeracy or mathematics. It is clear that what is to be taught in schools is vital. So, should we teach mathematics or should we teach numeracy? Are they the same or is one a subset of the other? Should we focus on mathematics or numeracy for employment or for the love of mathematics or both? Comparing literacy and numeracy again, most people do not forget how to read, to follow written instructions, or even how to add up simple numbers, but the ability to work out percentages, unless practised, for example, becomes relegated to 'something I did at school'. But even if agreement can be found about what should be taught, the problems of underperformance and underachievement in mathematics needs to be addressed; particularly so with girls and sections of the population from ethnic minority backgrounds or for those for whom English is not their first language. What does seem to be a self-evident truth is that the acquisition of mathematical skills is only worthwhile if children and young adults have the personal, social and moral education to make some sense of the world in which they live and thus know how to make use of those skills.

**Pause for thought** | mathematics, culture and underachievement

Consider this quotation from Zaslavsky (1981):

*It is the content and methodology of the mathematics curriculum that provides one of the most effective means for the rulers of our society to maintain class divisions.*

(p15)

With reference to the points drawn from Costello (1991) and Ernest (1991) presented below, to what extent do you believe this to be true?

- Mathematics is generally taught in a narrow context with little concern for its historical and cultural setting.

- Mathematics is presented as absolutist and the product of white middle-class males with decontextualised, abstract and formal mathematics most prized.

- Gender-biased texts reflect and presuppose the male-dominated cultural context.

- The mathematics curriculum in Britain is racist in the sense of discriminating against the needs, values and best interests of certain ethnic groups.

- IQ and other tests or means of assessment are culturally biased.

- Mathematics is used politically to promote certain values or social developments.

- School mathematics is remote from the experiences of many pupils and their own culture.

- Mathematics reflects a particular culture or society in a way that can be reasonably and productively understood.

- A lack of positive female and ethnic minority role models in mathematics serves to reinforce stereotypes.

## Summary and conclusions

There are many issues to be addressed when debating what is required of mathematics education for the twenty-first century. Pupils certainly need some basic mathematics as part of their life skills 'package' (or should this be considered numeracy?) and employers will increasingly require not only mathematical knowledge and understanding but also transferable skills such as the ability to apply mathematics in context, to reason logically and to be organised and systematic. How this combination of outcomes is to be achieved remains somewhat problematic.

## References

Anderson, J (2002) Being mathematically educated in the twenty-first century, in Haggarty, L (ed) *Teaching mathematics in secondary schools: a reader*. London: RoutledgeFalmer.

BSA (1997) *International Numeracy Survey: a comparison of the basic skills of adults, 16–60, in seven countries*. London: Basic Skills Agency.

Bynner, J and Parsons, S (1997) *Does numeracy matter?* London: Basic Skills Agency.

Costello, J (1991) *Teaching and learning mathematics 11–16*. London: Routledge.

DES (1982) *Mathematics Counts: Report of the Committee of Inquiry into the Teaching of Mathematics in Schools under the chairmanship of Dr WH Cockcroft* (the Cockroft Report). London: HMSO/Department for Education and Science.

DfES (2003) *The Skills for Life Survey: a national needs and impact survey of literacy, numeracy and ICT skills*. London: HMSO/Department for Education and Skills.

DfES (2004a) *Making Mathematics Count: Report of Professor Adrian Smith's inquiry into post-14 mathematics education* (the Smith Report). London: HMSO/Department for Education and Skills.

DfES (2004b) *The response to Professor Adrian Smith's inquiry into post-14 mathematics education*. London: HMSO/Department for Education and Skills.

Ernest, P (1991) *The philosophy of mathematics education*. London: The Falmer Press.

Hanson, M (2004) Learning and mathematics, in Ward, S (ed) *Education studies: a student's guide*. London: RoutledgeFalmer.

IEA (International Association for the Evaluation of Educational Achievement) (1995) *Third international maths and science study*. Available at **http://timesandpirls.bc.edu** (accessed 17 April 2009) (Includes reports from subsequent years.)

Kaiser, G, Luna, E and Huntley, I (eds) (1999) *International comparisons in mathematics education*. London: Falmer.

Lawlor, S (1988) *Correct core*. London: Centre for Policy Studies.

Letwin, O (1988) *Aims of schooling*. London: Centre for Policy Studies.

Mortimore, P, Sammons, P, Stoll, L, Lewis, D and Ecob, R (1988) *School matters*. Wells: Open Books.

National Research Council (1989) *Everybody Counts. Report to the nation on the future of mathematics education*. Washington, DC: National Academy Press.

PISA (2000) Knowledge and skills for life. Available at **www.pisa.oecd.org** (accessed 17 April 2009) (Includes reports from subsequent years.)

Skemp, R (1971) *Psychology of learning mathematics*. Harmondsworth: Penguin Books.

Tall, D (1995) Can all children climb the same curriculum ladder?, in Mond, D (ed) *The mathematical ability of school leavers*. Gresham Special Lecture. London: Gresham College.

Tout, D (1997) *Some reflections on adult numeracy*. Proceedings of the Third International Conference of Adults Learning Maths – a Research Forum (ALM-3). London: Goldsmiths College.

Zaslavsky, C (1981) Mathematics education: the fraud of 'Back to Basics' and the socialist counter-example. *Science and Nature*, 4: 15–27.

# Chapter 9

# Science and society

## Richard Walton

### Introduction

Modern society is largely defined by the products of science and its applications. Consequently, an understanding of science is now regarded as essential for the educated individual. Whether applying scientific ideas as an expert or making decisions as a layman, there is an increasing need for the public to have at least a minimum level of scientific literacy. Yet why should science be given such a preferred position in the curriculum that it is treated as a compulsory subject at school with all pupils conscripted to its cause? Science education, that is to say the teaching and learning of science, has become one of the great influences upon the wider world of education. In part, this is because it has stimulated some of the most innovative research of recent decades, but also because it is seen as underpinning the economic and technological future of the nation. This chapter touches upon science's historical roots, to consider what it is about the nature of science that makes it stand out, not only as such a remarkably successful human enterprise, but also what differentiates it from other competing subjects. It also discusses the many challenges and opportunities currently faced by those at the chalkface.

# What is science?

From the time of Aristotle during the fourth century BC, an attempt has been made to draw a distinction between scientific knowledge and technical skill. In doing so, Aristotle identified scientific knowledge (*episteme*) as a means of providing truths that can be demonstrated about the world as opposed to technical skill (*techne*) which he regarded as the ability to create new materials and artefacts. This distinction provided a relatively clear and simple view of the nature of science and its purpose. The Aristotelian view that the world can be systematically examined and understood strongly influenced the development of science, first of all in the Muslim world and then in Christian Europe. In the thirteenth century, Robert Grosseteste and Roger Bacon drew upon Aristotelian ideas to construct a scientific method through which knowledge was generated by an inductive–deductive pattern of scientific enquiry. The processes of induction and deduction have always been seen as central to the way in which scientific knowledge is obtained. Induction begins with making observations and leads the scientist to construct explanatory principles from them. By contrast, deduction takes the process in reverse. Beginning with general principles, the scientist is able to predict specific instances that might then be observed. The importance of practical observation in science education was stressed in the seventeenth century by Jan Comenius.

So, from the earliest days, the teaching of science has not simply been a matter of transmitting facts to be remembered and recalled, it has also included the need to teach and make full use of various skills, including observation and how to make reasoned judgements. Science education, therefore, focuses upon the following elements.

- *Knowledge* – science has a canon of facts and principles which forms the basis of our shared understanding of how the world works.
- *Practical skills* – the skills of observation and measurement need to be learned through engagement with apparatus and equipment.
- *Evaluatory frameworks* – scientific ideas are built up using logical processes by which evidence is evaluated, predictions made and hypotheses tested, often using the application of mathematics.

Science is, in simple terms, an intellectual, practical, creative and social endeavour that seeks to help us better understand and make sense of the world in which we live. In more recent years, there has been a recognition that scientific understanding is not simply a one-way process. Science and its associated technologies have the power to interact with and change our surroundings and this requires children and young adults to acquire an awareness of humankind's ecological impact (Walton, 2000). Similarly, it is increasingly the case that the wider role played by science in shaping our attitudes as members of society is being recognised through the inclusion of citizenship as an element in the school science curriculum (Ratcliffe and Grace, 2003).

The place of science in a compulsory core curriculum has long been argued along with significant discussion of the reasons why it important for the general public to have greater levels of scientific understanding (White, 1982). Millar (1996), for example, has argued that the school science curriculum should aim for public understanding in which the notion of understanding includes science content, science methods of enquiry and science as a social enterprise. The point has also been made by Wellington (1990) and Walton (2002) that not all science is learned in the formal environments of schools and classrooms but that informal sources (e.g. television, museums and science centres) have an increasingly important role to play as the pace of scientific and technological change increases.

---

### *Pause for thought* | justifying science

According to Millar (1996), the five arguments that justify the place of science in the curriculum are:

- cultural – science is a major achievement of our shared culture and it is as important to know about science as it is about the arts;
- economic – science forms the basis of many careers such as engineering, medicine and research;
- democratic – many decisions that must be made by the general public (e.g. whether to eat GM foods, use nuclear power or have our children vaccinated) are informed by scientific ideas;
- utilitarian – the application of science is useful to people living in a technologically-based society;
- social – it is important to maintain links between science and wider culture to prevent alienation of the individual.

What do you think about Millar's views? Is Newton as important a cultural figure as Shakespeare? It is really the job of schools to ensure that a supply of scientifically trained individuals is maintained? Can the public really make scientifically informed choices in complex situations? What do you regard as the most useful scientific knowledge or technical skills? Is there already a division between the scientific and technical haves and have-nots?

# Science education and cognitive development

In her seminal work arising from the Children's Learning in Science Project (CLISP) at Leeds University, Driver (1983) was led to the philosophical position that one could not apply simple induction to the methods adopted by children in learning science. This is because the prior knowledge and understandings that form a child's personal interpretation of phenomena may run counter to the accepted scientific view. These alternative explanatory frameworks are neither capricious nor transitory but, as Driver's mapping showed, are tenacious and follow consistent patterns of development. For Driver this meant that when constructing new explanatory frameworks in science, children have to be challenged to overcome what they believe to be true. Driver interpreted this shift in pupils' thinking as being akin to the paradigm shift put forward by Kuhn when scientific thought undergoes a revolution taking it from one pattern of orthodoxy to another (Kuhn, 1996). Driver's work removed from science education the myth of the *tabula rasa* where the minds of the young are empty slates or vessels waiting to be filled with knowledge. Her central theme was that new knowledge must be constructed and that this personal and social process of construction is strongly rooted in the use of language and appropriately structured tasks. In part, the findings of CLISP only served to confirm what one might expect, that as children grow older and mature intellectually so too does their capacity to understand increasingly more abstract ideas.

## Research box

### Vygotsky and the ZPD

Vygotsky (1934) drew a distinction between *spontaneous* concepts, which arise through a child's everyday practical activity and social interaction, and *scientific* concepts, which are the product of systematic instruction. As children grow, and 'the development of scientific concepts outstrips the development of spontaneous concepts', this transition places greater emphasis upon the intervention of the teacher in promoting learning through instruction (Sutherland, 1992). Central to Vygotsky's approach was the notion of the zone of proximal development or ZPD:

> The zone of proximal development of the child is the distance between his actual development, determined with the help of independently solved tasks, and the level of the potential development of the child determined with the help of tasks solved by the child under the guidance of adults and in cooperation with more intelligent partners.

> (Van der Veer and Valsiner, 1991, p337)

Children can, therefore, learn how to progress in their scientific knowledge and understanding through the intervention of the teacher or through working with more experienced peers.

The notion that through exposure to appropriately structured tasks a child may be helped to advance in terms of cognitive development has been one of the major outcomes of the work of Shayer and Adey (1981). Their Cognitive Acceleration in Science Education project (CASE), based at King's College London, has played an important role in British science education, and the influence of Shayer and Adey's work has extended into other subject areas and to the broader realm of standardised assessment and testing. Interestingly, Shayer and Adey recently repeated their original study only to find a general deterioration in the performance of British school children when compared to that of their predecessors a generation earlier. At present, it is not clear what causative factors are responsible for this decline (Crace, 2006).

Recent insights into science education and cognitive development have tended to move away from a simple constructivist model for science education into more complex fields of enquiry (Solomon, 1994; Osborne, 1996; Ogborn, 1997; Jenkins, 2000). Lave and Wenger (1991), for example, have employed the notion of 'situated cognition' to indicate the importance of the context in which learning takes place, while Engeström (1991) has explored Lave and Wenger's own notion of 'legitimate peripheral participation' even further. By contrast, Sharp and Kuerbis (2006) have drawn upon recent evidence from cognitive neuroscience to maintain that children's mental models of certain scientific phenomena are formed through a process of chaotic thought.

# Science in primary and secondary schools

The primary classroom has long operated as an environment in which subject integration is often the norm. Indeed, the boundaries between subject areas have usefully been blurred where class teachers have decided to organise pupils' work around themes or through project activity. Also, the training of primary teachers generally continues to encourage a broad and balanced view not just of science but of the curriculum as a whole, which, at its very best, can present the pupil with a highly coherent educational experience. Science, however, poses particular problems in that many primary teachers either lack confidence in teaching scientific ideas (Harlen and Holroyd, 1997) or that the faulty transmission of scientific ideas from teacher to pupil takes place because primary teachers themselves retain significant misconceptions and alternative explanatory frameworks (Jarvis et al., 2003). These can be addressed by more effective training and mentoring in science during the pre- and post-service training of primary teachers (Sharp, 2004; Hudson, 2005). In secondary schools science is essentially taught in isolation.

The fact that there are very different environments in which science is taught in primary and secondary schools raises problems of it own. Speering and Rennie (1996) have suggested that, rather than being an entirely positive experience, the transition from primary to secondary school can be a time of unfulfilled expectation for pupils who often move from a stimulating child-centred environment in the primary school to the less motivating *teacher-centred, blackboard-directed learning* of the secondary school. Of course, recent years have seen the development of a National Curriculum in schools in England and Wales. The introduction of a common core of science ought to have addressed some of the problems of continuity and progression faced by children as they move through the school system and particularly at the transition from primary to secondary. Gorwood (1991) has suggested that the difficulty of transition was not entirely solved by the introduction of the National Curriculum since primary and secondary teachers do not always communicate with each other effectively. This view is consonant with the more general findings of Galton et al. (1999), who stated:

*The most striking evidence of a drop in pupil performance emerges in OFSTED's data around the time of transfer from primary to secondary schooling with a steep rise between the end of Key Stage 2 (KS2) and the early stages of Year 7 in the proportions of schools where pupil attainment was judged to be 'unsatisfactory' – a figure of 50% of all secondary schools is reported.*

(p13)

Clearly, difficulties of transition are not restricted to science alone but science does have the particular problem of pupils often facing disappointment on entry to secondary schools, where their high expectations of secondary science classes are not realised when faced with the often pedestrian way in which secondary science is sometimes presented when compared with the more motivating experience of science teaching at primary level.

Science teaching in secondary schools has long been dominated by its division into three subject disciplines, physics, chemistry and biology, with the implication that these subjects are supported by a working knowledge of mathematics. Science teaching in many secondary schools is built around an infrastructure of laboratories and departmental organisation that supports this way of arranging the curriculum. Such subject divisions seem to reflect the natural organisation of the world. Physics reveals the fundamental forces and relationships between bodies; chemistry applies these to the interactions between atoms and molecules; biology studies the complex relationships between living organisms. Critics of this separate subject model see science as an integrated discipline in which interpenetrating subject areas should be taught in a co-ordinated, thematic manner. This, it is felt, more accurately reflects the way in which science is met in the world. But, as Atkin and Black (2003) have pointed out, there is no simple middle ground between advocacy of a separate subject approach and that of integrated science. This has led to a situation in which the content of science has been structured in different ways in secondary schools today. These include:

- as separate sciences with physics, chemistry and biology taught by separate specialist teachers (may lead to individually certificated awards in each of the subject areas);
- as co-ordinated science with physics, chemistry and biology taught as part of a scheme in which linking themes are developed and teaching expertise shared (certification is likely to be a double award in science).
- as integrated science all delivered by perhaps one individual (certification is likely to be a double award in science).

There are advantages to delivering science as an integrated subject. By not tying science teachers to separate subject disciplines, schools have greater flexibility in deploying their staff and timetabling and resourcing of science is made easier, particularly for smaller schools where a limited pool of science staff may not support separate subject work. However, such an approach only highlights the problem that much physics teaching in particular is delivered by non-specialists. This is due to the relatively small numbers of physicists entering the teaching profession when compared to those with backgrounds in chemistry and the life sciences.

Within the National Curriculum, the end of Key Stage 4 marks the end of compulsory education. It is the point at which young people first gain the qualifications in public examinations that they will carry with them throughout their lives. In this regard, science education must fulfil a double purpose: preparation for further study and also preparation for the world of work. It used to be that curriculum content was decided in a top-down manner. Universities decided what was required for matriculation and this, in turn, determined the content of A levels taken at age 18. A level requirements then determined the content of O level examinations at age 16. This was a system driven by the need to provide a single academic route from school to university. This produced a system in which A level examinations were regarded as the 'gold standard' for education as high quality, intellectually demanding, objective tests. The difficulty was that a system designed to produce an academic elite was ill-suited to a system of mass education with important vocational needs. Science education from nursery to university is perhaps more complicated now than ever before and still undergoing change (e.g. with the introduction of 21st century science at GCSE).

# Science, education and the world of work

There is a growing crisis in the supply of scientists (Roberts, 2002). Many reasons have been given for this state of affairs. Some relate to the nature of the subject disciplines themselves, with the physical sciences in particular perceived as being more difficult than others because of the knowledge base required, some to the need to show proficiency in mathematics, and some to the abstract nature of many scientific concepts which makes study intellectually demanding. In addition to this is the belief that scientific careers do not provide the high levels of remuneration that are enjoyed by those working in other fields such as law or finance. It has also been the case that the public image of the scientist has generally been associated with character types that young people do not find particularly attractive. The media still portray stereotypical views of scientists as gauche, rather socially inept individuals: the 'boffins' of yesteryear transmuted into the 'nerds' of today. There has also been a tendency to portray science as a white, male and middle class pursuit, a state of affairs which has served to exclude on grounds of gender, class and race (Bevins et al., 2003). On the other hand, and with the rise of new subjects such as information technology, media production, sports science and the paramedical disciplines, which bring together a wide range of cross-curricular areas, the cultural divide that was once held to exist between the sciences and the arts is now no longer so prevalent. And, even if fewer people are moving into the traditional pure sciences, this is offset by people moving into a wider range of careers that require some level of scientific literacy.

In order to address the need to provide more scientists, increasing efforts are being made to supplement the experience gained in the classroom through curriculum enrichment activities giving pupils access to science and applications in industrial and other 'real-world' contexts (Parvin et al., 1997), although Osborne (2000) casts doubt upon the efficacy of placing so much emphasis upon providing 'pre-professional training' when so few pupils actually progress to take up science-based careers. Despite Osborne's reservations, significant central government and regional development investment has been placed into providing networks to support and supplement the science curriculum.

Recent years have seen the rise of the *public understanding of science movement* (Gregory and Miller, 1998). In part, this is a response to the duty laid upon scientists to communicate their work more effectively but it is also a response to a perceived need for improved scientific literacy. This has led to the development of government policy to support programmes of informal science education. Informal programmes mean that significant science learning can take place outside the physical environment of the school classroom and outside the structure of the formal curriculum. However, Jeffs and Smith (2005) have emphasised the point that both formal and informal education are not mutually exclusive terms in that they reflect a *shared concern for learning* on the part of formal and informal educators. The motivational effect of learning in informal settings such as zoos, museums or hands-on science centres, or through curriculum enrichment activities such as competitions, drama and role-play, is so strong that, increasingly, activities such as these that were once thought to be peripheral to the science curriculum are now widely seen as part of the mainstream (Walton, 1997).

## Summary and conclusions

Science plays a central role in the school curriculum. It provides the groundwork of knowledge, skills and attitudes that enables individuals not only to understand the world around them but also to play a full part as members of an increasingly technological society. The growth of science since the mid-twentieth century has been driven in part by the economic and strategic necessity to provide a technically literate workforce. However, increasingly in recent years the emphasis has shifted towards a view of scientific literacy that places greater emphasis upon the individual's need to make informed choices within a democratic society. This has produced a concomitant shift away from the uncritical acceptance of the authority of the scientist as expert. The public is now expected to enter into more informed debate and, in so doing, draw upon some understanding of the nature of the scientific enterprise, including its content and its methods.

Alongside this growth in science, parallel developments in science education have been at the forefront of promoting change in teaching and learning. The influence of constructivist approaches to pedagogy, for example, has extended far beyond the boundaries of the school science curriculum. This has had for some the unsettling effect of removing the old certainties that science seemed to provide by questioning the objectivity of scientific knowledge itself, a situation which may in turn challenge the authority of the science teacher.

The future of science education seems to present the prospect of a more complex relationship between the intrinsic need to provide a critically aware and more scientifically informed public, and the extrinsic factors that require pupils to be adequately prepared for the world of work and a career in science. This will be a challenge for science teachers, not only to be able to develop their own skills as scientists but also as counsellors and advisers. This will require them to acquire many more of the 'soft skills' that were previously the province of the informal educator.

## References

Atkin, JM and Black, P (2003) *Inside science education reform: a history of curricular and policy change*. Buckingham: Open University Press.

Bevins, S, Harrison, W and Jordan J (2003) *Ethnicity and underachievement in science and mathematics education*. A Report to the Royal Society. Sheffield Hallam University: Centre for Science Education.

Crace, J (2006) Children are less able than they used to be, *Guardian*, 24 January.

Driver, R (1983) *The pupil as scientist?* Milton Keynes: Open University Press.

Engeström, Y (1991) Non scolae sed vitae discimus: towards overcoming the encapsulation of school learning. *Learning and Instruction*, 1: 243–59.

Galton, M, Gray, J and Ruddock, J (1999) *The impact of school transitions and transfers on pupil progress and attainment*. DfEE Research Report No. 131. London: HMSO.

Gorwood, B (1991) Primary–secondary transfer after the national curriculum. *School Organisation*, 11(3): 283–90.

Gregory, J and Miller, S (1998) *Science in public: communication culture and credibility*. New York: Plenum Trade.

Harlen, W and Holroyd, C (1997) Primary teachers' understanding of concepts of science: impact on confidence and teaching. *International Journal of Science Education*, 19(1): 93–105.

Hudson, P (2005) Identifying mentoring practices for developing effective primary science teaching. *International Journal of Science Education*, 27(14): 1723–39.

Jarvis, T, Pell, A and McKeon, F (2003) Changes in primary teachers' science knowledge and understanding during a two year in-service programme. *Research in Science and Technological Education*, 21(1): 17–42.

Jeffs, T and Smith, MK (2005) *Informal education: conversation, democracy and learning.* Nottingham: Educational Heretics Press.

Jenkins, E (2000) Constructivism in school science education: powerful model or the most dangerous intellectual tendency? *Science and Education*, 9: 599–610.

Kuhn, TS (1996) *The structure of scientific revolutions.* Chicago: University of Chicago Press.

Lave, J and Wenger, E (1991) *Situated learning: legitimate peripheral participation.* Cambridge: Cambridge University Press.

Millar, R (1996) Towards a science curriculum for public understanding. *School Science Review*, 77(280): 7–18.

Ogborn, J (1997) Constructivist metaphors of learning science. *Science and Education*, 6: 121–33.

Osborne, JF (1996) Beyond constructivism. *Science Education*, 80(1): 53–82.

Osborne, J (2000) Science for citizenship, in Monk, M and Osborne, J (eds) *Good practice in science teaching: what research has to say.* Buckingham: Open University Press.

Parvin, J, Key, M and Mapletoft, M (1997) Industry as a resource for teaching science, in Thompson, DL (ed) *Science education in the 21st century.* Aldershot: Arena.

Ratcliffe, M and Grace, M (2003) *Science education for citizenship: teaching socio-scientific issues.* Maidenhead: Open University Press.

Roberts, G (2002) *SET for Success: Report on Sir Gareth Roberts' review of the supply of people with science, technology and mathematics skills.* HM Treasury: HMSO.

Sharp, J (ed) (2004) *Developing primary science.* Exeter: Learning Matters.

Sharp, JG and Kuerbis, P (2006) Children's ideas about the solar system and the chaos in learning science. *Science Education*, 90(1): 124–47.

Shayer, M and Adey, P (1981) *Towards a science of science teaching: cognitive development and curriculum demand.* London: Heinemann.

Solomon, J (1994) The rise and fall of constructivism. *Studies in science education*, 23: 1–19.

Speering, W and Rennie, L (1996) Students' perceptions about science: the impact of transition from primary to secondary school. *Research in Science Education*, 26(3): 283–98.

Sutherland, P (1992) *Cognitive development today: Piaget and his critics.* London: Paul Chapman.

Van der Veer, R and Valsiner, J (1991) *Understanding Vygotsky: a quest for synthesis.* Oxford: Blackwell.

Vygotsky, LS (1934) Thinking and speech, in Rieber, RW and Carton AS (eds) (1987) *The collected works of LS Vygotsky: vol. 1 Problems of general psychology.* New York: Plenum.

Walton, RJ (1997) Improving the image of science, in Thompson, DL (ed) *Science education in the 21st century.* Aldershot: Arena.

Walton, RJ (2000) Heidegger in the hands-on science and technology centre: some philosophical reflections. *Journal of Technology Education*, 12(1): 50–61.

Walton, RJ (2002) *Science teaching and the public understanding of science.* Sheffield: Sheffield Hallam University Press.

Wellington, JJ (1990) Formal and informal learning in science: the role of interactive centres. *Physics Education*, 25: 247–57.

White, J (1982) *The aims of education restated.* London: Routledge and Kegan Paul.

# Chapter 10

# The nature of higher education

## Stephen Ward

### Introduction

University education in the UK used to be for an intellectual elite, but policies for expansion and widening participation are leading to a mass higher education system. The university is now said to be a business in the higher education market and higher tuition fees mean that its entrants might become more like customers than students. Unlike schools, universities have traditionally enjoyed autonomy from government control and academic freedom for their staff. This chapter examines higher education in universities, and its role in UK society today. It looks at the ways in which universities have traditionally defined knowledge, what counts as knowledge, and how this has changed with increasing government intervention. In particular, it examines the ways in which market forces have affected what universities do and the ways in which they are run. The term 'university' is used as shorthand for the various higher education institutions and the courses operating therein.

## What is higher education?

Higher education (HE) is a level of study that begins after A Levels or their equivalents. It is taught in higher education institutions (HEIs) such as universities and colleges of higher education. A basic hierarchy of awards at different levels, with the usual length of full-time study includes:

- the one-year Certificate in Higher Education (CertHE);
- the two-year Diploma in Higher Education (DipHE);
- the two-year Foundation Degree (FdA, FdSc);
- the three-year Bachelor of Arts (BA) and Science (BSc) degrees;
- the one-year Master of Arts (MA) and Science (MSc) degrees;
- the three- or four-year Doctorate (PhD).

There are also vocationally oriented degrees with specialist professional titles such as Bachelor of Education (BEd) or Masters in Business Administration (MBA). Higher education is sometimes confused with further education (FE), which is the term used to refer to education after the statutory school leaving age of 16 but at a lower level than higher education. This is complicated by the fact that further education colleges often teach higher education degrees and other HE courses. These are validated and awarded by a separate university or other body. It is unusual for further education courses to be taught in a university or college of higher education.

*Pause for thought* | why do a degree?

Higher education is an expensive business. Many people give up jobs and earning money in the short term to pay university fees. What are their reasons for doing this? Is it to have a better career and to earn more money later, or is it about education for its own sake? What made you decide to go into higher education and do a degree? Was it because your friends and family expected you to do it? Was it because of your own drive to better yourself or advance your career prospects?

# Ancient and medieval origins of universities

The Academy of Plato founded in 387 BC in ancient Greece might be said to have been the first university. Plato was a pupil of Socrates who was committed to a philosophy of rational argument that was contrary to the culture of the times. Found by the Court of Athens to be guilty of neglecting the established gods and corrupting the young, Socrates was sentenced to death and chose to accept execution rather than recant his commitment to rational truth. Socrates's principles, the fearless pursuit of truth in the face of irrational belief and bigotry, are fundamental in the modern university.

The term 'university' is derived from the Latin *universitas*, meaning 'a community'. So the original notion was of a universal kinship of scholars. China had universities in the seventh century. The Al Azhar Islamic University began in Cairo from AD 1000. In Europe, the first universities were in Bologna and Paris in the twelfth century for the teaching of Roman Catholic theology. As Haddad (2000) has explained, the medieval European universities were internationally linked. The lack of national frontiers in the medieval period, and the use of Latin as a *lingua* franca, allowed academics to interact freely across geographical areas and there was recognition of awards across institutions. The early universities were exclusively for men. Teachers were known as 'Masters' and wore hoods and gowns, and degrees were awarded 'with honours'. These medieval traditions continue in university life today and most strongly at Oxford and Cambridge. Established in the thirteenth century, these were the first universities in England. While they still have the highest reputation built on long history and tradition, their students did not always live up to expectations:

*Trevelyan describes the early days as 'riotous, lawless and licentious'. The typical student, he says, was 'miserably poor; he often learnt very little for want of books and tutoring, and left without taking a degree… Some of these old Oxonians, apparently, were as young as 14, but took easily to the tavern and the brothel. They even had a tendency to roam the countryside in robber bands.*

(Ellis, 1995, p54)

Things rapidly improved with the founding of the Oxbridge college system and the two universities went on to supply the nation's political and administrative leaders for centuries.

The Renaissance began to draw universities away from the control of the church, with tutors increasingly recruited from civil society, and with the fermentation of new ideas. The seventeenth century saw the formation of nation states, border controls and the use of national languages in education. The result was that universities lost their universal, borderless quality and became enclosed within national systems. The European Union's Socrates Scheme now funds students and staff to make links between European universities. However, van der Wende and Huisman (2004) have pointed out that attempts to develop a common university curriculum across Europe have been frustrated by government resistance to change.

It would be a mistake, though, to see the medieval period as a golden age of academic freedom. The knowledge the universities were allowed to share was still determined very much by the church. The Sorbonne in Paris, for example, was based upon a contract between the college and the crown to teach theology, and church control over university knowledge remained powerful, even throughout the Renaissance. There was no original research, and privileges were only guaranteed as long as the teachings of the Roman Catholic Church were not questioned. Universities were still supporting the church in 1633 during Galileo's trial for heresy, with the sentence against him read publicly in every institution. The role of the university at this time, then, was restricted to preserving and deepening the officially recognised knowledge of the church, or 'revealed' rather than 'verifiable' knowledge.

# The modern university

The modern university began with the Enlightenment and the industrial revolution of the late eighteenth and early nineteenth centuries. The entrepreneurial society turned to the university for scientific knowledge and trained professionals to fulfil the needs of national economies. The University of Berlin became the prototype for the modern university, a national institution with academic freedom to pursue truth. Its principles were based on the philosophy of Immanuel Kant and the humanist ideals of its founder Wilhelm Humboldt. Kant differentiated between knowledge that should be controlled by the state, such as law and medicine, and the pure academic truth of philosophy. In creating the University of Berlin, Humboldt's ingenuity was to resolve the conflict between the state and the academic community. He emphasised that the state needed a common cultural identity and that the role of the university was to reinforce this through the advancement of culture, reason, learning and teaching. So the Humboldt university model provided the highly educated professionals required by industry in exchange for freedom and autonomy in the knowledge it produced. Neave (2000) showed that the university contributed to a definition of the nation state itself in the form of the transmission of national culture and particular knowledge traditions:

*In von Humboldt's notion of academic freedom, the state itself served as a 'buffer organ' against outside pressures, not least of which was the utilitarianism associated with the rising industrial classes.*

(p35)

Towards the end of the nineteenth century, the university evolved into a research facility because industrial production began to need scientific knowledge and academics trained in experimental methods. It is the nineteenth-century Humboldt university model on which the civic universities of the UK were based. In this model:

- the state funds the university;
- the university has autonomy to define and codify knowledge and its staff have the freedom to pursue truth and to engage in a critique of the *status quo*;
- the university provides the skilled professionals and the new knowledge and research required by industry;
- the university contributes to the definition of the nation state through the knowledge and culture which it defines.

> *Pause for thought* | academic freedom
>
> The model of the Humboldt university is an attractive one for academics as they have complete freedom to determine what counts as knowledge and what should be learned. In contrast, the school curriculum is heavily controlled by the state. What are the advantages and disadvantages of university staff having unrestricted academic freedom? Do you agree with the Humboldt university model, or should governments have more control and accountability for tax-payers' money? Should students have the right to decide what is taught at university?

# The university and the state in the UK

In Britain, the relationship between universities and the state has always been ambiguous. Kogan and Hanney (2000) have detailed the various influences and directions which have been in place since the nineteenth century. Compared with most other countries, and compared to other sectors of the state, UK universities have had a high level of autonomy for much of evolution, enjoying legal status and freedom in:

- their mission;
- their finances;
- the employment of staff;
- student admissions;
- the content of courses;
- deciding on what counts as knowledge.

Neave (1988) has suggested that the universities of continental Europe became firmly embedded into national bureaucracies over this period, whereas in Britain *the status of universities as a property-owning corporation of scholars ... was preserved*. The philosopher John Stuart Mill argued that government intervention in universities should be limited in order to avoid the evil of adding to government power. Mill's formulation leads to the notion of a *facilitatory state which would provide resources to universities whose freedom would be enjoyed within an area of negotiation largely controlled by the universities themselves* (Kogan and Hanney, 2000).

# The binary system in the UK

The first part of the twentieth century saw the development of 'red-brick' universities in the urban centres of Britain such as Liverpool, Birmingham, Bristol, Leeds and Glasgow to respond to the local need for knowledge and technology. All universities were well funded by the government but remained free from state control. In many ways, this was an ideal higher education system, except that it was for a small elite with only about 5 per cent of each school cohort progressing to university, fewer than most of Europe and the United States. The Robbins Report (1963) recommended an immediate expansion of higher education with new universities to be built and colleges of advanced technology to be given university status. This led in the 1960s to the development of the so-called 'plate-glass' universities such as Warwick, Bath, Lancaster, Essex and York, all with royal charters to award degrees.

At the same time, higher education began in other colleges of technology and education which, like schools, were mostly run by local education authorities (LEAs). Their degrees were awarded by other universities. During the 1970s, many of these colleges were merged to form large polytechnics and the Council for National Academic Awards (CNAA), a national body for the approval and awarding of degrees in the colleges and polytechnics, was founded.

These developments gave Britain a 'binary' system of higher education including universities with a royal charter and polytechnics and colleges whose degrees were awarded by the CNAA and which were funded by the LEAs. Anthony Crosland, the Labour Education Minister at the time, had proposed the system with the ambition of creating separate branches of higher education to serve different purposes, with the universities providing 'academic' education and the polytechnics providing more 'vocational' and technical higher education over which the state would have more direct control.

---

*Pause for thought* | academic and vocational higher education

The 'binary' higher education system was designed to create universities providing 'academic' degrees and polytechnics providing 'vocational' studies. Kogan and Hanney (2000) have pointed out that this was in contradiction to the Labour government's policy for schools, which was to move to a 'unitary' system of comprehensive secondary education with the abolition of grammar schools. Do you agree with the principle of there being two types of university: those which teach purely 'academic' subjects such as philosophy or the arts, sciences and humanities, and those which teach 'vocational' subjects such as teaching and nursing?

---

The heads of the polytechnics, however, resisted being treated like schools with their finances controlled by the LEAs and fought for financial independence. This was granted by the Secretary of State for Education in 1989 with the incorporation of polytechnics as independent institutions, although the request for the title of 'polytechnic universities' was refused. But things were to change rapidly. The 'binary' system was soon abolished when all polytechnics were given full university status in 1992. Britain suddenly had a single higher education system of universities, with some colleges of higher education, many of which later attained university status as 'teaching-led' institutions.

# Universities in the twenty-first century: mass higher education in the market place

Although most HEIs are now referred to as universities, the hierarchy of university status continues with the ancient universities of Oxford and Cambridge, and the London universities, at the top. These and other elite universities identify themselves as 'the Russell Group' because their vice chancellors regularly meet together in the colonial surroundings of the Russell Hotel in London. The hierarchy of institutions is now formalised through league tables of university quality and student satisfaction surveys in which, interestingly, the traditional high status universities are not always rated highly by their students. Just as companies rate their products through satisfaction surveys, the state now tests market opinion in the same way. So, while not directly controlling the knowledge taught in universities, the state controls universities through the market.

The market is the massively increased numbers of students in higher education, which has risen from 5 per cent of the university-going age cohort in the early 1960s to some 40 per cent now, with a government-set target of 50 per cent by the year 2010. In fact, this is a target for the whole of the European Union (EU) and was determined at the EU Lisbon agreement in 2001 to equip Europe to compete in global markets. Coulby (2005) has noted four features of this new global economy:

- *accessibility* of knowledge through increased technology;
- *superabundance* of knowledge;
- *marketisation* of knowledge bought and sold as a commodity;
- *internationalisation* of knowledge which is readily developed and exchanged over continents.

Mass higher education, then, is now seen as one of the mechanisms for Europe's survival in the race for prosperity and knowledge at a time when countries like China are opening a new university every few months. The debate about universities has moved away from academic autonomy to 'who pays'. This creates its own problems:

- increased state funding for universities as a result of mass higher education means higher taxation;
- political parties who propose higher taxation do not get elected;
- high-tax economies tend to be less successful.

---

### *Pause for thought* | higher education and the economy

Successive governments and the European Union argue that economies need more higher education, although Wolf (2002) provides evidence that economies across the world do not necessarily benefit from higher education in the sense of increasing production or raising a country's position in the international economic league tables. Do you agree with expanding higher education to a wider audience, or does it just lead to the prospect of unemployed and disaffected graduates? Does the economy need so many graduates?

---

With the onset of mass higher education in the UK, the state was no longer able to fund universities as it had done for the elite universities of the past. So funding needed to come from elsewhere. In the late 1990s, the Dearing Report on higher education (NCIHE, 1997) recommended the introduction of substantial tuition fees payable by individual students, together with a system of student loans, repayable on employment. This was accepted after fierce political controversy, to be followed by further increases in student fees. There is every indication that tuition fees will continue to rise as the demand for high-quality higher education increases. Tuition fees transfer the funding of higher education from the state to the individual and form part of the UK government's attempts to reduce the control of the state and to allow the market to control development and quality. The rationale for market-driven higher education is outlined as follows.

- Students have a choice of university.
- Students pay their fees for a degree which will secure them more remunerative employment.
- Universities have to compete for students.
- Increased competition raises quality in higher education.
- The state can reduce its financial commitment and keep taxes low.

- Low-tax economies are more successful.
- Businesses and employers will have more resources to pay high salaries to well-educated graduates.

This 'virtuous' circle was reinforced by Wolf (2002), who showed that the introduction of tuition fees in other countries has not deterred university entrants, and by the argument that graduates' earnings over a lifetime exceed those of non-graduates (the implication being that graduates can afford to pay for it).

---

**Pause for thought** | who pays for university degrees?

Some people argue that higher education should be free. Others argue that graduates benefit from their degrees and should contribute financially to their own education. What are the economic arguments for and against these positions? Should there be a special case for those graduates who go on to perform particular public functions (e.g. teachers, doctors, dentists) or should all graduates be treated the same? See Stevens (2004) for further discussion of the politics of university fees.

---

# Widening participation and the world of work

Despite all the efforts to increase the number of places in universities from the 1960s, those taking up the opportunity remained predominantly from the middle classes. The extreme end of this was the way in which the Universities of Oxford and Cambridge took relatively high proportions of students from public schools and then supplied government and businesses with its leaders. This has been depicted by Ellis (1995) as 'the Oxbridge conspiracy'.

The higher education system of progression from school at 18 also worked against those who were already in employment and not successful in education earlier. In order to allow more working-class people to penetrate higher education, UK governments have instituted a policy of 'widening participation' designed to extend access. This has been realised through a variety of strategies.

- The Open University began in the 1960s to allow part-time degree study by correspondence.
- Access courses began in the 1980s as a bridging year to higher education for mature people without formal entry qualifications.
- Foundation degrees began in the late 1990s for those in work to study on a part-time basis while continuing in employment.
- Links between universities and secondary schools have been developed to raise working-class pupils' awareness of the possibilities of higher education.
- The Office for Fair Access to Higher Education (OFFA) was set up to ensure equality of entry to universities.

As well as widening the social class of students entering university, governments have also moved to ensure that the university curriculum is directly linked to students' employability. To this end, the Quality Assurance Agency (QAA) was established in the 1990s with a remit to approve, and improve, teaching and learning in higher education. A kind of government inspection agency, the QAA did not have the remit to approve curriculum content in degree courses – governments are not allowed to interfere in academic autonomy. It was designed to ensure that students were taught properly and that their studies equipped them with 'transferable skills' which could be used in employment.

Research box

### the decline of the intellectual

Furedi (2004) has argued that the government control of universities has become stronger through academic auditing by the QAA. Academics from different universities are employed by the QAA in policing subject quality. This makes it appear that the universities retain autonomy, but Furedi has suggested that this process has converted academics into 'professionals' who serve as inquisitors on behalf of the QAA and others who act on behalf of the university. This leads to the denigration of intellectual life, a diminished level of individual freedom and a decline in the search for 'objective truth'. According to Furedi, intellectuals should influence the politics of the real world; instead they are trapped as professionals in the institutional bureaucracy of the university:

> *Professionalism promotes values and forms of behaviour that may well be inconsistent with those of the intellectual. Activities such as offering a critique of the status quo, acting as the conscience of society, or pursuing the truth regardless of the consequences are not what the job of a professional is all about.*

(p39)

The shifting balance between state control and control by the institution results in the diminishing of the academic freedom and the independence of university knowledge.

# Postmodern higher education: the university in ruins

The case for marketised mass higher education has its critics. Some argue that mass higher education has had a 'dumbing-down' effect: degrees have been devalued and standards in universities have fallen. Others raise more serious academic concerns about marketisation and the decline of the state. In the 'modern' university, the state played a strong role in funding and, by holding on to its autonomy, the university was able to define the cultural identity of the nation. With marketisation and privatisation in the 'postmodern' world, the state is weakened (Green, 1997).

One impact of marketisation on the university curriculum is that more and more students, rather than academics, make decisions about degrees and their content. As a result, popular degree subjects such as media studies, sports science, drama, dance, commercial music, football, golf and astrology thrive, while traditional subjects close down because they are no longer economically viable. Recently, some universities have closed down departments such as mathematics and chemistry, which were found to be 'uneconomical' to run. The government has found itself unable to prevent these closures, firstly because it is unable to control the university curriculum directly and secondly because it is unable to find additional funding simply to subsidise a university department not 'paying its way'. Readings (1996) has argued that on this basis the very foundations of the traditional western university are crumbling into postmodern chaos. The 'hollowing out' of the nation state through global capitalism and transnational corporations has led to the ruin of the modernist university:

*The modern university was conceived by Humboldt as one of the primary apparatuses through which this production of national subjects was to take place in modernity, and the decline of the nation-state raises serious questions about the nature of the contemporary function of the university.*

(p46)

The commodification of knowledge as information to be bought and sold, and the infantilisation and proletarianisation of the student population, mean that the university ceases to reflect the state culture, becoming nothing more than an economic instrument, like an airline. Decisions about which subjects are taught are similar to decisions about which routes to fly, and decisions about which subjects to study are similar to decisions about what people will pay to get there. A vice chancellor becomes the chief executive of a private company. Higher education is also no longer to be the exclusive preserve of universities and colleges. Recent changes to HE provision make it possible for private organisations such as Microsoft to award HE qualifications, and provision exists for even schools to offer higher education level courses.

Barnett (2000) has also noted the university disappearing as a tangible entity that defines and codifies knowledge:

*The contemporary university is dissolving into the wider world … The postmodern university is a distributed university … It is a multinational concern, stretching out to and accommodating its manifold audiences. It [is] … no longer a site of knowledge, but, rather a site of knowledge possibilities … The university is no longer to be understood in terms of the category of knowledge but rather in terms of shifting and proliferating processes of knowing.*

(pp20–21)

Barnett makes another point about the university curriculum. It is not simply that subjects are determined by the market, but that the nature of university knowledge has changed from the pursuit of truth to the teaching of 'performative skills'. Students' learning in a subject is now depicted in terms of the skills they will learn to equip them 'to perform' in the world of employment. History graduates, for example, are no longer historians, but those with the transferable skills for industry. As Barnett has suggested: *as an institution with rules of its own that governed what it is to know, the university is no more.* Of course, it is the world that is changing around the university. Barnett has argued that we are in a world of 'fragility' and that the university must acknowledge uncertainty, unpredictability, challengeability and contestability. Scholarship should take on a worldly role, there should not just be self-indulgent private debates between academics. The postmodern university should help people to live without fear in an uncertain world. Delanty (2001) has argued a new role for the university in the context of cultural and epistemological changes in society with the democratisation of knowledge:

*Given that the university is no longer the crucial institution in society for the reproduction of instrumental/technical knowledge and is also no longer the codifier of a now fragmented national culture, it  can ally itself to civil society. No longer the privileged site of particular kinds of knowledge, it can become a key institution in a society that is coming to depend more and more on knowledge …*

(p6)

## Research box

### the university in the twenty-first century

Despite the concerns raised by Barnett (2000), the possibilities for the future of the university in which it may be able to retain its modernist role are endless if only it would wake up to this. Although there is an overwhelming call for skills, he has argued, wider society calls for knowledge, breadth, critical reason and freedom:

> *society is hesitantly intimating that it needs the universities to live up to their rhetoric of guardians of reason. The university seems intent on constructing itself in narrower frames of self-understanding. A trick is being missed.*

(p34)

In The ignorance explosion, Lukasiewicz (1994) has suggested that the proliferation of knowledge is text-based and that there is more of it than can be comprehended. Knowledge production far exceeds knowledge comprehension and the relationship between academics and their audience has broken down. There is, then, a new illiteracy. Students are reduced to having data-handling skills and the human mind is reduced to processing data. The paradox becomes that knowledge production creates ignorance. Increase in academic fields also increases illiteracy and produces the need for academic literacy courses. We are ignorant of the world we have created. It is an unknowable world.

## Summary and conclusions

This chapter has outlined the changes that have taken place in higher education with the move from the 'modern' to the 'postmodern' university in relation to changes in the market place. Higher education continues to be in a state of rapid and perhaps irreversible flux, with more to come as the student population increases and successive governments enable the influence of the market on education to continue. Debates on the future of higher education will no doubt focus around several key questions.

- How do market forces affect the nature and status of university knowledge?

- How does higher education relate to the economy and should it be academically or more vocationally inclined?

- Does mass higher education lead to improvements in the global as well as national economy?

- Does the expansion, massification, commodification and infantilisation of higher education lead to 'dumbing down'?

- Do changes to higher education as a whole necessarily lead to loss of academic freedom and the decline of the intellectual?

Such questions, and the inevitable debates that will follow, however, mask one of the virtues of higher education, the development and self-realisation of the individual through academic study. That this is now open to more people must itself be a matter for celebration.

# *References*

Barnett, R (2000) *Realising the university in an age of supercomplexity*. Buckingham: Society for Research into Higher Education/Open University Press.

Coulby, D (2005) The knowledge economy: technology and characteristics, in Coulby, D and Zamabeta, E (eds) *World yearbook of education: globalisation and nationalism in education*. London: RoutledgeFalmer.

Delanty, G (2001) *Challenging knowledge: the university in the knowledge society*. Buckingham: Society for Research into Higher Education/Open University Press.

Ellis, W (1995) *The Oxbridge conspiracy: how the ancient universities have kept their stranglehold on the establishment*. London: Michael Joseph.

Furedi, F (2004) *Where have all the intellectuals gone? Confronting 21st century philistinism*. London: Continuum.

Green, A (1997) *Education, globalisation and the nation state*. London: Macmillan.

Haddad, G (2000) University and society: responsibilities, contracts, partnerships, in Neave, G (ed) *The universities' responsibilities to society*. International Perspectives Series. Oxford: Pergamon Press.

Kogan, M and Hanney, S (2000) *Reforming higher education*. London: Jessica Kingsley.

Lukasiewicz, J-F (1994) *The ignorance explosion*. Ottawa: Carleton University Press.

Neave, G (1988) On being economical with university autonomy: being an account of the retrospective joys of a written constitution, in Tight, M (ed) *Academic freedom and responsibility*. Buckingham: Society for Research into Higher Education/Open University Press.

Neave, G (2000) Universities' responsibilities to society: an historical exploration of an enduring issue, in Neave, G (ed) *The universities' responsibilities to society*. International Perspectives Series. Oxford: Pergamon Press.

NCIHE (National Committee of Inquiry into Higher Education) (1997) *Education in the Learning Society: Report of the National Committee* (the Dearing Report). London: HMSO.

Readings, B (1996) *The university in ruins*. Cambridge, MA: Harvard University Press.

Robbins, Lord (1963) *Higher Education: Report of the Committee on Higher Education appointed by the Prime Minister ... 1961–1963* (the Robbins Report), Cmnd 2154. London: HMSO.

Stevens, R (2004) *University to uni: the politics of higher education in England since 1944*. London: Politico's.

Van der Wende, M and Huisman, J (2004) Europe, in Huisman, J and van der Wende, M (eds) *On cooperation and competition: national and European policies for the internationalisation of higher education*. Bonne: Lemmens Verlags and Mediengesellschaft.

Wolf, A (2002) *Does education matter? Myths about education and economic growth*. Harmondsworth: Penguin.

# Part 2

# Themes in education

# Chapter 11

## Lifelong learning

### Steve Bartlett and Diana Burton

**Introduction**

This chapter looks at the meaning of lifelong learning and outlines the influence on it of economic development, advances in information and communication technology and globalisation. The importance of lifelong learning within current education policy is discussed. Some consideration is given to whether lifelong learning really is essential in ensuring the future economic and social development of society or if this term is simply part of the rhetoric that is used in maintaining the social compliance of the workforce.

## What is lifelong learning?

Lifelong learning is a comparatively new term that has often been used to describe the formal learning that takes place after the compulsory phases of education. It includes what has variously been described as adult education, continuing education, continuing vocational education, continuing professional development and recurrent education (Kogan, 2000). However, lifelong learning needs to be seen as something much wider than this. Learning is something we do all of the time. We learn from birth, through school, to the workplace. We learn continually as our lives change from one phase to another, from childhood, through adolescence and into adulthood. The learning process takes many forms and there is a multitude of theories attempting to explain how it happens but, certainly, it takes place throughout our lives. Thus we are all engaged in lifelong learning.

We learn during our normal social interaction, so, for example, a sports fan will continually discover new information about developments in their favourite game through going to competitions, watching TV, reading newspapers and talking to friends and colleagues. Sometimes we make a deliberate effort to become involved in formal learning situations such as when we decide to take evening classes in cooking or a foreign language. Here there is a conscious attempt to 'better oneself as a person' or perhaps we may enjoy the social activity involved in being part of the class. We may take a particular course of learning in order to gain a specific qualification to help our career and employment prospects. Here the learning is undertaken for clear economic gain. Edwards (2000) has suggested that the concept of lifelong learning *could provide a framework, like health, for considering learning from the cradle (or earlier) to the grave.*

# Some ideologies of lifelong learning

All aspects of education can be seen as ideologically shaped in some way and this is also the case when analysing the meanings and policies that shape developments in lifelong learning (Bartlett *et al.*, 2001). For instance, a progressive or learner-centred view of lifelong learning sees the needs and wishes of the learners as foremost. Learning is viewed in its broadest sense, being both informal as well as formal, and as happening in all areas of life. Lifelong learning is part of attaining self-fulfilment, and individuals should explore life in their own way following their own interests. Thus a learner-centred approach to lifelong learning covers all kinds of learning and may actually stress the informal and unintentional. An important element of this process is the involvement of learners and their willingness to go further in their learning. Much of this learning, though personally rewarding to learners, may or may not benefit them or the wider society economically. Qualifications are not considered as the primary driver since the inner satisfaction and achievement of the learner does not necessarily have to be proved to, or measured by, others. Followers of this ideological approach may prefer the term 'lifelong education' to lifelong learning, where the latter has come to signify a narrower vocational purpose (Edwards, 2000; Crowther, 2004).

Alternatively, an instrumental approach considers how lifelong learning can bring tangible benefits to the individual and also the wider society (Bartlett, 2003). Here the learning is not an end in itself but is done for the economic benefits it brings. This view looks at how certain forms of learning may enhance employability and add to productivity. As such it is concerned with learning outcomes that are often linked to some form of qualification. An instrumentalist standpoint sees lifelong learning as usually taking place after the compulsory phase of education has been passed through by the learner. This learning is closely associated with the career development of the individual and the updating of the skills and capabilities of the workforce as a whole. There is a tendency here to emphasise a planned approach to learning that is monitored and accredited.

The two ideologies of lifelong learning presented here can, of course, coexist. Many accounts of lifelong learning use aspects of both of these ideological approaches, perhaps emphasising one and then the other, at different times.

# How we learn

In small-scale communities, especially those that are relatively self-sufficient and dependent for survival upon their own skills of, for example, herding, hunting or farming, learning often takes place in the family and small group setting. Individuals learn all the knowledge and skills they will need from living and working closely with older members of the community. They in their turn will pass this knowledge on when they become adults. The learning is informal and practical and involves all members of the group. This learning is a lifelong process (see early anthropological texts, such as Mead 1942, for interesting functional accounts of small-scale societies and the learning processes in which members take part).

In larger-scale societies where individuals earn a living from paid labour, more formal education systems emerge. As the economies within these societies develop and they become more affluent, the education systems themselves become more complex, and the length of time spent in formal education is extended. It is easy when living in such societies to assume that formal education is where we do our learning and to forget the concept of lifelong learning.

> ***Pause for thought*** | the site of learning
>
> Consider the two main phases of compulsory education and schooling, primary and secondary. What are the main things you learned at each stage that have remained with you? How will they help you (or not) live your adult life? Are educational institutions such as schools the best places to learn such things?

# The increasing pace of change

If we learn throughout our lives, why has the term 'lifelong learning' become so significant in recent years? Over the past 50 years or so, perhaps since the birth of our grandparents' generation, there has been rapid and continuous change in our society that has affected all areas of our lives. Patterns of employment, housing conditions, healthcare, leisure activities, individual mobility and forms of transport have all changed. If we examine forms of information and communication technology (ICT) used in the home we can see the extent of these changes. Forty-five years ago, few households had a TV. Those sets that existed were black and white with only one channel. Twenty years ago, very few households had a personal computer (PC) and these were large and very slow. Ten years ago, few houses had internet access. If they did it was often through a shared phone landline. Broadband did not exist. Video recorders have appeared in every home and disappeared again. Your children in their time will probably wonder how anyone could have lived their lives using tape technology.

These advances and developments are taking place in all areas of our lives. We have only to walk through modern multinational chain stores and retail outlets to see how commodities that service every part of our lives are continually being updated or replaced as they become redundant. This rapid and accelerating pace of change can be seen as a result of a combination of developments in economic production, ICT and globalisation. These are very much interlinked forces and their rapidity and diversity create a huge range of choice within our lives generally and for learners in particular.

## Development of economic production

Methods of production have changed rapidly over a comparatively short time from labour-intensive methods to mass production to a level of automation that now requires few people, if any, in the actual manufacturing process. Goods can be produced more quickly and cheaply than previously. A greater variety of products are made in larger numbers than ever before and consequently the standard of living for the majority of people has risen.

## Development of ICT

While the development of factories employing early mass production techniques revolutionised industry, the invention of modern computer and robotic-driven systems has produced a further revolutionary leap forward. ICT now plays an important part in all areas of our lives. This has meant that new skills and knowledge are required by us all, both in our daily lives and at work. At the same time, many of the old working skills have become rarer and even obsolete, given that they are no longer in demand as part of the production process (e.g. panel beaters or shipbuilders). The technology is advancing so quickly that it becomes very difficult to keep up, and the need for workers to be able to update becomes more important than the skills they currently possess. One of the key factors in creating such rapid change is the revolution in communications. It is now possible to access information and communicate instantly and at any time via the internet and the world wide web. It is as though the world has shrunk and time has been compressed into smaller units (Edwards, 2000). This can be seen as an important part of the globalisation process.

# Development of globalisation

Burbules and Torres (2000) have proposed that globalisation can be seen as having a range of meanings. If by globalisation one means the movement of people, ideas and products around the world, then it has always existed. From the earliest times there have always been migrations of people. There have been voyages of discovery, wars of conquest and the development of trade overland and by sea. What has changed is the speed and ease by which labour and goods can now be transported in response to fluctuations in supply and demand around the world. Thus markets have been able to expand until we have what can be termed a global economy.

While there are many benefits to be derived from globalisation, such as greater choice of goods at lower prices resulting from market forces, there are also many potential problems. While competition may benefit the wealthier parts of the globe, those who are poor and forced to sell their labour and economic assets cheaply remain disadvantaged. There is the distinct possibility that the market will result in the dominance of the culture of the rich at the expense of the rest as, for example, the 'McDonaldisation' of the world as western, predominantly American, tastes spread and the demand for their products increases globally while smaller cultures and languages are lost (Ritzer, 2000).

Beck (1992) has concluded that these forces of the market, modern technology and globalisation are creating changes in the very nature of society, an evolution from modernity to reflexive modernity. This reflexive modernity is characterised by an increased lack of certainty in our lives and consequently individuals have to make constant decisions about how they act as they go about their daily business. Their choices concern how they work, what they spend their money on and personal relationships with family, friends and others. We will benefit, or not, according to the decisions we make, and so each choice involves an element of risk. Beck sees us as living now in a 'risk society' where rapid changes in our social environment mean that we can no longer be sure of our social structures, such as the family, work or even the government itself, since they are in a state of constant flux. Market forces, which are beyond individual or state control, are seen to have increasing power. In tandem with this is the stronger emphasis on individualisation. Beck notes a growing variation in the ability of individuals to manage their positions in this risk society. Some sections of the population benefit from greater choice, wealthier lifestyles and the latest technology. For others, those who do not have the marketable skills required for regular employment, this increasing choice brings the risk of them losing out even more, resulting in widening social division. These divisions occur within countries but can also be seen as happening globally with great differences between the wealthy and poor areas of the world.

Research box

## the third way

The impact of global markets and the profound social changes that have accompanied them has led many social commentators such as Giddens (1998, 2000) to suggest that the policies of the traditional left with their emphasis on state control are no longer feasible. However, while there appears little doubt as to the power of the global market and the inability of governments to maintain total control over their own economies, Giddens has made the point that we should not assume that governments now have nothing to offer against the forces of globalisation. He posited a complex two-way interaction between the global and the local. While nations are influenced by global forces, governments can operate to promote, protect and support where appropriate. Rather than withering away under the growth of the global market, governments can play an active part in helping their people respond. Thus Giddens proposed a third way that lies between the old forms of state socialism and the tyranny of totally free markets. It involves the state promoting competitiveness and efficiency while encouraging inclusion by ensuring the provision of services such as education, health and social security. These structures will provide individuals with the support they need to operate freely in the global 'knowledge' economy. Governments also have an important part to play in the development of the civil society that gives individuals identity, security and belonging in an increasingly uncertain world.

For government, Giddens's third way ideology (1998, 2000) has been manifested in the desire to provide vital services such as education, health and social security for every individual, and the creation of opportunity for all to succeed in life, whilst at the same time stressing the duty of everyone to play their part in society. There is a strong emphasis on social justice and the rights and responsibilities of each citizen (Lawton, 2005). The language of partnership is used to describe the relationship between government and citizen. It is this third way ideology that has come to influence the thinking of a number of world governments.

# Lifelong learning and the response of government

The Fryer Report (NAGCELL, 1997), drawing on the discourse reflected by Beck (1992) and Giddens (1998, 2000), adhered to the view that the UK is going through a period of profound social change that characterises it as a risk society.

*Pause for thought* | analysis of change

The Fryer Report identified 12 key aspects of the changes taking place within our society. These are:

- accelerating change in many dimensions of life, from work to the family, driven in part by powerful and often remote global forces;
- increasing diversity and fragmentation of experiences and institutions and a greater willingness to tolerate, even celebrate, such features of the modern world;
- changing identities, loyalties and aspirations;
- much greater emphasis upon consumption and its pleasures, including too some democratisation of inventiveness and creativity;

- more focus upon choice, lifestyle and individuality;

- the increasing variety and pluralism of popular culture;

- the pervasive and growing role of information and knowledge in many arenas of economic, social, political and working life;

- the growing importance of communications and information technology to many aspects of our lives;

- the development of new dimensions of political participation, in the realms of constitutional reform and active citizenship;

- the emergence of new agendas in politics, concerned with issues as diverse as race and gender equality, disability rights, the environment, food and transport;

- widening of key social divisions, experienced in fields of income, employment, housing, health and education, including access to information;

- evidence of the growth of social exclusion, despair and even a sense of hopelessness, resulting from the impact of multiple deprivations.

Take each of the above points in turn and reflect upon their accuracy. Consider media reports, your personal experiences and those of your peers in relation to the 12 points. Identify what actual evidence exists for each of these changes.

This report noted changes in employment through the introduction of new work practices, the application of new technologies, the production and delivery of new products and services, and the reduced size of workplaces. These changes have significant effects upon the type of worker required and the report suggested that in the future there will be diminishing opportunities for unskilled and semi-skilled employment, and those with only 'one industry' or task-specific skills will be increasingly at risk. Today, therefore, we are in the midst of changes in the time, location and forms which work takes.

After coming to power in 1997, the Labour government published its Green Paper, *The learning age: a renaissance for new Britain* (DfEE, 1998) in response to the Fryer Report. It saw the greatest challenge for the country as the need to equip people with new skills, knowledge and understanding. To remain competitive in this new world, many of our traditional social and economic institutions needed to be modernised and reformed. The Green Paper described lifelong learning and the creation of a learning culture as a key part of the wider process whereby individuals work together, with the help of government, in forging a better and more inclusive society. Lifelong learning is thus important on two levels. On the individual level, if people are not to be excluded from society they will need to upskill to maintain their employability. At a national level, if the UK economy is to compete in the new global market we need to maintain a 'flexible' labour force that is adaptable and able to respond immediately. Lifelong learning is portrayed as of central importance within a transformed, globalised economy (Taylor, 2005).

## Lifelong learning and education policy

Arnove (2003) has suggested that the development of a global economy and the increasing interconnectedness of societies pose common problems for education systems around the world. The government placed education as a central plank in its policy agenda of modernisation, with the concept of lifelong learning as an important element within that policy. Taylor (2005) felt that government policy on lifelong learning can be divorced neither from its general education policy nor from its broader human capital approach to education, within an ideology of 'marketised welfarism'. The government felt a need to build on the existing strengths of the education system but also to overcome the spiral of disadvantage whereby 'alienation from, or failure within, the education system is passed on from generation to generation' (DfEE, 1998). Thus the importance of education, both in the compulsory years and throughout life, has been stressed. The theme that runs through government policy is the developing of human capital in order to compete in the knowledge economy.

It is worth considering some of the significant developments that have been taking place in education and how they relate to encouraging an ethos of lifelong learning.

- The development of quality assurance measures aimed at monitoring performance in all phases of education, such as testing of pupils, compiling league tables of performance and regular inspection of all educational institutions, has been designed to raise the currency of educational qualifications.
- Nursery provision has been expanded rapidly on the premise that a good start is more likely to lead to a positive view of learning throughout the compulsory phases of education and beyond.
- In primary education, the emphasis on 'essential basic skills' is manifest through the literacy and numeracy strategies (consolidated in the National Primary Strategy and Excellence and Enjoyment) and a focus on the use of ICT.
- At secondary level, the emphasis has remained on basic skills but in addition there are attempts to raise standards with initiatives to increase parental choice of school and competition between schools, thus specialist schools and academies have been established and there are proposals to allow schools and parents to establish independent trust schools.
- The National Curriculum was reformed for all pupils, becoming more flexible and relevant to vocational needs at Key Stage 4 particularly.
- Citizenship has been introduced into the curriculum to help address rapid social change and the potential fragmentation of established communities. While lifelong learning does apply to all stages of education, post-compulsory and adult learning are the phases that most clearly fit under its banner.
- The reforms in post-16 education have seen a dramatic increase in the number of pupils who now stay on in education after 16. Vocational A levels were introduced and GNVQs accorded parity of esteem, on paper at least.
- The number of students taking first degrees has increased with the expansion of higher education. The aim is that by 2010, 50 per cent of young people in the 18–30 age group will take part in higher education. The development of foundation degrees has emphasised a vocational application.
- A range of measures has been introduced to improve education and training opportunities in the workplace. There are programmes to develop the basic literacy, numeracy and ICT skills of those in low paid jobs, the long-term unemployed and young offenders. The need to update older workers in modern ICT skills and other new forms of working is also recognised. Those on welfare benefits are provided with suitable skills training after an assessment of their needs. Financial support is also available for the low paid.

Policies of lifelong learning do not just involve the domain of education and training. They are part of wider social policies that are aimed at inclusion, such as Excellence in Cities, which was aimed at reinvigorating whole areas that were run down and had disadvantaged populations. There is an overlap between social, economic and education policy in what supporters of the third way would portray as 'joined-up government'. Strategies that take a broader approach to child and family welfare, such as Sure Start, have aimed at improving the future chances of children and their parents by involving education, health and social agencies. These strategies have led to the multi-agency approach currently being developed in the area of child welfare with the creation of child centres and extended schools. Evaluations of the impact of Sure Start have not been positive, with London University researchers reporting that *possibly the utilisation of services by those with greater human capital left others less access to services than would have been the case had they not lived in Sure Start areas* (Ward, 2005).

# Criticisms of policy on lifelong learning

Biesta (2005) has commented that *the dominant policy discourse nowadays sees adult education first and foremost as a lever for economic growth and global competitiveness*. The very instrumental approach to education taken in recent decades involves a narrow view of the purposes of education and can lead to a very restricted curriculum with an unhealthy emphasis on measurable outcomes. Rather than raising educational standards and encouraging involvement of students, this may actually lead to the increasing alienation of certain groups from the education system.

The human capital approach assumes that educating the workforce to a higher level will lead to increased economic performance. However any causal link between educational qualifications and production has never been clearly established. In fact, whether increasing educational provision, particularly in HE, does have a significant economic impact has been increasingly questioned (Wolf, 2002). Gorard (2003) has suggested that the government strategies for the retraining and upskilling of the workforce, with the emphasis on basic low-level skills, have so far had very little impact in spite of the media hype that has surrounded them. Work-based training does not appear to be rising in uptake.

*Pause for thought* | the value of higher education

In the light of differing views on the value of higher education, discuss the following with your colleagues:

- why you came into higher education;
- why you chose the course you are on at this particular institution.

How might your degree enhance (or not) your quality as a future employee?

It may be that the existence of a risk society and the need to develop an adaptable workforce have been greatly exaggerated and are really little more than social myths encouraged by those with vested interests in capitalist production (Hughes and Tight, 1998). Why might this myth be perpetuated? Crowther (2004) has portrayed lifelong learning as a *deficit discourse*. By this he meant that responsibility for retraining is placed upon the individual rather than on government. Thus any failure is seen as individual rather than systemic. It is individuals who need to adapt to a lifetime of increasing occupational insecurity, as a consequence of changing employment conditions with more part-time and temporary work. The political rhetoric of lifelong learning involving individuality, adaptability and operating in the 'knowledge economy' may be drawing attention away from real structural inequalities in society by emphasising the importance of individual action.

Also the current emphasis by government, educationalists and employers on acquiring formal qualifications through education, whether part- or full-time, and the requirement of enrolment in vocational or skills training as a prerequisite of entitlement to welfare benefits, means that lifelong learning may actually be a form of compulsion and control over the workforce (Tight, 1998; Minter, 2001; Coffield, 2002). Crowther (2004) saw it as *a new disciplinary technology to make people more compliant and adaptable for work in the era of flexible capitalism*. Most recently this is seen in the policy arena of FE funding where the Foster Review advocated the cessation of funding for adult learning that was not skills-related (Foster, 2005).

This ideology of lifelong learning does not inevitably have to be the dominant discourse. There are calls for individuals and local communities to have greater involvement in the development of a broader approach to lifelong learning that would encourage informal as well as formal networks (Tight, 1998; Crowther, 2004; Taylor, 2005). This would allow learning to move from being mainly for instrumental purposes alone to becoming an enriching experience for individuals and their communities.

## Summary and conclusions

In this chapter we have seen that lifelong learning can have a variety of contestable meanings. It may be used for learning that takes place after the compulsory phase of education. It may be primarily about formal learning and vocational education or it may involve all aspects of learning in an adult's life. In its broadest sense it may be about all the learning that takes place from our birth until we die. Your own personal perspective on lifelong learning is likely to depend upon your ideological stance. You may regard it as being for economic purposes, as a form of social control or as a means to achieving individual fulfilment. You may however reach a compromise position and see a combination of all three purposes in operation in different degrees at different times.

## *References*

Arnove, R (2003) Introduction: reframing comparative education: the dialectic of the global and the local, in Arnove, R and Torres, C (eds) *Comparative education: the dialectic of the global and the local*. Oxford: Rowman and Littlefield.

Bartlett, S (2003) Education for lifelong learning, in Bartlett, S and Burton, D *Education studies: essential issues*. London: Sage.

Bartlett, S, Burton, D and Peim, N (2001) *Introduction to education studies*. London: PCP.

Beck, U (1992) *Risk society: towards a new modernity*. London: Sage.

Biesta, G (2005) The learning democracy? Adult learning and the condition of democratic citizenship. *British Journal of Sociology of Education*, 26(5): 687–703.

Burbules, N and Torres, C (eds) (2000) *Globalisation and education: critical perspectives*. London: Routledge.

Coffield, F (2002) Breaking the consensus, in Edwards, R, Miller, N, Small, N and Tait, A (eds) *Supporting lifelong learning*. London: RoutledgeFalmer.

Crowther, J (2004) 'In and against' lifelong learning: flexibility and the corrosion of character. *International Journal of Lifelong Education*, 23(2): 125–36.

DfEE (1998) *The learning age: a renaissance for a new Britain*. London: Department for Education and Employment/HMSO.

Edwards, R (2000) Lifelong learning, lifelong learning, lifelong learning: a recurrent education?, in Field, J and Leicester, M (eds) *Lifelong learning education across the lifespan*. London: RoutledgeFalmer.

Foster, A (2005) *Review of the future role of FE colleges*. London: DfES/HMSO.

Giddens, A (1998) *The third way: the renewal of social democracy*. Cambridge: Polity Press.

Giddens, A (2000) *The third way and its critcs*. Cambridge: Polity Press.

Gorard, S (2003) Patterns of work-based learning. *Journal of Vocational Education and Training*, 55(1): 47–63.

Hughes, C and Tight, M (1998) The myth of the learning society, in Ransen, S (ed) *Inside the learning society*. London: Cassell.

Kogan, M (2000) Lifelong learning in the UK. *European Journal of Education*, 35(3): 343–59.

Lawton, D (2005) *Education and Labour Party ideologies, 1900–2001 and beyond*. London: RoutledgeFalmer.

Mead, M (1942) *Growing up in New Guinea*. London: Pelican.

Minter, C (2001) Some flaws in the common theory of widening participation. *Research in Post-compulsory Education*, 26(3): 303–19.

NAGCELL (1997) *Learning for the twenty-first century: first report of the National Advisory Group for Continuing Education and Lifelong Learning* (the Fryer Report). London: NAGCELL.

Ritzer, G (2000) *The McDonaldization of society*. Thousand Oaks, CA: Pine Forge Press.

Taylor, R (2005) Lifelong learning and the Labour governments 1997–2004. *Oxford Review of Education*: 31(1):101–18.

Tight, M (1998) Lifelong learning: opportunity or compulsion? *British Journal of Educational Studies*: 46 (3): 251–63.

Wolf, A (2002) *Does education matter? Myths about education and economic growth*. Harmondsworth: Penguin.

Ward, L (2005) Sure Start sets back the worst placed youngsters, study finds. *Guardian*, 1 December, p5.

# Chapter 12

## Leadership in education

## John Sharp and Graham Meeson

### Introduction

Considerable interest in educational leadership over recent times has resulted in a period of unprecedented growth and research in the field. This in turn has led to a rise in the popularity of leadership as a study option on undergraduate and postgraduate university courses and an increase in the provision of professional leadership qualifications. Indeed, it is unlikely that you won't have experienced either leading or being led, whether at school, college, university or the workplace. It would therefore be highly worthwhile for you to reflect and build upon these experiences. The realisation of leadership potential is now widely recognised as a fundamental contributor towards people's personal and professional development and effectiveness and, eventually, their career satisfaction. In this chapter the concept of leadership is introduced and leadership models within a range of educational contexts are presented and explored.

# Historical background

Most companies and other organisations remain heavily managed and largely hierarchical in structure, despite some rhetoric to the contrary. Of course, management brings order, control and authority to a hierarchy. The acceptance of this, as a legacy of the European Industrial Rsevolution, is perpetuated implicitly and explicitly throughout our own systems of education and training. The German sociologist Max Weber (1864–1920) was perhaps the first to systematically consider the links between social structure and human behaviour in the industrial world (Bush and Bell, 2003). For Weber, the processes involved in industry necessitated the promotion of certain principles, values, beliefs and ideals in the interests of efficiency. This model of industrial efficiency was concerned with the maximisation of output and profit such that the needs of the individual were, at best, of only secondary importance. Problem-solving was applied, which owed more to scientific method and pragmatism than to a deep-rooted understanding of people as individuals. People were, in fact, little more than the human component in an industrial machine. This so-called 'rationalist' approach was characterised by:

- a strong division of labour in the workforce;
- strict adherence to rules, regulations and bureaucracy;
- goal-oriented and autocratic management;
- minimal opportunities for learning;
- meeting production targets;
- external accountability.

The opposite of 'rationalism' might be 'collegiality', a term whose origin can be traced to the colleges of Oxford and Cambridge Universities. Systems that operate 'collegially' do so on principles of collectivity, equality, mutual trust and shared goals; they adopt flat rather than hierarchical management structures (Bush and Bell, 2003). The independence of the organisation and the autonomy of the individual within the workforce are protected at all costs. Decisions are reached and problems solved by way of discussion, compromise and agreement. Opportunities for learning and innovation are maximised. Of course neither approach is perfect, since principles, values, beliefs and ideals can be compromised within each. Nevertheless, many companies and other organisations are constantly reconsidering the ways in which they operate as they come to terms with the pace of life and expectation in today's world. The principle of hierarchy, entrenched though it is, is slowly giving way to other forms of organisational structure, and the importance of management is slowly giving way to the importance of leadership.

---

**Pause for thought** | the nature of education organisations

The 'politicisation' and external control of education at all levels throughout the UK is seen by many leading authorities on education as a regressive rather than progressive step. Concerns abound over the erosion of academic freedoms, the marginalisation of proper educational debate and the apparent reduction in the status of education to nothing more than a commodity bought by consumers and driven by the forces of a market economy. According to Furedi (2004):

> *Increasingly, every aspect of education is subjected to rule-making and regulated through inspection and auditing. As a result of a highly centralised system of education managed by an interventionist bureaucracy little is left to chance. It has been noted that even primary school teachers are allowed little initiative to exercise their professional judgement... In the university sector, a system of auditing has succeeded in influencing the minutiae of teaching and even of research. The expansion of bureaucratic control is justified on the grounds that it ensures the maintenance of standards of institutions. It is argued that it helps hold teachers, lecturers and their institutions to account.*

(p9)

Why do you think successive governments have set about intervening and taking more and more control of education? Is the imposition of a 'rationalist' approach, driven as it is by targets, short-term goals, performance indicators and streamlining, the best way forward? Do you feel that criticisms of government intervention and control, particularly where these are seen as attempts at social engineering, are justified? Are the notions of 'rationalism' and 'collegiality' in their purest forms realistic models for any educational organisation to adopt? To what extent have today's educational organisations arrived at compromise or contrived solutions? What role do you think educational leaders might have in resolving some of these issues?

---

# Leadership *vs* management

The words 'leadership' and 'management' are often used synonymously or interchangeably but most authors now agree that leadership and management are quite separate constructs. The precise differences between them, however, remain at times blurred and hotly debated. It is often said that the difference between leadership and management is the difference between inspiration and perspiration. But what exactly does this mean? Owen *et al.* (2004) propose a range of behavioural and operational factors that differentiate management from leadership.

- Managers build organisational structures while leaders build organisational cultures.
- Managers maintain systems while leaders challenge them.
- Managers focus on structures and doing the right thing while leaders focus on people and doing things right.
- Managers concern themselves with performance indicators and targets while leaders inspire with shared visions.
- Managers maintain low levels of emotional attachment while leaders ask for hearts and minds.
- Managers are programmatic and follow fixed paths while leaders are innovative and find paths.
- Managers control while leaders empower.
- Managers are taught by organisations while leaders learn from them.
- Managers ask how and by when while leaders ask what for and why.

According to Gronn (1999), however, the importance of leadership and what leadership means in educational settings often suffers from a 'naïve realism' driven by a series of implicit theories or received wisdoms.

- Leaders tend to be formal position holders or figureheads in a hierarchical system and therefore hold more power.
- Leadership enjoys a status which is different from and more important than management.
- There exists a qualitative difference between the minority who lead and the majority who follow.
- The leader–follower relationship is directional in that leaders act on behalf of and in the best interests of followers.
- Outcomes can be attributed to the actions of individual leaders.
- The variability and uniqueness of contexts in which leadership is exercised are of little significance.
- Leadership involves the individual rather than the team.

> **Pause for thought** | the characeristics of leadership
>
> What do you think about the differences between leadership and management presented by Owen et al. (2004)? Are these constructs really separate things or simply either end of a behavioural and operational continuum? In other words, could there be a place for manager-centred leadership or leadership-centred management? Do good leaders necessarily make good managers and vice versa? Reflect upon your own experiences of leadership and management and discuss these with a colleague. Do any other defining features or characteristics of leadership and management occur to you? Is there any substance to the 'implicit theories' view of Gronn (1999)? What might be the implications or consequences of letting 'implicit theories' go unchallenged?

The function of educational leadership in an organisation is, of course, primarily to direct action. As a general rule, individuals become leaders because they are influential among their peers. The ability to influence others, however, is not something that people are born able to do, but is something they learn to do. This means that everyone has leadership potential even if they never actually aspire to being a leader. One of the pressures associated with realising leadership potential in any organisation is knowing when to accept leadership and when to offer it. Barriers to expressing leadership or to realising leadership potential may come in many different forms (Law and Glover, 2000). These might be associated with elements of your own personality, where you work and who you work with. To a large extent leaders can only lead with the consent of those who follow. Trust is an essential component of this often fragile relationship. If the power invested in the leader by virtue of their role is not wielded in an ethically appropriate way that trust will soon be lost. The misuse of power associated with leadership can be problematic. Those who find themselves with power may choose to use it to control people, to get their own way or to advance themselves rather than the interests of those they lead. Leaders who use what power they have in such ways can, in extreme circumstances, become dangerous and damaging individuals.

---

***Pause for thought*** | assessing your own leadership potential

MacBeath and Myers (1999) offered a self-evaluation protocol which can be used as a starting point for discussion. A modified version appears below. As MacBeath and Myers pointed out, self-evaluation is context-dependent and there may be a difference between how you evaluate yourself and how others might see you. Complete and score the form below yourself and compare outcomes with a colleague. Is this how you really are or how you would like to be? While there may be issues over the nature of certain elements, high overall scores tend towards positive leadership potential.

| | | |
|---|---|---|
| Are you a rule breaker? | Never 1 2 3 4 5 | Always |
| Are you efficient? | 1 2 3 4 5 | |
| Do you have radical views? | 1 2 3 4 5 | |
| Do you share power? | 1 2 3 4 5 | |
| Are you democratic? | 1 2 3 4 5 | |
| Are you charismatic? | 1 2 3 4 5 | |
| Do you pursue long-term goals? | 1 2 3 4 5 | |
| Are you forgiving? | 1 2 3 4 5 | |
| Are you competitive? | 1 2 3 4 5 | |
| Do you delegate a lot? | 1 2 3 4 5 | |
| Do you embrace change? | 1 2 3 4 5 | |
| Do you confront bad practice? | 1 2 3 4 5 | |
| Are you reliable? | 1 2 3 4 5 | |
| Are you open-minded? | 1 2 3 4 5 | |
| Do you attend to detail? | 1 2 3 4 5 | |
| Are you gregarious? | 1 2 3 4 5 | |
| Are you demanding? | 1 2 3 4 5 | |
| Are you a team player? | 1 2 3 4 5 | |
| Are you flexible? | 1 2 3 4 5 | |
| Are you an optimist? | 1 2 3 4 5 | |
| Do you fight for what you believe in? | 1 2 3 4 5 | |
| Are you entrepreneurial? | 1 2 3 4 5 | |
| Are you unpredictable? | 1 2 3 4 5 | |
| Are you a risk-taker? | 1 2 3 4 5 | |
| Can you make decisions? | 1 2 3 4 5 | |

| | |
|---|---|
| Do you take responsibility? | 1  2  3  4  5 |
| Are you straightforward? | 1  2  3  4  5 |
| Are you idealistic? | 1  2  3  4  5 |
| Do you listen? | 1  2  3  4  5 |
| Do you lead by example? | 1  2  3  4  5 |

Overall score: _____

Take some time to consider the charismatic, situational, transcendental and transactional leadership characteristics presented earlier. Do you recognise any of these qualities in you or those around you? Is it likely that you would see them all exhibited in one person? Would that one person be easy to work with or for?

# Contemporary models of educational leadership

As an emergent field, educational leadership has tended to borrow its models from elsewhere (Coleman and Briggs, 2002; Anderson and Bennett, 2003). This approach has not always been helpful as the theoretical frameworks, principles, values, beliefs and ideals involved do not always reside easily in educational circumstances or pay due attention to the constraints within which some educational organisations operate. (Recall 'rationalism' and 'collegiality'.) Models of educational leadership fall into four main categories, each underpinned by its own collection of theories and principles (e.g. Bennis and Nanus, 1985; Mitchell and Tucker, 1992; Bush, 2003; Bush and Middlewood, 2003). While language and terminology may vary, these include:

- charismatic leadership;
- situational leadership;
- transcendental leadership;
- transformational leadership.

Of course, no one model of leadership is completely independent of any other, for no two individuals who subscribe to any particular view of leadership ever exhibit exactly the same leadership style, make use of exactly the same leadership strategies or operate within the same context. Effective leaders are, however, generally flexible and adaptable individuals who remain conscious of what is going on around them and respond accordingly and appropriately at all times (Golemane, 2000).

## Charismatic leadership

Charismatic leadership concerns itself with individual traits. Individuals, through their charisma and actions are identified as 'great leaders' who then become national role models to inspire others. Such traits often reflect the idealised masculine heroic myth and, traditionally, the most well-known charismatic leaders have been men (Lingard *et al.*, 2004). Charismatic leaders are well known for being successful at finding ways forward in particularly stressful situations or succeeding against all the odds. Models of leadership based upon the charisma or traits of individuals do have disadvantages as they oversimplify the complexity of human relationships and the situations and events that occur in everyday life. Though now regarded with some cynicism, and for reasons that may be obvious, studying charismatic leaders:

- helps to identify our own notions of what is important in leadership;
- provides an understanding of more sophisticated models of leadership.

---

### Research box

## leadership and gender

Much has been written about the differences between men and women as leaders and whether gender has any impact on leadership style and even career progression. On style, women appear to do well. Some 'typical' female characteristics often said to be aligned with effective leadership include the capacity to listen, communicate and share power, a genuine concern for personal and emotional well-being and a person-centred and interactive approach. Rosener (1990) has suggested that women who have broken through the 'glass ceiling' in what is often regarded as a 'man's world' and who have succeeded in certain leadership roles, have done so as a result of, rather than in spite of, their gender. They have not had to 'masculinise' themselves to conform. They have not had to alter how they dress and behave, for example. Gray (1993) has also noted that the similarities in how men and women actually operate in leadership roles are, in reality, far greater than differences, with both genders adopting what might be described as 'feminine' as well as 'masculine' characteristics.

Experience, it would seem, is more important in terms of role fitness than gender stereotyping. The study of leadership in English primary schools, however, is of particular interest (although the ratio of female to male professors in university departments would provide an equally valuable alternative). According to MacBeath and Myers (1999), for example, women make up about 80 per cent of the primary teaching profession at any one time, but only about 50 per cent of head teachers are women (though more women than men occupy middle management positions). Women also lag behind men when age is included as a factor and women from ethnic minority groups are worst affected. As MacBeath and Myers pointed out finding an overall explanation is difficult because some of the same causal factors also appear to apply to some men though not to the same degree. These can include access to relevant role models, perception of teaching as a career, devotion to the job, mobility in the job market, maternity and career breaks.

---

## Situational leadership

Situational leadership is essentially task-driven. It concerns itself with what a leader can attempt to achieve democratically by ensuring the optimal performance of a team in relation to the knowledge and skills base available. Situational leaders are, therefore, good problem-solvers with a talent for matching different individuals to different stages of a project at different times. Leadership is contingent on the environment or situation or task at hand. The characteristics they demonstrate include an understanding of when to delegate, support, coach or direct (Blanchard *et al.*, 1994):

- when delegating, the leader gives responsibility for day-to-day decision-making away to the able and willing (assumes a high competence and high commitment and enthusiasm on the part of the team member);
- when supporting, the leader listens, praises and facilitates (assumes high competence and some commitment and enthusiasm on the part of the team member);
- when coaching, the leader trains, directs and supports (assumes some competence but mixed commitment and enthusiasm on the part of the team member);
- when directing, the leader structures, controls and supervises (assumes low competence and low commitment and enthusiasm on the part of the team member).

The disadvantages of situational leadership lie in it being seen as simply a way of getting things done, another form of management. This criticism is particularly evident when situational leaders are viewed as in complete control and overly authoritative when coaching or directing. Situational leadership may easily result in transactional predicaments where work is undertaken in response to 'payback' or to avoid punishment. Opportunities for learning may be stifled.

## Transcendental leadership

Transcendental leadership is essentially relationship- and empathy-driven and may be strongly associated with individuals with high emotional intelligence (Greenleaf, 1996; Cardona, 2000; Goleman *et al.*, 2002). Emotional intelligence concerns itself with our ability to understand our own emotions and how they make us feel and react, as well as the emotions, feelings and reactions of those around us. Recognising what triggers emotional responses helps to maximise the positive aspects of our behaviour and relationships with others (e.g. trust, openness, honesty, motivation, commitment, collaboration) while minimising those that are negative and destructive (e.g. jealousy, resentment). Positive emotions can help to achieve goals, complete tasks and solve problems. Transcendental leadership concerns itself with addressing and supporting the needs and growth of individuals and organisations together and with promoting a strong sense of ownership. By adopting such an approach, individuals are empowered by their leader quite literally to transcend themselves, that is to become more knowledgeable and capable team members while at the same time becoming more autonomous in what they do. Transcendental leaders, who serve their organisations well, can often be identified by the sorts of questions they ask:

- What can I/we (the organisation) do to … ?
- How can I/we (the organisation) enable you to … ?
- Where would I/we (the organisation) benefit from … ?

The disadvantage of transcendental leadership can be found in its rather woolly and diverse approach which may lack sufficient focus and direction. Transcendental leaders may be seen as easily manipulated or as a 'soft touch'.

## Transformational leadership

Transformational leadership is essentially change-driven and particularly suited to education (Burns, 1978; Gronn, 1996). Transformational leaders have the vision to identify a need to bring about change or to create something different or new, however large or small that change or creation might be, in order to achieve a particular goal. Transformational leadership concerns itself with teamwork and to understanding the needs of the individual but in different ways to situational and transcendental leadership. Transformational leaders know how teams are built and maintained and operate and perform. Teams work on the synergy of ideas, practices and responsibilities that allow them to achieve results where individuals or groups might perform less well or fail. Effective team leadership focuses attention, maintains motivation and enthusiasm, and coordinates activities. Within a team, leadership may be transferred from one member to another if particular expertise is required or needs to be brought in from an external source at any point in time. Transformational leaders not only adapt to a situation, and in doing so exemplify the same empathy and emotional awareness as transcendental leaders, they also transform it. Effective transformational leaders can shape the principles, values, beliefs and ideals of a whole organisation. Executed well, transformational leadership can be pivotal in helping to tackle feelings of helplessness within an organisation and improve morale in a disenfranchised workforce by lifting and empowering individuals to higher levels of motivation and commitment. Transformational leaders:

- recognise and encourage an expression of views;
- encourage individual and organisational learning;
- acknowledge and reward effort;
- strive towards achieving sustainable growth;
- relish in and respond positively to uncertainty.

Transformational leadership suffers from some of the same disadvantages as situational and transcendental leadership. It tends to rely on a single individual as the driving force behind determining change and direction with followers in what might still be described as a compliant role. It is possible to lose sight of goals to be achieved when developing people and maintaining teams. Weak transformational leadership can, for example, lead to the rationality and acceptability of key decisions being called into question and the time taken to reach decisions becoming protracted, all of which can cause progress to falter.

---

***Pause for thought*** | approaches to leadership

Consider how you might respond to the following situations. Put yourself in the role of leader and identify strategies that might bring about an appropriate conclusion.

*You are part of a group of four on placement (school or other). You have been tasked with organising a drama production. The criteria and expectations are clear. No one else in the group appears prepared to work together to take things forward.*

*As an active member of your student union you have been asked to plan a series of activities for charity week in order to raise money for a local community project. There are seven other people involved and you have been nominated as leader. All are willing to work for you as their turn will come. Time is short and there is still much left to do.*

*As part of a departmental summer school project, you have been put in charge of a small group of paid students and other volunteers. For this additional responsibility you receive a small amount of money more than everybody else. The others appear quietly to resent this. Payment is conditional on maintaining and developing the project.*

How does your approach to each of these situations relate to the models of charismatic, situational, transcendental and transformational leadership?

---

### Research box

### complexity, chaos and the emergence of distributed leadership

According to Morrison (2002), the tendency towards globalisation, increasing organisational diversity and interdependency, the speed and ease with which we communicate, and the rise of an ever-more confident, educated and demanding work force, requires a new model of educational leadership which breaks with current practices. Morrison has anticipated that this paradigm shift in thinking about educational leadership will emerge from the application of complexity and chaos theories, which together provide a means of analysing and making sense of how organisations operate as open, dynamic, self-regulating and adaptive systems and the ways in which they fail to conform to simple and deterministic cause-and-effect relationships and linear predictability. Handling such everyday variation, in whichever organisation it occurs, requires distributed leadership or leadership at source.

## Summary and conclusions

The formal study of leadership within an educational setting is a relatively new and emerging field of enquiry. While there have been several attempts to appropriate models of leadership drawn from outside education, few have been entirely successful. Education is varied, it takes place in a great many different sorts of environment, and educational organisations are usually under a great many internal and external constraints. Educational leaders, therefore, need to be flexible, adaptable, trustworthy and emotionally literate individuals who have the strength and vision to delegate responsibility where appropriate and to be able to motivate and inspire whole teams of people. Seeking out or developing suitable models of educational leadership within which different practices can be analysed and reflected upon is clearly of some importance. Transformational leadership, with its associated principles, values, beliefs, ideals and focus on change, the individual and the team, is perhaps a good place for aspiring educational leaders to look for inspiration. Whether it be in school, college, university or some other place of work, accepting responsibility for the deployment of staff, resources or funding on even the smallest of scales brings with it opportunities to demonstrate leadership potential, opportunities which should be grasped in the interests of personal and professional development and effectiveness. Only trained, educated and visionary educational leaders will ever be in a position to challenge orthodoxy and to liberate citizens of the future.

## *References*

Anderson, L and Bennett, N (eds) (2003) *Developing educational leadership: using evidence for policy and practice*. London: Sage.

Bennis, W and Nanus, B (1985) *Leadership: the strategies for taking charge*. New York: Harper Row.

Blanchard, K, Zigarmi, D and Zigarmi, P (1994) *Leadership and the one-minute manager*. London: Willow.

Burns, JM (1978) *Leadership*. New York: Harper Row.

Bush, T (2003) *Theories of educational leadership and management*. London: Sage.

Bush, T and Bell, L (eds) (2003) *The principles and practice of educational management*. London: Sage.

Bush, T and Middlewood, D (2003) *Leading and managing people in education*. London: Sage.

Cardona, P (2000) Transcendental leadership. *The Leadership and Organisation Development Journal*, 21(4): 201–6.

Coleman, M and Briggs, A (eds) (2002) *Researching educational leadership and management*. London: Paul Chapman.

Furedi, F (2004) The formalisation of relationships in education, in Hayes, D (ed) *The RoutledgeFalmer guide to key debates in education*. London: RoutledgeFalmer.

Goleman, D (2000) Leadership that gets results. *Harvard Business Review*, 78 (2)–90.

Goleman, D, Boyatziz, R and McKee, A (2002). *The new leaders: transforming the art of leadership into the science of results*. London: Bloomsbury.

Gray, HL (1993) Gender issues in management training, in Ozga, J (ed) *Women in educational management*. Buckingham: Open University Press.

Greenleaf, RK (1996) *On becoming a servant leader*. San Francisco: Jossey–Bass.

Gronn, P (1996) From transactions to transformations: a new world order in the study of leadership? *Educational Management and Administration*, 24(1): 7–30.

Gronn, P (1999) *The making of educational leaders*. London: Cassell.

Law, S and Glover, D (2000) *Educational leadership and learning*. Buckingham: Open University Press.

Lingard, B, Hayes, D, Mills, M and Christie, P (2004) *Leading learning*. Buckingham: Open University Press.

MacBeath, JEC and Myers, K (1999) *Effective school leaders: how to evaluate and improve your leadership potential*. Harlow: Prentice–Hall.

Mitchell, G and Tucker, S (1992) Leadership as a way of thinking. *Educational Leadership*, 49(5): 30–5.

Morrison, K (2002) *School leadership and complexity theory*. London: RoutledgeFalmer.

Owen, H, Hodgson, V and Gazzard, N (2004) *The leadership manual: your complete practical guide to effective leadership*. London: Pearson–Prentice Hall.

Rosener, JB (1990) Ways women lead. *Harvard Business Review*, 6(6): 119–25.

# Chapter 13

# Race and education

## Nasima Hassan

### Introduction

This chapter addresses the issue of race in education through reference to historic and contemporary research and consequent initiatives. Some of the wider issues associated with black and minority ethnic pupils in the classroom are reviewed through an exploration of race and identity. Successive government initiatives to combat racism in schools in response to the socio-political conditions in Britain from the early 1960s onwards are considered. A discussion of the race and achievement nexus draws together conclusions as reflected in the experiences of black pupils in inner London schools which might be considered representative of other geographical locations within the UK.

# Educational initiatives to combat racism in education

Successive governments have proved unable to deliver a coherent philosophy and policy to combat racism in education and this has been at an undeniable cost to the nation, its education system and its fragile race relations. Critics argue that the very deracialisation of education policies has failed to address the growing cancer of low expectations of teachers, racist stereotyping and inadequate provisions for children learning English as a second language (Troyna and Williams, 1996). Indeed, the term 'learners of English as an *additional* language', for example, was not formally accepted in place of 'learners of English as a *second* language' by the Training and Development Agency for schools (TDA) until 2002. This can be taken to demonstrate the power of language to perpetuate low teacher expectations and implicitly devalue pupils' diverse skills. A series of reactive recommendations following several major high profile incidents might not have been necessary had diversity been embraced earlier (MacPherson, 1999; Cantle, 2001; Ousley, 2001).

### Research box

#### the roots of racism in the playground

The assumed innocence of children hinders informed debate about children's notion of 'race'. Many studies have identified awareness among even very young children of racial differences and therefore of different values placed upon different skin colour. In addition, the incidence of racial name-calling is an increasingly common feature of the primary school environment, more damaging perhaps than physical acts (Cohen, 1989; Wright,

1992). Swann (DES, 1985) has observed that racial abuse is reference not only to the child but also by extension to their family and indeed more broadly to their ethnic community as a whole. Troyna and Hatcher (1992) have argued that children respond to specific situations more in anger at times than as 'racists'. Interestingly, their research along with that conducted by Gaine (1995) took place in predominantly white primary schools. The discussion therefore explores the socialisation processes on children in their understanding of 'race' and how this impacts on the friendships and relationships they form.

Historically, and in response to the need for successful integration of immigrant children, three policies that have received most criticism for their lack of thought and appropriateness include:

- assimilation;
- integration;
- cultural pluralism.

These policies were designed to make grassroots impact in textbooks and teaching strategies, as well as addressing the wider notions of race and equal opportunities characterised by legislation in their time. For example, the Race Relations Act 1976 has been heavily criticised for not going far enough to stamp out direct acts of racial discrimination in practice.

# Assimilation

To assimilate means to merge and become part of something. It is about the denial and rejection of individuality. The policy of assimilation, which lasted up until the end of the 1960s, was more in reaction to a perceived problem rather than attempting to stabilise and strengthen race relations within the classroom environment. It was understood to calm the concerns of white parents alarmed at the presence of large numbers of immigrant children in their local schools, a state of affairs created by a system of dispersal designed to spread the problem of immigration throughout the country. The implementation of this dispersal policy required statistical data on immigrant pupils, such as their linguistic abilities and the socio-economic status of their parents. This important information was used to secure access to additional funding via Section 11 of the Local Government Act 1966. Local education authorities (LEAs) could access this fund to aid their dispersal and assimilation work.

This assimilation phase existed against a background of the rise of the political far right and the growing strength of the National Front. It proved a hopelessly problematic policy however, almost impossible to implement, administer or measure in terms of success. It had been created on the very negative assumption that black pupils in the classroom were a problem to be dealt with through their inability to speak English. Research has shown that bilingual and multilingual immigrant children in America, Canada and Britain opt for a 'silent period' when at first exposed to a new language (Cummins, 2001). This silence can be understood in terms of response to a culture shock. However, in terms of language acquisition it marks a crucial listening period which varies in length, allowing children to learn at their own pace. Assimilation strategies actually pressurised immigrant children to learn English quickly in order to solve the problem of their very presence.

# Integration

The dawn of the 1970s, and of a new era of diversity, offered the policy of integration as a suitable replacement to assimilation. Quite simply, integration meant to become part of a bigger picture and to become fully absorbed into it (e.g. the American ideal of throwing everyone together in a melting pot to substitute a new identity of 'coffee coloured people' for the mishmash that had gone before). Integration introduced the first sighting of multiculturalism in education by way of an acknowledgement of cultural diversity (Parekh, 2000). Defining multiculturalism is no exact science. Literally, multiculturalism is about pluralism engaged in social theory. Alleyne (2002) concluded that multiculturalism celebrates difference as an end in itself. Powell and Schwartz (2003) opted for an unambiguous link to racism: *The notion of multicultural diversity entails exactly the same premise as racism – that one's ideas are determined by one's race and that a source of individual identity is [one's] ethnic heritage.* For some, there exists no incompatibility between multiculturalism and Britishness. For others, however, multiculturalism suggests 'separateness' and is often mistaken to mean that different cultural communities should live their own ways of life in a self-contained manner (Parekh, 2000).

The clear emphasis in developing integration policies was on absorption into the mainstream, while conceding that cultural differences could, when used selectively, be of interest to others. LEAs were expected to develop and implement multicultural strategies in schools, to facilitate the process of integration. This was done through a 'bolt-on' approach, as something else to push some schools to implement. The anxiety felt by teachers forced into unfamiliar territory was in direct response to ill-considered multiculturalism, resulting in shallow, superficial and barely recognisable global education. This particular brand of multiculturalism had the aim of *institutional hybridity – a fusion of myriad cultures, Bhangra, Afro, Asian and South Indian with Britishness … in order to ethnicise schools into integration* (Kundnani, 2001). In an attempt to redress the impact of racial stereotyping and growing prejudices based on ignorance, aspects of the immigrant life experience were to be shared. These included food, music, costumes, rituals, faith practices, festivals and traditional ways of life. Critics summarised this approach as the '3 Ss' – saris, steel pans and samosas – as these were the least threatening elements of cultural diversity that might be shared. Exotica was the only way to go to integrate successfully, it seemed (Sarup, 1991). Swann (DES, 1985) was also openly and vehemently critical of integration and multiculturalism in this form. Although some initial barriers were overcome by this first phase of multiculturalism, the strategy was tokenistic and devalued the wealth of heritage that immigrants held so dear. Allowing British society to select elements of cultural diversity that they found particularly palatable, for example the curry, now as British as a bulldog or a pint of beer, could never facilitate social cohesion in the classroom or indeed anywhere.

# Cultural pluralism

The principle of cultural pluralism was introduced in the 1980s to find a resolution for the continuing dilemma of racism in education. Two groundbreaking government publications, *West Indian children in our schools*, or the Rampton Report (DES, 1981), and *Education for all*, or the Swann Report (DES, 1985), both cited earlier in this chapter, left no doubt that the issues of underachievement as experienced by West Indian pupils in particular were now firmly included on the educational agenda. The Swann Report reflected a period of growing social unrest and signified a need to address deeply-rooted ideologies of prejudice and discrimination, thus marking a transition. The title *Education for all* identified the intent to redress the balance, not only in education policy but in society as a whole. Swann was clear about how we had arrived at this important transition point:

*All in all, central government appears to have lacked a coherent strategy for fostering the development of multicultural education and thus to have been unable to play a leading role in coordinating or encouraging progress in this field. We regard both the assimilationist and integrationist educational responses to the needs of ethnic minority pupils as, in retrospect, misguided and ill founded.*

(1985, p198)

Acknowledgement of recommendations made by Rampton and Swann was of foremost consideration, although traces of assimilation and integration still survived from the troubled 1960s and 1970s. The expectation that shared values and ideals should unite all citizens of the now multiracial, multiethnic Britain of the time was paramount. A sense of belonging was to be cultivated in the sharing of these values. Cultural pluralism rode on the wave of anti-racism policies in all LEAs and schools. Funding from central government sought to employ bilingual support staff where possible. However, a controversial enforced ban on mother tongue in the classroom hindered linguistic progression. When coupled with advice to parents only to 'speak English with your children at home', this compounded the apparent value and status of mother tongue as worthless in the eyes of the education system. As with assimilation, all-white schools were not required to engage with such approaches and often remained oblivious to the need for them. This was no longer acceptable.

The Education Reform Act of 1988, which prepared the ground for the National Curriculum, promoted cultural pluralism through the buzzwords of 'choice and diversity', incorporating non-statutory guidance on multicultural education for all teachers. Despite the rhetoric of antiracism and equality of opportunity, strategies to combat racism in practice continued to prove inadequate. The foundations of successive policies were so deficient in structure and philosophy that they became a self-fulfilling prophecy by virtue of their inevitable failure. Introduced in response to a perceived crisis in education – the presence of immigrant children in schools, the urban race riots in Liverpool and Birmingham, the underachievement of black boys as signalled by league tables – it is difficult to see how could they ever hope to impact positively. The National Curriculum, which made its first appearance in schools in 1989, provided direct strategic guidance to permeate all schools and provide *a broad and balanced curriculum … an entitlement of all pupils* regardless of their catchments. In the spirit of shared values, the religious education syllabus was to dedicate 50 per cent study time to Christianity and 50 per cent to the main religions represented in Britain, namely Buddhism, Hinduism, Islam, Judaism and Sikhism. This measure was widely perceived as insufficiently progressive to offer a truly multicultural curriculum. The absence of black scientists, artists, poets and role models in general contributed to the mis-education of black pupils throughout the 1960s and 1970s, and it appeared that this institutional racism in education might continue. How could ideals such as the fostering of intelligence and mutual understanding take place within a blanketing white, western worldview? It became important to question the notion of tolerance, a word used happily in school mission statements the length and breadth of Britain. Tolerance means to put up with, perhaps reluctantly. It means to endure or permit grudgingly. It is not about acceptance, understanding and most significantly it is not about equality.

More recent government policy in the 1990s led to various initiatives championing equality of opportunity and high standards for all through parental choice, standards and diversity, bringing cultural pluralism into the political mainstream. MacPherson (1999) recommended Ethnic Minority Achievement Grants (EMAG) to replace Section 11 funding of the Local Government Act of the 1960s and all LEAs were directed to appoint EMAG co-ordinators and teams to make grassroots impact. These teams would be subject to the same accountability through inspection criteria as other sections of education. MacPherson emphasised the continued destructive impact of racism (endemic in the operations of the Metropolitan Police) and condemned *the collective failure of an organisation to provide a professional service to people because of their colour, culture or ethnic origin*. Racism can be seen in processes which discriminate through unwitting prejudice, ignorance, thoughtlessness and stereotyping.

The incorporation of citizenship as a compulsory secondary curriculum subject in the new millennium, supported by GCSE qualifications in citizenship studies, has helped the 'inclusion' agenda, the replacement for cultural pluralism. A report on 'community cohesion' in the aftermath of race riots in Bradford, Oldham and Burnley was hailed as a race manifesto advising *black people to develop a greater acceptance of principal national institutions*, including citizenship (Cantle, 2001). Through the embedding of antiracist and multicultural elements into citizenship as a formally assessed and accredited discipline, a sea change has taken place which can, at this stage at least, only be considered a start in the battle to combat racism in education (Kundnani, 2001).

# Race and achievement

Of the many powerful, commonplace generalisations about 'race' and achievement, those around African-Caribbean boys as the lowest-achieving group in comparison to their white and Asian peers, are the most tenacious (DES, 1981, 1985; Troyna, 1984; Gillborn and Mirza, 2000):

*West Indian children as a group are underachieving in our education system.*

*There is no doubt that West Indian children as a group, and on average, are underachieving, both by comparison with their fellows in the white majority as well as in terms of their potential.*

*The underachievement of West Indian children is a reinforcement of a stereotype that black people are academically challenged.*

*Race, gender and class all impact on achievement. The lowest achieving ethnic groups (Bangladeshi, Pakistani and Caribbean) are disproportionately overrepresented in the lowest socio-economic groups.*

These comments reflect the complexity of the debate on race and underachievement, while at the same time reinforcing the central discourse that the underachievement of black pupils, in particular black boys, has continued to raise the greatest concerns. As with multiculturalism, underachievement has been defined in fluid terms depending on the subject (ethnic group) and context. The very use of the word 'underachievement' is synonymous with the many stereotypes associated with racial characteristics of black people: that they are lazy, lacking mental capacity, and inclined to challenging behaviours, conflict and aggression (particularly boys). However, in terms of educational achievement such powerful stereotypes have been applied both to black pupils and to their rates of learning. Gillborn and Mirza have noted that:

*[i]t is vital to identify differences in attainment but we must be careful to avoid wider beliefs that reinforce wholly stereotypical perceptions that some ethnic groups are naturally talented in some areas or inherently culturally disposed to learning whilst others are not. Thus, simply replacing 'underachievement' with the more recent notions of 'difference' needs to be carefully considered.*

(2000, p56)

It is vital to point out that the underachievement of black boys is just one facet of the multiplicity of issues when the question of race and achievement is raised. The all-encompassing nature of this debate has preoccupied politicians, journalists and educational professionals alike, with crime, gang culture, binge drinking, the wearing of hoodies, gun restrictions and sink schools all featuring prominently. Since the 1960s when the education system was said to be responding to a crisis in relation to growing numbers of immigrant children in the classroom, institutional racism in its various forms has been blamed for the systematic and consistent failure of Britain's education provision to address the issue of underachievement. Activists within black communities became increasingly vocal in the 1970s, spurring the government to set up its inquiry chaired by Lord Rampton (DES, 1981), which noted that *whilst we cannot accept that racism alone accounts for the underachievement of West Indian children, we believe that taken together with negative teacher attitudes and an inappropriate curriculum, racism does play a major part in their underachievement.*

## Research box

### black pupils' expectations and experiences of schooling

There are many factors that contribute to underachievement as experienced by black pupils. They include the lack of recreational options, high levels of unemployment in the family and poor housing (Modood and Berthoud, 1997), other material deprivation (Modood, 1994; Gillborn and Gipps, 1996), and experiences of racism in wider society (Maughan and Dunn, 1988). However, the mismatch between the expectations and experiences of black pupils compounds the entire underachievement debate. Parents from the Indian subcontinent who were educated in English, usually in larger teaching rooms and with the utmost respect for their teacher in a culture that valued discipline, found clear areas of difference in their children's schooling. The 'migrant effect' did not anticipate such lowering of expectations in terms of educational provision. Eade (1995) concluded that parental lack of knowledge about the systems in place might also be a factor in the mismatch experience. Among African-Caribbean pupils, the raising of aspirations aimed to combat notions of cultural inadequacy rooted in patterns of disaffection. Coard's (1971) report, *How the West Indian child is made educationally sub-normal in the British school system*, was endorsed by Swann (DES, 1985) who noted that *research evidence and our own findings have indicated that the stereotypes teachers tend to have of West Indian children are often particular with generally negative expectations of academic performance.*

African-Caribbean pupils continue to bear the brunt of concerns about underachievement. A review of inner London LEAs concluded that African-Caribbean pupils were the lowest achieving ethnic group. In 2002, when the national average achieving five GCSEs grades A*–C was 51 per cent, African-Caribbean pupils were the lowest achieving ethnic group with 30 per cent. Follow-up inspection visits to the LEAs involved in the sample study uncovered a sense of helplessness regarding strategies to raise the achievement of black boys.

Sewell (1997) attempted to demystify the issue, reporting that *underachievement is strangely decontextualised from wider societal issues such as negative media representations and poverty.* Sewell explored many factors that have exacerbated the dilemma of underachievement, including violent and anti-school masculine culture, the absence of male role models in the classroom, challenging behaviour patterns and the mismatch of masculinity as a process of socialisation linked directly to academic underachievement. For some boys, masculinity means 'hardness', antagonism to school-based learning, sporting prowess and fashion. However, this cannot be interpreted as a standard for all, which is the immediate danger when considering the power of media stereotypes.

Successive studies have also noted *inter alia* low teacher expectations, inappropriate and inconsistent discipline systems leading to increased incidents of disruption and exclusion, misunderstanding about black identity and expressions of culture, lack of role models, the impact of institutional racism in society as a whole and the comprehensive failure of LEAs to embrace inclusion and diversity (Saunders, 1996).

Educationalists in America have reported a similar linked pattern of black boys and underachievement in external examinations, with higher exclusion rates and labelling as the lowest-achieving ethnic group, markedly in comparison with bilingual Latino students. Research has offered a range of possible explanations, including differences in cognitive abilities, aversion to intellectual competition, genetic difference, economic disadvantage and manifestations of racism in society. A comparative 'whiteness study' has had limited impact in Britain. 'Whiteness', it was argued, should be considered not as a biological fact but as a social construction, encouraging white teachers to explore how their ethnicity impacts on their work (Pearce, 2003). As with the American research into black underachievement, the ultimate aim of this study was to ensure equality of educational provision for all. Fundamentally, the impact of negative stereotyping and the lack of cultural identification with the system of schooling (and indeed the curriculum) are considered the most powerful of those socio-cultural factors that have contributed to the consistent disaffection and thus underachievement of black boys in American schools (Katz, 1993). American approaches include the successful mass recruitment of black teachers with international teaching qualifications and the delivery of training on black culture in all schools as two initiatives to attempt to understand the 'gangsta' street culture. Ethnic minority teachers make up only 7 per cent of London's teaching cohort, whereas ethnic minority pupils make up 44 per cent of the total school population. This has prompted some commentators to note that this is unacceptable in the twenty-first century school (Education Commission, 2004).

---

### *Pause for thought* | cultural racism – a new phenomenon

Multicultural education policies combined with antiracist education policies are now charged with addressing an evolving phenomenon. Identified as 'cultural racism', the emergence of this development is illustrated in the rise of 'Islamophobia' since the Twin Towers disaster in New York in 2001. The classifying of such a cultural group prompted Gilroy (1992) to conclude that such *a form of cultural racism, which has taken a necessary distance from the crude ideas of biological inferiority now seeks to present an imaginary definition of the nation as a unified cultural community.*

Cultural racism may suggest that ethnic groups have a very defined culture that is distinct and easily identifiable. What evidence can you find to support cultural racism in the media? Which other groups are subject to this emerging racialised identification theory? Could it be argued that globalisation challenges such notions of ethnic identification? What should be the response of educationalists to the rise of Islamophobia? Consider the guidance given by the teaching unions, for example the National Union of Teachers (NUT) and the National Association of Schoolmasters and Union of Women Teachers (NASUWT), in response to incidents of Islamophobia in schools. Can multicultural and antiracist education policies have been effective in countering ethnic stereotyping?

## Summary and conclusions

This chapter has considered historic government strategies to embrace difference and has reviewed their relative success rates. The ways in which race impacts on language, deciding who belongs and who does not, has added to the notions of identity. In addition, the focus on achievement and attainment in this era of heightened concern around league tables has confirmed the need to celebrate diversity and acknowledge individual needs in order to promote high aspirations and challenge deeply help stereotypical assumptions.

The contemporary socio-political debate around 'race' and education attempts to address the historic 'island race' notion associated with being British. Not surprisingly, second- and third-generation immigrants are experiencing their own journeys of discovery, illustrating the complexity and at times controversy of the very nature of the debate. New ethnicities, identities and cultures are a common feature of every town and city, and education policy and governmental initiatives in education need continually to bear this firmly in mind.

## References

Alleyne, B (2002) An idea of community and its discontents: towards a more reflexive sense of belonging in multicultural Britain. *Ethnic and Racial Studies*, 25: 607–27.

Cantle, E (2001) *Community Cohesion: a report of the Independent Review Team* (the Cantle Report). London: Home Office.

Coard, B (1971) *How the West Indian child is made educationally sub-normal in the British school system*. London: New Beacon Books.

Cohen, P (1989) *Tackling common sense racism*. University of London: Institute of Education, Centre for Multicultural Education.

Cummins, J (2001) Cultural and linguistic diversity in education: a mainstream issue? *Educational Review*, 49(2): 105–14.

DES (1981) *West Indian Children in Our Schools* (the Rampton Report). London: HMSO/Department of Education and Science.

DES (1985) *Education for All: report of the Committee of Inquiry into the Education of Children from Ethnic Minority Groups* (the Swann Report). Cmnd 9453. London: HMSO/ Department of Education and Science.

Eade, J (1995) *Routes and beyond: voices from educationally successful Bangladeshis*. London: Centre for Bangladeshi Studies.

Education Commission (2004) *Educational experiences and achievements of black boys in London schools, 2000–2003*. The London Development Agency. Available at **www.lda.gov.uk** (accessed 18 April 2009)

Gaine, C (1995) *Still no problem here*. Stoke on Trent: Trentham.

Gillborn, D and Gipps, C (1996) *Recent research on the achievement of ethnic minority pupils*. London: OFSTED/Institute of Education.

Gillborn, D and Mirza, HS (2000) *Inequality*. London: OFSTED.

Gilroy, P (1992) The end of anti-racism, in Donald, J and Rattansi, A (eds) *Race, culture and difference*. London: Sage.

Katz, M (1993) *The urban underclass*. Princeton, NJ: Princeton University Press.

Kundnani, A (2001) From Oldham to Bradford: the violence of the violated. *Race and Class*, 43(2): 105–31.

MacPherson, W (1999) *The Stephen Lawrence Inquiry*. Cm 4262-I. London: The Stationery Office.

Maughan, B and Dunn, G (1988) Black pupils' progress in secondary school, in Verma, G and Pumfrey, P (eds) *Educational attainments: issues and outcomes in multicultural education*. London: Falmer Press.

Modood, T (1994) *Not easy being British*. London: Runnymede Trust.

Modood, T and Berthoud, R (1997) *Ethnic minorities in Britain*. London: Policy Studies Institute.

Ousley, H (2001) *The Bradford District Race Review*. Bradford: Bradford Vision.

Parekh, B (2000) *The future of multi-ethnic Britain – the Parekh Report*. London: Profile Books.

Pearce, S (2003) Compiling the white inventory: the practice of whiteness in a British primary school, *Cambridge Journal of Education*, 33(2): 62–9.

Powell, T and Schwartz, B (2003) The struggle to define academic multiculturalism. *Cultural Critique*, 55: 152–81.

Sarup, M (1991) *Education and the ideologies of racism*. Stoke on Trent: Trentham.

Saunders, P (1996) A British bell curve? *Sociology Review*, (6)2: 81–8.

Sewell, T (1997) *Black masculinities and schooling*. Stoke on Trent: Trentham.

Troyna, B (1984) Fact or artefact? The 'educational underachievement' of black pupils. *British Journal of Sociology of Education*, 5(2): 153–66.

Troyna, B and Hatcher, R (1992) *Racism in children's lives*. London: Routledge.

Troyna, B and Williams, J (1996) *Racism, education and the state*. London: Croom Helm.

Wright, C (1992) *Race relations in the primary school*. London: David Fulton.

# *Chapter 14*

# From special needs to inclusive education

## Carol Smith

### Introduction

All students of education studies bring their own experiences of special needs and learning difficulties to their studies, whether through setbacks they themselves have experienced or through learning alongside peers with a diversity of needs. Few of us have entered higher education without experiencing reverses in learning at some point in our compulsory schooling, perhaps with quadratic equations in mathematics or with coordination when attempting the triple jump in athletics. So, the accompanying feelings of frustration and low self-esteem are familiar to all, but especially to those who find difficulty in accessing the curriculum daily. When analysing policies and practices for including young people with learning difficulties in the education system, it is essential to draw on this personal experience to evaluate provision and consider how issues could be resolved. This chapter critically reviews developments in provision for pupils and students with special educational needs (SEN) in England and Wales, focusing on the period from the late 1970s to the present day, as this has been a time of rapid change. It includes consideration of the historical perspective in order to understand the rationale behind the change in emphasis from SEN provision to inclusive education and particularly the models and discourses underpinning these developments.

# The historical perspective: from 1870 to 1970

From 1870, elementary education became compulsory for all children. However, its provision did not account for children who, for a variety of reasons, were considered ineducable or difficult to educate. The provision of schooling for young people with physical or sensory disabilities developed gradually, and may have been hampered by the system of 'payment by results', by which teachers' wages were determined by the results of tests in the basic subjects. If children with disabilities were likely to lower these results there was no incentive for teachers to include them in their classes or schools. Young people with more severe learning disabilities were labelled as 'idiots' or 'imbeciles' and therefore considered unfit to be included within the education system, while the 'feeble-minded' were considered to have sufficient ability to benefit from attendance at a special school. The assessment and diagnosis of such people was the responsibility of the medical profession and so a medical discourse evolved, not only to consider those who were ineducable but also anyone who had a disability or learning difficulty. Therefore, a medical model of disability, where the problem was seen to be with the individual, prevailed until the latter half of the twentieth century.

*Pause for thought* | the medical model and attitudes to disability

The medical (or clinical) model of disability is a product of the nineteenth and early twentieth centuries, but how does it influence our thoughts and language today? In medical discourse, the term 'assessment and diagnosis' was used. Perhaps 'assessment and provision' would have been preferable in an educational context! Support assistants sometimes speak of a child they 'look after', rather than 'support'. Concern is often expressed that certain young people will not cope in the school environment because of a physical disability and that they should have the advantage of a special setting, offering them 'the care they need'. Such thoughts and terms locate the difficulty that individuals experience in school within themselves. It is a deficit model. Take a few minutes to reflect about things you have said, or heard, that suggest individuals' inabilities to participate in school or society are because of a personal deficiency.

Although the 1914 Elementary Education (Defective and Epileptic) Act legislated that local education authorities (LEAs) must provide for these categories of children, and successive legislation made their education compulsory, the move towards provision of compulsory schooling progressed slowly, and continued to be underpinned by a medical and deficit model. Not until 30 years later were *defective* children removed from medical care and into education, frequently but not exclusively in special schools. However, health authorities retained the responsibility for individuals who were deemed ineducable until legislation in 1970 acknowledged all children's rights to receive an education and the label was abolished.

# From 1970 to the new millennium: a shift away from deficit models

If the previous 100 years had seen slow progress in the educational provision for individuals who were considered difficult to teach, these three decades provide a marked contrast as changes in provision became radical and extensive. Human rights movements, at a national and international level, championed the rights of all children and adults to be fully included in society. The disabling barriers created by society, rather than disability, were seen as main causal factors in their marginalisation or exclusion. Legislation has promoted equal opportunities in society and in education. Yet it is important to recognise 'the tensions created between a public rhetoric of equal opportunities and activated government policies which in all areas of public life are deepening inequalities rather than reducing them' (Armstrong *et al.*, 2000).

The Warnock Report (1978) was the first response to dissatisfaction with the education of individuals who were 'handicapped', 'maladjusted' or 'educationally subnormal'. The majority were being educated in day or residential special schools and therefore segregated from their community. A key finding of the Warnock Committee underpinning recommendations in the subsequent report was the anger felt by young people on being isolated from their local community by segregated schooling, a sense of separation which was compounded on leaving school. The main recommendations of the report identified by Armstrong (1998) were:

- the abolition of previously used categories in favour of pupils' special educational needs (SEN) being described using educational rather than medical criteria;
- recognition that up to 18 per cent of pupils in mainstream schools experience difficulties in learning because of SEN;

- that more emphasis should be placed on multi-professional assessment and on parents' involvement in decision-making about their children;
- that assessment and provision should be extended to include pre-school children;
- that provision should be extended to include the needs of young people in further education.

A further recommendation was that, wherever possible, pupils with SEN should be educated in mainstream settings. The 1981 Education Act contained many of the recommendations of the report. However, within the teaching profession it was frequently referred to as 'Warnock without resources'. The downturn in the economy and lack of funds to support implementation of the recommendations resulted in 'patchy' integration of pupils into mainstream settings. Nevertheless, the recommendations influenced subsequent legislation and continue to be strongly reflected in policy-making today.

While the aim of the Warnock Report was to remove all but a minority of pupils from segregated settings, discourse revolved around 'integration' rather than 'inclusion'. Unfortunately, these terms are frequently used synonymously in educational discussion. However, integrating individuals into mainstream settings implies their readiness and willingness to change in order to fit into the setting. Three main types of integration were identified by Warnock, namely:

- locational integration, where pupils are located in a special class or unit, but on the same site as a mainstream school;
- social integration, where pupils are again located in a special class or unit on the same site as a mainstream school, but where they are also given the opportunity to socialise with mainstream pupils, perhaps at break or by eating together at lunch-time;
- functional integration, where pupils with SEN are taught for part, or all, of the timetable in mainstream classes.

---

**Pause for thought** | are functional integration and inclusion the same?

Functional integration is often confused with inclusion. But are individuals necessarily fully included if they are being taught in a mainstream classroom alongside individuals who do not experience any difficulties in accessing the curriculum? Think of a classroom you have spent time in recently, either in the role of teacher (in its widest interpretation) or learner. Were all pupils equally included and able to share the same experiences? Were pupils with special needs supported in a separate area of the classroom, or were they receiving support alongside and engaging with peers who were not experiencing learning difficulties? Did some pupils choose not to be fully included in the activities or tasks? What do you think was the impact of the level of functional integration or inclusion on the individuals' self-esteem or sense of belonging in the different situations? Is it possible, or in the best interests of all learners, for full inclusion to take place all of the time?

---

The post-Warnock period has continued to be one of considerable change. The human rights discourse has influenced policy on inclusion. Government legislation has created tensions between a commitment to inclusion and the problems this brings because of the introduction of market forces into the education system. In order to avoid confusion over the use of the term 'inclusion' it must be pointed out that, at the level of government policy-making and legislation, inclusion refers to being included in a mainstream, as opposed to a segregated, setting. To teachers, it can refer to the degree of in-class inclusion. However, the term is frequently used in close proximity in both contexts in discussion.

Two key documents promoting the rights of the child to equal opportunities and inclusion in mainstream education are the UN Convention on the Rights of the Child (United Nations, 1989) and the Salamanca Statement (UNESCO, 1994). The latter was agreed by representatives of 92 governments, of which the UK was one, and 25 international organisations at the World Conference on Special Needs Education at Salamanca in Spain. Lindsay (2003) saw the 'moral imperatives' in the Statement as deriving from *an assertion that children's characteristics, interests, abilities and learning needs are unique to each child and collectively diverse* and that regular schools are the most effective form of provision. And, with regard to governments' responsibilities, Rustemier (2002) stated that:

*These international human rights texts are not simply guidelines but place obligations on governments to reform education. One of the main strengths of a human rights approach to education is the recognition that the rights of children and young people to enjoy inclusive education are accompanied by the responsibilities of governments to provide it.*

(p10)

Successive UK government legislation acknowledged the rights of all children and young people to an inclusive education. The Education Reform Act 1988 introduced a National Curriculum for all children. This development affirmed children's rights to receive a curriculum that was broad and balanced, and also differentiated to accommodate their needs. However, levels of attainment linked to age were introduced, with testing at the end of key stages to measure a school's success. This had an adverse effect on the willingness of mainstream schools to include those who would find it difficult to achieve.

Meanwhile, the Special Needs Code of Practice (DfEE, 1994) provided guidance to schools to support inclusion. This identified eight areas of SEN:

- learning difficulties;
- specific learning difficulties (e.g. dyslexia);
- emotional and behavioural difficulties;
- physical disabilities;
- sensory impairment (visual);
- sensory impairment (hearing);
- speech and language difficulties;
- medical conditions.

This was accompanied by a multi-stage approach to the identification and assessment of need, with differentiation of work and monitoring by teaching staff as the first stage and the use of an Individual Education Plan (IEP) as the second. Later stages included the involvement of outside agencies and a Statement of Need outlining provision. It was recommended that IEPs could have a varying number of targets and should be reviewed at least every six months.

Mittler (2000) described the Code of Practice as a 'landmark document' as it promoted inclusion *by setting out as clearly as possible the principle that all schools and all teachers, without exception, were responsible for the teaching of all children* and that schools were responsible for adapting provision to meet the needs of all individuals. The Code also reflected the social model of disability, locating difficulties encountered by individuals with SEN within society. If barriers created by society and schools were removed, this would improve access to the setting and the curriculum. This was the first time such structured provision had been required and teachers found their workload increased considerably with additional paperwork, while also lacking confidence and expertise in writing IEPs.

To overcome initial difficulties and criticism and to meet the requirements of the Special Needs and Disability Act 2001, a new SEN Code of Practice (DfES, 2001) was introduced into schools in 2002. This attempted to reduce bureaucracy through the reduction of the number of areas of SEN and also the number of stages of intervention. The eight areas of SEN were reduced to:

- communication and interaction;
- cognition and learning;
- behavioural, emotional and social development;
- sensory and/or physical.

However, a comparison with the areas of need in 1994 shows that categories have simply been combined, while the same range of need is still included. The three-stage approach of this later Code is clearer, with:

- School Action (Early Years Action for the Foundation Stage) provided by the school with support from the Special Needs Co-ordinator (SENCO);
- School (or Early Years) Action Plus involving outside agencies (e.g. the educational psychology service);
- statemented provision.

Clearer guidance was provided to support the writing of IEPs. No more than three or four short-term and achievable targets now needed to be set, but teaching strategies and resources should be identified and success or exit criteria stated. It now became a requirement that IEPs must be reviewed at least every six months, but preferably every term.

While this clarified teachers' responsibilities, of more significance was the strengthening of the rights of pupils and parents to be involved in any decision-making about their provision. So, parents and children had the right to be involved in target-setting and the reviews to assess the extent to which targets had been met, and in any other decision-making regarding provision. Research (Armstrong and Galloway, 1992; Brown, 1999) has shown that parents often experience difficulty in making their voices heard. While professionals might listen, parents frequently express concern as to whether their views are taken seriously. In discussing parents' role in the assessment that forms part of the statementing process, Armstrong and Galloway (1992) found that *many parents felt that their own contribution to the assessment was only taken seriously when it supported what the professionals were saying*. In illustration of the complexities involved, an interesting situation arose with a parent who was also a wheelchair user. She found that with increased school security it was more difficult to make appointments and then obtain entry to the school if a responsible adult was not available to unlock the main door. Her difficulty was further compounded by being in her wheelchair and unable to reach the buzzer.

If parents find it difficult to make their voices heard, it must be more difficult for children, and especially young children with learning difficulties. Yet, pupils can participate in decision-making at two levels. They can contribute to decisions about the effectiveness of their own provision (*I need more time to change for PE so perhaps I could come in from break a few minutes earlier; Because I'm left-handed it would be better if I sat ...*). However, individuals need to be taught how to contribute by developing an understanding of how they learn. Without this understanding they are likely to focus on their own difficulties rather than social barriers. Quicke (2003) expressed some concern about participation in review meetings, where he saw a danger in individuals being asked *to collude in their own negative labelling*. But pupils can also participate in decision-making at a wider level and thus influence school policy.

*Pause for thought* | pupils making a difference

In higher education, all students have the opportunity to influence practice and initiate change. This could be by articulating their views to staff at an individual level, constructive suggestions in module reviews, student union representation on committees (e.g. Equal Opportunities Committee) and representation on programme committees. How can pupils in early years, primary and secondary schools make their voices heard and thus make a positive contribution to developing an inclusive setting?

Booth (1999) has defined inclusion as *the process of increasing the participation of learners in and reducing their exclusion from the curricula, cultures and communities of neighbourhood mainstream centres of learning*. If learners are not given the opportunity to express what they believe prevents or could facilitate their full inclusion, how can this be achieved?

## Research box

## listening to young people who have been marginalised

Rose and Shevlin (2004), along with a team of researchers from the UK and the Republic of Ireland, attempted to find out the extent to which young people from marginalised groups, such as minority ethnic groups, young people with disabilities, members of gypsy traveller groups and refugees, had been included in educational settings. They wanted them to relate their experiences in order to *inform teachers and education policy makers about the steps which may be taken to enable the inclusion agenda to be more thoroughly addressed*. Part of their rationale was a concern that, despite claims of substantial progress in young people's views being recognised, the reality is that their voices frequently go unheard, as it is assumed that immaturity and a lack of competence would prevent them from participating successfully in decision-making. The project's findings were that physical access was still an issue for those with disabilities, and, to a certain degree, access to the curriculum. Negative peer attitudes and low teacher expectations were also mentioned. It also emerged that *students were expected to assimilate and adapt to mainstream norms*. The research concluded that professionals can still learn from the experiences and opinions of young people, and that as well as listening, must act on their views, removing obstacles to inclusion that still exist within education.

In addition to the Special Needs Code of Practice (DfES, 2001), a Disability Code of Practice (Disability Rights Commission, 2002) was introduced to support the implementation of the Disability Discrimination Act (DDA), which placed new obligations on education providers. Riddell (2003) described these as being:

- not to treat disabled pupils/prospective pupils less favourably;
- to make reasonable adjustments to avoid putting disabled pupils at a substantial disadvantage.

Reasonable adjustments do not include the provision of auxiliary aids and services, because these would be provided by other support services, or the duty to make alterations to the physical features of the school. Nonetheless, the vagueness of the term, and indeed of the term 'less favourably', gives rise to concern that providers could unwittingly act illegally, as only through the build-up of case law will these terms be clarified. However, as with the SEN Code of Practice, the Disability Code reflects the social model of disability in that it seeks to ensure that barriers to inclusion are removed.

# Promoting exclusion

Despite the commitment of recent legislation and policy to the ideal of inclusion, its success in breaking down barriers and its potential to continue developments towards inclusion for many years to come, it is interesting that the same legislation has, in many ways, created exclusionary pressures and issues for some.

- Is the social model of disability adequate for our understanding of the needs of and pressures on all people with disabilities?
- Does the National Curriculum and the ways in which it is provided exclude certain groups who have special needs or who are on the margins of society?
- Does the effect of market forces exclude those who are less able?

Crow (1996), a disabled feminist activist, has applauded the success of the social model of disability in enabling people with disabilities to overcome exclusion and discrimination, suggesting that its contribution *now and in the future, to achieving equal rights for disabled people, is incalculable*. So influential is this model, however, that Crow has also suggested we are at risk of overlooking the impact of impairment on the lives of those with disabilities. While social barriers can be removed, pain or fatigue cannot. Fears for the future are both different and greater for many disabled people. Yet she states that, because of this predominant model of disability, discussion of these is 'taboo'. Swain and French (2000) have concluded that a model, which they call an 'affirmation model', is emerging by building on the social model. This too acknowledges the presence of impairment, but focuses on *the positive experiences and identity of disabled people from being impaired and disabled*.

The National Curriculum was promoted as an entitlement curriculum for all children. It applies to special schools as well as mainstream settings. Because of this it can be said to be promoting equal opportunities. However, it was also established in order to raise standards in education, both in primary and secondary settings. To this end, it introduced attainment targets and level descriptors, and linked these to age. Furthermore, Standardised Assessment Tasks (SATs, now Standard Assessment Tests), were also created to measure achievement in English, mathematics and science at the end of Key Stages 1 and 2 in primary schools and Key Stage 3 in secondary schools, with GCSEs being the mode of assessment at the end of Key Stage 4. While this curricular framework was welcomed, the pressures of 'delivering' the National Curriculum and enabling pupils to achieve the appropriate levels often led to less flexible styles of teaching and a focus on more whole-class teaching. And, although there was government acknowledgement that not all children would achieve the intended levels, there was also an assumption that teachers would teach with a view to all children achieving (Swann, 1992). With schools being encouraged to move towards more flexible approaches again in their teaching styles, the problems experienced by children with special needs, such as coping with the demands placed on concentration by whole-class teaching and the frustration of copious written recording, may be reduced. However, 'curricula have always been a means of exclusion' (Clough, 1998) and frustration in finding it difficult to cope with the curriculum, or in understanding its relevance, leads to exclusion through withdrawal and avoidance strategies, truancy or enforced exclusion as a result of disaffection and anti-social behaviour.

This question, of course, is again related to the pressures of the National Curriculum and testing. However, the emphasis here is on the publication of results. School performance data based on National Tests (SATs) and GCSE results is available to parents, and many wish to send their children to a school which achieves exemplary outcomes. This has led to pressures on schools to achieve more and more in order to compete for pupils with other schools. This 'marketisation' of education is particularly important at a time when numbers on roll are falling, but is seen as detrimental to the inclusion of some children with SEN (Barton, 1995; Ballard, 1999; Armstrong *et al.*, 2000). The process can exclude children with special needs in two distinct ways. The first, as we have seen, is by the approach taken to delivering the curriculum in order that schools can achieve good results, which may be inappropriate for many pupils. The second is in mainstream schools' reluctance to accept children from special schools who may adversely affect their positions in the league tables. Stobbs describes the publication of league tables as *one of the features of current educational policy that most frustrates and undermines a ready welcome and the development of appropriate provision* (cited in Pyke, 2003). Not until school effectiveness is measured only in terms of value-addedness, where success is calculated on how far individuals have progressed from a base-line assessment, will these exclusionary pressures be overcome.

# Future directions

In the past, strategies to support pupils with SEN have been reactive rather than proactive. Initiatives have been directed towards providing for those who have difficulties rather than aiming to prevent them. The influence of the social model has encouraged the removal of barriers to access, and policy has become more proactive in that often barriers are no longer there to be taken down. However, there is a need for early intervention, and for support agencies to work together, to ensure that all children achieve their potential. This proactive approach, particularly in areas of high social deprivation, would reduce the need for intervention as a reaction to problems.

In Scotland, services work together through Integrated Community Schools to provide for the needs of pupils through an integrated approach involving teachers, social workers and health professionals (Tett, 2005). This approach is developing well in England, and can be seen in early intervention programmes such as Sure Start, where not only young children but also their families receive support. Early intervention can support the early identification of and provision for needs, and this may then lessen their impact at a later date. However, the expansion of such schemes depends for its effectiveness on support with adequate resources.

## Summary and conclusions

Provision for pupils with SEN has developed from segregated schooling, where a medical model of disability underpinning provision located the problems within the individual. The last 30 years of the twentieth century witnessed a move first of all towards integrating individuals with special needs within mainstream settings and then to encouraging their inclusion in mainstream classes. These changes were driven by local and international human rights movements and also by the recognition that many barriers to inclusion were created by society. If removed, these would increase the degree of access for people with a variety of difficulties. This recognition reflects the social model of disability which is now criticised as not going far enough.

While much emphasis is placed upon the inclusion of individuals with SEN it is important to stress that inclusion goes further and includes all marginalised groups in society. Concerns have been expressed that policy aimed at promoting inclusion in education can also be exclusionary and that future policy should look towards lessening the disadvantage that excludes individuals from accessing and achieving their potential in education.

However, inclusion is about more than compulsory schooling. If a society is to be promoted where all groups, regardless of ability, ethnicity, faith or culture are to be given equal opportunities, their differences must also be accepted and celebrated. In inclusive schools we see this acceptance and celebration of diversity in the curriculum and the ethos of the setting. In such settings children are able to develop confidence and self-esteem. While there is still a long way to go in the education system as a whole to create such enabling cultures, it is only by doing so that a tolerant and inclusive society will evolve.

# References

Armstrong, D (1998) Changing faces, changing places: policy routes to inclusion, in: Clough, P (ed) *Managing inclusive education: from policy to experience*. London: Chapman.

Armstrong, D and Galloway, D (1992) On being a client: conflicting perspectives on assessment, in Booth, T, Swann, W, Masterton, M and Potts, P (eds) *Policies for diversity in education*. London: Routledge.

Armstrong, F, Armstrong, D and Barton, L (2000) *Inclusive education: policy, contexts and comparative perspectives*. London: Fulton.

Ballard, K (ed) (1999) *Inclusive education: international voices on disability and justice*. London: Falmer.

Barton, L (1995) The politics of Learning for All, in Nind, M, Rix, J, Sheehy, K and Simmons, K (eds) (2003) *Inclusive education: diverse perspectives*. London: Fulton.

Booth, T (1999) Viewing inclusion from a distance: gaining perspectives from comparative study, in Nind, M, Rix, J, Sheehy, K and Simmons, K (eds) (2003) *Inclusive education: diverse perspectives*. London: Fulton.

Brown, C (1999) Parents' voices on advocacy, education, disability and justice, in Ballard, K (ed) *Inclusive education: international voices on disability and justice*. London: Falmer.

Clough, P (1998) *Managing inclusive education: from policy to experience*. London: Chapman.

Crow, L (1996) Including all of our lives: renewing the social model of disability, in Nind, M, Rix, J, Sheehy, K and Simmons, K (eds) (2003) *Inclusive education: diverse perspectives*. London: Fulton.

DfEE (1994) *Code of Practice on the Identification and Assessment of Special Educational Needs*. London: HMSO/Department for Education and Employment.

DfES (2001) *Code of Practice on the Identification and Assessment of Children with Special Educational Needs*. London: HMSO/Department for Education and Skills.

Disability Rights Commission (2002) *Code of Practice for Schools – Disability Discrimination Act 1995; Part 4*. London: DRC.

Education Act 1981. London: HMSO.

Education Reform Act 1988. London: HMSO.

Lindsay, G (2003) Inclusive education: a critical perspective. *British Journal of Special Education*, 30(1): 3–12.

Mittler, P (2000). *Working towards inclusive education: social contexts*. London: Fulton.

Pyke, N (2003) Targets 'unfair' to inclusive schools. *TES Extra for Special Needs*, November.

Quicke, J (2003) Educating the pupil voice. *Support for Learning*, 18(2): 51–7.

Riddell, S. (2003) Devolution and disability equality legislation: the implementation of Part 4 of the Disability Discrimination Act 1995 in England and Scotland. *British Journal of Special Education*, 30(2): 63–9.

Rose, R and Shevlin, M (2004) Encouraging voices: listening to young people who have been marginalised. *Support for Learning*, 19(4): 155–60.

Rustemier, S (2002) *Social and educational justice: the human rights framework for inclusion*. Bristol: CSIE.

Special Educational Needs and Disability Act 2001. London: The Stationery Office.

Swain, J and French, S (2000) Towards an affirmation model of disability, in Nind, M, Rix, J, Sheehy, K and Simmons, K (eds) (2003) *Inclusive education: diverse perspectives*. London: Fulton.

Swann, W (1992) Hardening the hierarchies: the National Curriculum as a system of classification, in Booth, T, Swann, W, Masterton, M, and Potts, P (eds) *Curricula for diversity in education*. London: Routledge.

Tett, L (2005) Inter-agency partnerships and Integrated Community Schools: a Scottish perspective. *Support for Learning*, 20(4): 157–61.

UNESCO (1994) World Conference on Special Educational Needs (Salamanca Statement). Paris: United Nations Educational, Cultural and Scientific Organisation.

United Nations (1989) *Convention on the Rights of the Child*. New York: United Nations.

Warnock, M (1978) *Special Educational Needs: report of the Committee of Enquiry into the Education of Handicapped Children and Young People* (the Warnock Report). London: HMSO.

# Chapter 15

## Faith in education: what place for faith communities in schools?

### Kate Adams and Mark Chater

**Introduction**

In the British education system there is a long-established but rapidly changing presence of faith communities in schools, manifested not only in multi-faith classrooms, but also in chaplaincy support, a church presence on governing bodies, publicly funded church schools, more recently established Islamic schools and very recently founded city academies based on Christian principles. This chapter aims to enable readers to pose and explore questions about that presence and how it impacts on pupils, classroom teachers and other educational professionals. This is an important area of knowledge for teachers and students who may work in faith schools or multi-faith schools, or who may collaborate with them in clusters. It is also important for educators in other sectors who engage with members of faith communities.

## Religion in education: a historical overview

For a very long time, religious organisations and individuals have paid attention to education and involved themselves in it. They transmit their religious teachings to the young; they advise parents on raising their children; they use places of worship as sites to nurture and develop faith; they run schools; they campaign and advise on education policies; in the UK, churches and other religious groups run schools in the state sector; and business leaders with a personal religious commitment are investing in new Academies. Why all this effort? What is in it for the faith communities, and what is the nature of the evolving relationship between religious faith and education processes? Here, we summarise the historical interdependence in the west between pedagogical processes and the Jewish, Christian and Muslim systems of theology to show how deeply faith and education are intertwined, and raise issues about the effects that this mutual involvement can have.

The Jewish, Christian and Muslim traditions, known as the Abrahamic religions, spring from a common ancestral root in the Middle East and have all had major impact on the western European intellectual tradition. Despite their significant differences in theology, the three traditions face some challenges in common: how to express their faith content in intellectual terms; how to communicate their faith to children; how to adjust to a religiously diverse world; and how to respond to a society that is secularising (i.e. losing its explicit commitment to worship, belief and moral norms determined by faith). These four challenges remain paramount for today's followers of Judaism, Christianity and Islam in the UK. While other major faith traditions, such as Hinduism, Buddhism and Sikhism, also have significant communities in the UK, their historical presence in the west is more recent, and therefore has had less long-term impact.

A shared belief in God as creator, law-giver and Lord has common educational implications for Jews, Christians and Muslims. For example:

- there are things about God that children and young people need to be taught;
- parents and religious authorities should collaborate to do the teaching;
- growing up in the world involves discovering God's will and obeying it as best one can;
- God can be discovered through the ordinary things of life, such as intellectual study, friendship and nature, as well as through doctrinal and moral precepts.

Religions have grappled with these issues throughout their history and have generally been at their most educationally creative at times of the most intense theological change. When theology was relatively static, teaching was a matter of routine. When theology was in crisis or changing rapidly, as during the adjustment to scientific modernity of the nineteenth and twentieth centuries, teaching methods would become more intense and innovative (Westerhoff, 1981).

The religions' interest in education grapples with two conflicting and, at times, irreconcilable priorities. The first is their belief that God is revealed in the ordinary; the second is that God is obscured in the ordinary. The implication of the first priority, when considered educationally, is that whenever we educate children about this world we are, implicitly, helping them to discover ultimate meaning. Therefore education is a good thing in itself. But the implication of the second priority is that an ordinary secular education on its own is not sufficient, and that religious and moral issues must be taught explicitly. Therefore education is only a qualified good, and can be harmful.

The first of those two views may be seen as the more positive towards education, and examples are found historically in all three traditions, which have at various times developed models of education designed to affirm the ordinary. Judaism looks to Moses Maimonedes, the twelfth-century Spanish-born philosopher who undertook the gigantic task of integrating classical Greek learning with the teachings of the *Torah* (the Jewish law). Contemporary Jewish leaders recognise the need to embrace secular learning and to be in dialogue with it, even where they disagree (Neuberger, 1997). In Christianity, early theologians, including St Paul and St Augustine, saw themselves as practitioners of education, teaching through culture and experience (1 Corinthians 9: 20–23). Augustine advocated a learner-centred approach (Howie, 1969). Later Christian educators adopted prototypes of differentiation (Jungmann, 1959) and models of child-centred, pluralist learning (Gallagher, 1988). The tradition of Islam, in its earliest stages, invented the concept of universities, developed technological and legal learning independently from the Qur'an and, subsequently, gave the west its first translations of Aristotle (Southern, 1953).

The Christian churches, as the majority religion in Britain, had an additional reason to invest in public education during the nineteenth and early twentieth centuries. Opening schools for the poor and middle classes at a time when state provision was limited became an expression not only of the churches' sense of mission but also of their wider social duty in response to the industrial revolution. In the same period, Anglican, Methodist and Roman Catholic training colleges were established with the purpose of training qualified teachers for church schools. In the twentieth century, as an expanding state legislated to take over schools and teacher training, the churches' share of this work diminished. Church schools and higher education institutions still exist, working within an equal opportunities framework to provide education for all.

The shared insights of these religiously world-affirming educational communities may be summarised as a belief that there is little or no point in requiring children to memorise sacred texts, digest half-understood theological formulae or conform blindly to moral precepts; that such projects, when attempted, have no educational value and no effect on allegiance to faith. Instead, educational methods were developed that ensured independence of spirit and ownership of ideas, and many of these were later adopted by the state sector.

A belief that education is a good in itself has historically led members of these traditions to found schools and to maintain, when they can, schools in the public sector which advocate a religiously infused vision of learning. Learning is seen as a means to bring the whole person (physical, aesthetic, intellectual, social and spiritual) into being. This is a sacred duty in itself (Groome, 1991) and one that has influenced the curriculum, for instance through the development of a values statement (QCA, 1999).

The more negative view, that education is only a qualified good and that forms of education that do not explicitly address the religious dimension are harmful, is also present in all three western religious traditions. It is a view that places faith communities apart from, and in tension with, modern secular education. In the UK, where Judaism and Islam are minority faiths in a society that could be understood as post-Christian, the impulse is sometimes to resist absorption by conserving traditional values through separate religious and moral teaching, where it is available. To some extent, this impulse informs the growing Muslim interest in Islamic schools. However, it would be a mistake to conclude that all British Muslims wish to separate themselves and their children from state education. The reality is more complex. Muslims have both praise and criticism for British education and the society that evolved it, and they have differing response strategies in education, family life and politics (Seddon *et al.*, 2003). Church schools are being re-evaluated by Christian educators, with a view to making them more distinctive (Arthur, 1995). A new breed of city academies, some sponsored by Christian organisations or individuals, is emerging.

At the same time, educators of several faiths are concerned that the spiritual and moral dimensions of education should not be lost, or become invisible, in a school system that seems to favour skills over personal development. Partly for this reason, an interest in spirituality, as distinct from religious faith, has been seen as a more productive way forward.

# The spiritual development of children

The spiritual development of children is firmly on the educational agenda, being an area that teachers must plan for. It is also an area that the Office for Standards in Education (OFSTED) inspects. Yet spirituality – and spirituality within an educational context – is complex and there are underlying conceptual problems. Here, we explore some of these problems, with a particular emphasis on those that relate to faith communities.

Considering spirituality in the school is important because that is the first educational environment in which all students encounter the theme. However, the notion of whether or not spirituality can actually be taught in contemporary schools is open to question. Castelli and Trevathan (2005) have outlined three major arguments in the conceptualisation of spirituality. The first contends that spirituality can only be taught in the context of a faith tradition (e.g. Thatcher, 1999), while a second point of view suggests that spirituality is innate and thus not dependent upon a faith stance (e.g. Hay and Nye, 1998). The third is considered in the next section.

If teachers adopt either of these first two stances it will, of course, have major implications for their practice. For example, a Christian teacher who believes that spirituality can only be taught in the context of the Christian tradition is immediately faced with difficulties in the classroom. Even if they are working in a faith-based school, not all of the children will necessarily be from a Christian background. In situations where there is a small number of children with no religious upbringing, teachers will need to be fully aware of their own beliefs, and also not make assumptions about the secular children's ability or inability to be spiritual.

Conversely, a teacher who believes that spirituality is not dependent upon a faith stance may be better placed to ensure the spiritual development of children of all faiths and none. However, they would need to be aware of different religions' conceptions of spirituality, which may contradict their own ideas. Further, there may be conflicts if children or parents from faith traditions believe that spirituality can only be taught from a faith stance.

# Guidance for the teacher

Theoretical issues about the definitions of spirituality – more numerous than this section can accommodate – are important because a third view presented by Castelli and Trevathan (2005) proposes that it is unrealistic to expect schools to ensure children's spiritual development when there is no consensus over its definition. Until now, you may have paused to ask yourself what spirituality is, or you may have been quite comfortable with the terminology. At a national level, the definition of spirituality is an important one for educators.

Academics have long searched for a definition relevant to education, resulting in a range of answers and debates. Brown and Furlong (1996) have described spirituality as a *weasel word: … a convenient catch-all, suitably vague and elusive of definition*. As Best (2000) has suggested, the greater the attempts to define spirituality, the more elusive a definition becomes. These authors' comments offer little comfort for teachers, who are required to ensure that pupils' spirituality is developed. Before considering practical guidance for teachers, it is worth exploring your own definitions of spirituality.

*Pause for thought* | what is spirituality?

Consider answers to the following questions, ideally with colleagues: Would you describe yourself as a spiritual person? If not, who do you know of who could be described in this way? How can the spiritual dimension of the person be described to a Martian who has landed on Earth? Discuss these issues with your colleagues and consider the variety of answers that you have collected. Are there common themes? Are there significant differences? How can those differences be accounted for?

Many people throughout history have claimed to have had a spiritual experience. Have you? If so, how would you describe it? What was it that made the experience a *spiritual* one, rather than one which might be described as purely emotional or psychological?

In attempts to clarify the position for teachers, government bodies have published various guidelines. You will need to examine the current definitions and advice for teachers, but below is a selection of characteristics that OFSTED (2004) seeks to identify in pupils:

- a set of values, principles and beliefs;
- an awareness and understanding of their own and others' beliefs;
- a respect for themselves and for others;

- a sense of empathy with others, concern and compassion;
- an increasing ability to reflect and learn from this reflection;
- an appreciation of the intangible;
- an expressive and/or creative impulse;
- an understanding of feelings and emotions, and their likely impact.

Do these criteria match with your own descriptions of spirituality? If they are different, it is worth reconsidering why and how the differences have arisen. The fact that differences are probable does not imply that there are right or wrong answers. What is important is that the differences can reveal insights into your own conceptions, some of which you might not have previously articulated.

The concepts of spirituality and spiritual development need further consideration in view of the presence of faith communities within educational settings. Definitions of spirituality are often largely culturally defined, so in a multi-faith classroom there are additional factors of which teachers need to be aware. Given that different religions perceive spirituality in different ways, students may bring their own perceptions into the classroom with them, partly influenced by their own religious upbringing. For example, a Muslim teenager may experience Ramadan, the month of fasting, as a spiritual experience when they feel closest to Allah.

Further, even within what might be termed a multi-faith classroom in a school setting, there will be children who have not had any religious upbringing. Yet, their spiritual development needs to be attended to as well. This can be a daunting task for teachers, but it is important that adults do not make assumptions about children's capabilities to experience or express the spiritual. In particular, adults must not assume that children with no religious upbringing have no capability to express ideas and/or have experiences which other people might define as being religious.

# Children's spirituality

Alongside the positioning of spirituality in the curriculum runs research into pupils' spirituality. Contemporary research into children's and adolescents' spiritual experience has provided valuable insights into how young people experience this aspect of being human. At times, children describe their spiritual experiences in terms of their religious background. For example, Muslim children have told researchers how Allah communicates with them through dreams, sending them messages (Coles, 1990; Adams, 2004).

However, religion is not necessarily a factor in determining spirituality: people can be spiritual without being religious. For example, secular children may have spiritual experiences, such as seeing or sensing a deceased grandparent. Teachers need to be aware of the distinction between religion and spirituality in the classroom and, as Hay and Nye (1998) have observed, need to be able to distinguish between when religious talk is spiritual and when it is not.

Teachers must learn to listen with care to children, without imposing their views upon the interpretation of the children's talk, and without making assumptions about children's ability to be spiritual. Coles (1990) described a conversation with a 10-year-old girl from the Hopi culture, which illustrates this point perfectly. The girl told how she had not answered her teacher's questions on religion, because the teacher was Anglo-Saxon and, the girl feared, might reject her beliefs, or fail to understand them.

---

***Pause for thought*** | assumptions about children's spirituality

Imagine you are teaching a class of children or older students comprising Christians, Hindus and those of no faith. You are exploring their responses to the possibility that there may be life after death, seeking not only their ideas, but any justifications that they have for their views.

- List a series of questions that you would ask.
- Now, note down your own views about life after death.
- Reflect carefully on how your views have shaped the questions you intend to ask the children.
- Have your questions been influenced by your own beliefs in any way?
- Have your questions been influenced by your assumptions about children's or older students' capabilities to have and to express spiritual ideas?
- Have your questions been influenced by a knowledge of Christian, Hindu or other religious and non-religious views about life after death?

---

A key element to a successful approach will be to maintain an open mind and to create a forum for open enquiry. Children will need to feel that their views and their expressions of the spiritual, whether religious or not, will be respected by their teacher and by their classmates. The teacher has the capability and responsibility to ensure such an ethos. For some teachers with deeply held convictions, this may not be an easy road to travel. Deeply held convictions about religion can cause problems not only for spiritual development in education but also for much wider issues.

# Faith against education: the new religious extremisms and state education

In the world after the terrorist atrocities of 9/11 in America (2001) and 7/7 in London (2005) it is impossible to deny the existence of religious extremism, usually known as fundamentalism, but it also remains difficult to define it adequately. Several forms of fundamentalism are spreading globally, posing a threat to liberal pluralistic state education systems. Two important modifying statements are necessary. First, although extreme religious behaviour is as old as religion itself, fundamentalism is a more recent phenomenon, both a by-product of modernity and a reaction against it. And second, although fundamentalist groups are growing rapidly in many religions, and tend to attract publicity and attention, they do not represent all that religious traditions have to say, nor are fundamentalists about to 'take over' in any particular religion (Marty and Appleby, 1994; Muslim Council of Britain, 2002).

## what is fundamentalism?

There is no single definition of 'fundamentalism' but there are recurring characteristics that appear across several fundamentalist groups in many different faiths and cultures. For this reason, it is often more accurate to talk of 'fundamentalisms'. From the research available (e.g. Barr, 1977; Ali, 2002; Bendroth, 1993; Marty and Appleby, 1994; Bush, 2001; Muslim Council of Britain, 2002; Victor, 2005) a basic list of characteristics is presented as follows.

- Taking a sacred text literally, even if it disagrees with science, history or common sense (e.g. believing in a literal six-day creation story, sometimes called Creationism, or Intelligent Design – a related modern belief), or adopting a non-literal interpretation only when literal meanings become completely untenable.

- Resisting democratic, pluralist values such as the free vote, multi-party systems, freedom of speech and freedom of religion – except when these values will aid the advance of their own group, or when a democratic rhetoric can be used to disguise other motives.

- Strong, at times violent, opposition to feminism, gender equality and homosexual rights.

- Charismatic male leadership in small sects or cults, where the leader is highly respected and cannot be questioned or held to account.

- Dualistic thinking, dividing the world into people who are saved or not, righteous or not, the 'either you are with us, or you are with the terrorists' principle.

- In Christian fundamentalist groups, a belief that the world will end violently in a confrontation between good (the west) and evil (Islam), after which Christ will return to Earth – at times, a desire to see this destruction come soon, rather than to avert it.

- A willingness to use violence against the innocent, such as bombing, nerve gas or suicide attack, to advance their cause, in defiance of the mainstream teachings of their faith.

It is important to note how hard many religious leaders and educators are working to point out the dangers of fundamentalism within their own communities (El-Affendi, 2001; Sacks, 2002). It is ironic and instructive that fundamentalist groups, though enemies to each other, have so many key characteristics in common, and seem almost to feed off each other's extremisms (Ali, 2002). Our task is to analyse these characteristics for their impact on educational values such as free open enquiry.

At the very least, fundamentalist allegiance sits uncomfortably with any education system that intends to teach values of critical independent thinking, tolerance, commitment to diversity and equality, and democratic participation. In particular, if schools and universities teach specific scientific and technological propositions, such as that life on the planet has evolved, or that there is a gay gene, or that free access to information and entertainment is desirable, this is likely to encounter profound suspicion and opposition. Literacy, when seen as something more than functional and related to the flexible use of interpretive techniques, is implicitly in opposition to any tendency to privilege and protect one sacred text as being above any criticism.

Educational programmes that engage the young in participative democracy, fostering attitudes of acceptance of religious and moral diversity, may be unfairly suspected by fundamentalists of moral weakness or relativism (Finnis, 1991). Fundamentalists batten upon, or simply invent, narratives of declining morality in order to generate moral panics and sway public opinion in favour of conservative policies. Moral panics are often exploited as an expression of wider social or cultural tensions and so can be manipulated (Goode and Ben-Yehuda, 1994). A healthy political education, taking in aspects of history, psychology, religion and technology, offers young people the skills to engage in complex analysis in which crude dualisms of right and wrong have no place. Fundamentalist beliefs thrive on such dualism, and effectively require the young to suspend critical thought.

A late modern condition of uncertainty, in which many teachers shy away from explicit advocacy of moral or religious 'truths', creates fluidity and insecurity for young people. Into this vacuum fundamentalism comes, offering a security and certainty apparently based on reason, goodwill and authority.

*Pause for thought* | fundamentalism and education policy/practice

Reflect on the ways in which the education system should respond to fundamentalism. Consider the following options alongside your own ideas. Accept, reject or amend any of these options and explain your reasons:

- changing the law on collective worship in schools, so that it does not have to be Christian;
- making it possible to change the science curriculum, so that Intelligent Design can be taught as an alternative to Darwinism;
- restricting the rights of the public to set up a school, so that it becomes harder for extremist groups of any ideology to engage in educational work.

# Faith in education: new paradigms for an old relationship

Fundamentalism is not the whole of any religion, but it exists, and, like spirituality, is an area that educational professionals need to be informed about, particularly with reference to faith communities. So, while faith and education have a close relationship, there are tensions and the final part of the chapter poses the question: what might be the best way forward to secure an appropriate future for the presence of faith in education?

Whether or not faith schools are justifiable is not the issue under discussion here. This is a major debate which is dealt with elsewhere (see Gardner *et al.*, 2004 for arguments both for and against faith schools). Rather, we accept that faith schools exist, and that there are also increasing numbers of multi-faith communities within non-denominational schools and other educational settings.

In all schools, the coverage of religions must go beyond Christianity. The five other main religions which are represented in Great Britain must also be covered across all key stages. These are:

- Islam;
- Judaism;
- Buddhism;
- Sikhism;
- Hinduism.

For some pupils, teachers and parents, particularly those with a strong commitment to a faith, this may pose difficulties. Naturally, for some (though not all) devout religious people, the process of engaging with different religious beliefs may pose difficulties. Learning about different points of view can be uncomfortable, even painful, perhaps leading to reflection on one's own beliefs which may have been held for a lifetime.

However, the process of becoming a reflective practitioner is fundamental to an educator's job. As Pollard (2002) has written, it is essential that teachers are fully aware of their own identity. Pollard's view encourages teachers to reflect upon different aspects of themselves, including how they appear to others, their values, aims and commitments, and their perceptions of pupils. Given that religious beliefs – in addition to atheistic or agnostic views – form part of a person's identity, it is inevitable that teachers will have to confront other people's views on religion. This can occur in the course of either teaching about religion in a variety of educational settings or in conversations with members of faith communities in other contexts.

Educators seeking to offer a balanced, unbiased view of religion and spirituality in the classroom, must ensure that the fundamentalist tendencies of religion are reduced yet not ignored. Fundamentalist tendencies are best reduced by exposure to open enquiry of the sort that takes place within religious education and spiritual development in schools. For example, effective religious education moves beyond pupils simply learning facts about different religions, to learning from religion also. This latter concept includes pupils reflecting upon their own experiences and the experiences of others in light of what they have learnt about religion, and interpreting and evaluating what they have learnt.

Children and older students should be encouraged to:

- listen to the views of others;
- reflect on their own views;
- engage in debate with others;
- respect the view of others.

Exposure to other opinions and beliefs in such an environment of respect could aid a reduction in religions' potentially damaging fundamentalist tendencies. These attitudes and skills can then be taken into adult life.

## Summary and conclusions

This chapter has shown how the west and Britain have had a close historical relationship between faith and education, how schools need to ensure children's spiritual development, how fundamentalist tendencies in several religions pose a threat to secular education, and how educators can model open critical enquiry in matters of faith and spirituality.

Education has the power to change the potentially damaging fundamentalist tendencies of religions. If teachers in faith schools and non-denominational schools alike are aware of these tendencies and actively encourage open enquiry into them, this should help pupils develop into critical thinkers. By taking a critically reflective approach to views about religion and spirituality, educators can help students of all ages make informed judgements. While this process can at times present some with awkward challenges, it can also be a healthy way for the faith presence to raise issues that might not otherwise be given exposure. It is only through open discussion and genuine dialogue in which students and educators hear each other that pertinent issues can be raised and moved forward.

# References

Adams, K (2004) Scriptural symbolic dreams: relevant or redundant in the 21st century? *Sleep and Hypnosis: an international journal of sleep, dream and hypnosis*, 6(3): 11–118.

Ali, T (2002) *The clash of the fundamentalisms: crusades, jihads and modernity*. London: Verso.

Arthur, J (1995) *The ebbing tide: policy and principles of Catholic education*. Leominster: Gracewing.

Barr, J (1977) *Fundamentalism*. London: SCM.

Bendroth, M (1993) *Fundamentalism and gender*. New Haven, CT: Yale University Press.

Best, R (2000) (ed) *Education for spiritual, moral, social and cultural development*. London: Continuum.

Brown, A and Furlong, J (1996) *Spiritual development in schools*. London: The National Society.

Bush, G (2001) Address to joint session of congress and the American people. Available at **www.whitehouse.gov/news/releases/2001** (accessed 9 April 2006).

Castelli, M and Trevathan, A (2005) The English public space: developing spirituality in English Muslim schools *The International Journal of Children's Spirituality*, 10(2): 123–31.

Coles, R (1990) *The spiritual life of children*. Boston, MA: Peter Davison.

El-Affendi, A. (2001) (ed) *Rethinking Islam and modernity*. Leicester: Islamic Foundation.

Finnis, J (1991) *Moral absolutes: tradition, revision and truth*. Washington, DC: Catholic University of America Press.

Gallagher, J (1988) *Our schools and our faith*. London: Collins.

Gardner, R, Cairns, J and Lawton, D (2004) *Faith schools: consensus or conflict?* London: Routledge.

Goode, E and Ben-Yehuda, N (1994) *Moral panics: social construction of deviance*. Oxford: Blackwell.

Groome, T (1991) *Sharing faith: the way of shared praxis*. San Francisco: Harper Collins.

Hay, D and Nye, R (1998) *The spirit of the child*. London: Fount.

Howie, G (1969) *Educational theory and practice in St Augustine*. London: Routledge and Kegan Paul.

Jungmann, J (1959) *Handing on the faith*. New York: Herder and Herder.

Marty, M and Appleby, R (1994) *Fundamentalisms observed*. Chicago University Press.

Muslim Council of Britain (2002) *The quest for sanity: reflections on 9/11 and the aftermath*. London: MCB.

Neuberger, J (1997) *On being Jewish*. London: Arrow.

OFSTED (2004) *Promoting and evaluating pupils' spiritual, moral, social and cultural development*. London: OFSTED.

Pollard, A (2002) *Reflective teaching*. London: Continuum.

QCA (1999) *National Curriculum Handbook for primary teachers*. London: Qualifications and Curriculum Authority.

Sacks, J (2002) *The dignity of difference: how to avoid the clash of civilisations*. London: Continuum.

Seddon, M, Hussain, D and Malik, N (2003) *British Muslims: loyalty and belonging*. Leicester: The Islamic Foundation.

Southern, R (1953) *The making of the middle ages*. London: Hutchinson.

Thatcher, A (ed) (1999) *Spirituality and the curriculum*. London: Cassell.

Victor, B (2005) *The last crusade: religion and the politics of misdirection*. London: Constable.

Westerhoff, J (1981) *A faithful church: issues in the history of catechesis*. Wilton, CT: Morehouse Barlow.

# Chapter 16

# Education for citizenship and democracy

## Howard Gibson

### Introduction

In 1998, and under the guidance of Professor Bernard Crick, an Advisory Group on Citizenship issued its report on *Education for Citizenship and the Teaching of Democracy in Schools* (QCA, 1998). The outcome of this report was the introduction of citizenship education to primary-aged pupils from September 2000, and to secondary pupils from September 2002. Crick had concluded that there were three principal strands of the citizenship curriculum: social and moral responsibility, community involvement, and political literacy. The third of these, political literacy, or education for democracy, has had less attention than citizenship education and Crick acknowledged that his committee's recommendations for teaching politics were limited. This chapter looks at different versions of democracy and examines the causes of political apathy in young people. There is a critique of the citizenship education suggested by the Crick Report, which fails to recognise the power and influence of the media and the diminished role of the state in the global economy. An alternative curriculum is suggested which, through such areas as media studies, would make pupils aware of the constructed nature of political discourse and would encourage them to engage in political action.

## What does democracy mean?

The origin of the word democracy lies in the Greek *demos*, meaning 'people in a community'. The ending '...ocracy', from the Greek *kratos*, meaning power or strength, implies rule. So democracy is about the rule of the people. However, the concept of democracy is problematic and there are various versions and views of democracy in different societies and cultures. Some might say that democracy should involve having a parliament. But while the United States of America claims to be democratic, for example, it does not have a parliament (although it does have two elected legislative assemblies). Perhaps democracy has nothing to do with an institutional name but with having the right to vote for who represents you in that institution, in which case a more direct form of democracy might be appropriate, such as voting via the web. It might be argued that, instead of representative parliamentary democracy, where a party is elected for a period of time to make decisions, there should be a referendum where everyone votes on all the big issues as they come along. There are also worries about democracy when it can allow minority racist parties, such as that of Le Pen in France, to gain representation and influence. There are also problems with how democracy is implemented. General Pervez Musharraf, who carried out a military coup in Pakistan in October 1999, declared he was instituting:

*... not martial law, only another path to democracy. The armed forces have no intention to stay in charge any longer than is absolutely necessary to pave the way for true democracy to flourish in Pakistan ... what Pakistan has experienced in recent years has merely been a label of democracy, not the essence of it ... I shall not allow the people to be taken back to the era of sham democracy but to a true one.*

(Goldenberg, 1999)

It might be argued that states with military rulers are more effective than democratically elected governments. There is also a question as to whether we have a true democracy when members of the public have the right to participate in an election but do not bother to vote. In 1997, for example, Labour was elected by only 31 per cent of those qualified to vote. In 1932, Hitler's Nazi Party came to power in Germany with 37 per cent support among the democratic electorate. For these reasons, some question whether democracy is always a good thing. It is not easy to talk about democracy with clarity, let alone define it. Saward (2003) has suggested that it is *an enormously rich, suggestive, evocative political term, and it is partly this fact that makes it such a potential political weapon*.

# Democracy and the curriculum

While a clear definition of democracy is not easy to give, from the Crick Report (QCA, 1998) and the curriculum documentation for citizenship education we get glimpses of how it is represented.

- *Participation*. There is a concern for the problem of apathy and dwindling commitment of young people in political life and the need to reverse this lack of interest and engagement. These worrying levels of apathy, ignorance and cynicism about public life need to be tackled at every level.
- *Communication*. There is a need to communicate views and opinions and engage in open discussion with others. Talk or discourse is obviously fundamental to active citizenship. Thus, to the need for pupils to participate in their community and become active in politics, we can now add the important skill of learning how to debate and engage with others.
- *Rule of law*. There is the requirement for members of a democratic community to obey the law. The assumption is that once debate has progressed sufficiently and decisions reached, however unpopular they may be with some individuals, the rule of law should apply. Respect for the rule of law is a necessary condition of social order and a necessary component of education.

But this apparently self-evident account of what democracy is, and how schools should prepare pupils for it, is both questionable and contentious.

---

*Pause for thought* | political apathy

Political apathy is said to be a key problem for democracies and one of the reasons for citizenship becoming mandatory in primary and secondary schools in England. However, while the government's response has been to emphasise the need to increase participation by encouraging the democratic involvement of pupils in school councils and the like, an alternative could have been to investigate why British democracy might be producing apathetic citizens and what consequences this might have for the teaching of citizenship in schools. Discuss political apathy with friends and colleagues. Do you think it really exists? Do you vote yourself, or take an active part in politics at any level? Why are governments interested in the political views of a nation's youth?

# Participation

The claim about the need for more commitment and participation is unconvincing because, although it rails against the problem of apathy, it fails to examine the historical decline of political commitment and ignores the huge changes to the nation state in recent years. These have come primarily from the effects of globalisation:

- the idea of national autonomy which used to define the democratic state can no longer be assumed;
- cultural pluralism and multiple identities in societies present complex challenges for national governments;
- the inability of states to deal with global problems, such as the environment, inequality and poverty makes them appear ineffective and powerless.

These are some of the issues that affect modern democracies and which may account for apathy. James Anderson (2002) has described the stark effects of globalisation on national democracies:

*Globalisation is putting democracy in question and is itself being questioned as undemocratic. Its border crossings are undermining the traditional territorial basis of democracy and creating new political spaces which need democratising. 'Global forces' are disrupting the supposedly independent, sovereign states and national communities which have provided democracy's main framework. And these 'global forces' are apparently beyond control or, more specifically, beyond democratic control. The political implications are wide reaching and far from clear … National democracy's problems are experienced most immediately in perception that the national state is losing its sovereignty to 'outside' bodies and is being infiltrated by them. Actions taken in or by other states are having increasing impact on supposedly 'sovereign' neighbours. State electorates are more directly affected by decisions made in other jurisdictions, including supra-state bodies like the EU. Private multinational corporations have become more powerful, and foreign-owned ones may determine the success or otherwise of national economies. States are losing some of their autonomy, as power 'goes upwards' to other, supra-state, political institutions, 'sideways' to privatised operations, or in some respects 'goes nowhere' or just 'evaporates', as economics outruns politics and political control is simply lost to the global market.*

(pp6–9)

By putting much of the decision-making processes beyond the borders of individual countries, there has been a decline in the economic, political and social effectiveness of the national state. As private multinational corporations have become more powerful they have affected the success or otherwise of national economies. Hertz (2001) went so far as to suggest that modern democracies are now resigned to the fact that multinationals are taking the place of elected governments and that shopping may be now more effective than voting: *This is the world of the Silent Takeover … Governments' hands are tied and we are increasingly dependent on corporations.* Since the Thatcher era of government in the 1980s, 'rolling back the state' has been policy in the UK, relaxing regulation on business and encouraging private health care and education. Bottery (2003) has argued that a consequence is the undermining of loyalty to the state. Put another way, as the nation state's influence on its citizens withers, so does their allegiance to it.

Democratic theory, from Locke to Rousseau and Bentham to Mill, has always been vigilant in separating the public from the private realm, and liberal democracies have tended to preserve free market economies. Within the walls of a factory or beyond a nation's borders can be found the economic freedoms for individuals to innovate, produce, market and sell. The point for democracies is this, while those economic freedoms that accompany capitalism whet consumers' appetites for more products, dealing with the less pleasant by-products, such as global warming, becomes problematic. To reduce global warming, for example, it might be considered sensible to reduce dramatically the use of private motor vehicles (though the link remains subject to intense scientific debate), but a government which does this will probably not be elected the next time round. A democratically elected government finds it difficult to limit the freedom of its voters.

## Research box

### market sovereignty or democracy?

The historian Eric Hobsbawn (2001) has argued that *democracy can be bad for you* and that the market and democracy are mutually exclusive. Is he right?

> *Market sovereignty is not a complement to liberal democracy; it is an alternative to it. Indeed, it is an alternative to any kind of politics, as it denies the need for political decisions, which are precisely decisions about common or group interests as distinct from the sum of choices, rational or otherwise, of individuals pursuing private preferences. Participation in the market replaces participation in politics. The consumer takes the place of the citizen ... [We] face an age when the impact of human action on nature and the globe has become a force of geological proportions. Their solution, or mitigation, will require measures for which, almost certainly, no support will be found by counting votes or measuring consumer preferences. This is not encouraging for the long-term prospects of either democracy or the globe.*
>
> (p26)

Because of colonisation, globalisation and increasing mobility, many citizens within national states now have multiple identities. One can, for example, be a UK citizen, British, a Muslim, a member of the EU, have a commitment to another country by birth or marriage, and so on. The state today is plural and diverse and no longer consists of a single people. In consequence, according to Parekh (2002), the state *cannot claim to embody and legitimate itself in terms of [its inhabitants'] sense of collective identity either, both because many of them no longer place much emphasis on their national identity or privilege it over their other identities, and because some of them increasingly cherish trans-national ties and identities.* The publication of Salman Rushdie's *Satanic Verses* in 1988, for example, produced a strong reaction from some members of the Muslim community and led to a conflict which lies at the heart of modern democracies: freedom of speech versus blasphemy.

Such issues as these place great pressure on democratic governments. It was suggested earlier that the citizenship education curriculum (QCA, 1998) recognises the need to engender participation and commitment to counter the alienation and cynicism of the young, but it skirts around the causes. To say that 'trust in society's core institutions has been falling steadily' does not explain the phenomenon. Given the complexity of issues attending globalisation, including the expansion of corporate capitalism, the withering power of the nation state, the proximity within single nations of people with diverse and sometimes conflicting identities, it seems reasonable to explain dwindling participation not simply in terms of individual apathy but in recognition of the challenges that face modern, complex democracies.

> **Pause for thought** | spin, sleaze and political apathy
>
> It is sometimes argued that voter apathy is the consequence of spin and the so-called 'dumbing-down' of modern political life. In Britain, examples of political sleaze are easy to come by and you can use the internet to remind yourself. You might research the questions that arose about the legality of the 2003 war with Iraq. Allegations about lies in political life and the spoon-feeding of the public with sound bites all perhaps contribute to political apathy. Pupils' trust in politics and politicians remains constantly at 'low levels' according to attitude surveys (Cleaver et al., 2005). Furedi (2004) has suggested that the government's response to such claims has only reduced its credibility:
>
> > *Apathy and disengagement breed both anti-political and apolitical reactions. The political class is aware of this: but instead of attempting to address the underlying malaise and disillusionment through developing challenging political ideals that could inspire the electorate to vote, its response has been to acquiesce in dumbing down.*
> >
> > (p80)
>
> It might be argued that rather than instead of merely reminding young citizens of their duty to participate in their local community or to become more charitable (QCA, 1998), there should be a curriculum that attempts to explain the complex causes of apathy and the actions of government. What do you think?

# Communication skills

Earlier it was suggested that political literacy or the education for democracy component of the citizenship education curriculum emphasises debate and discussion: *Talk or discourse is obviously fundamental to active citizenship … [because] open and informed debate is vital for a healthy democracy.* For some, echoing John Stuart Mill (1806–73), free communication is one of the central pillars of liberal democracy. For Mill (1969) there was no test for the adequacy of a claim to a good idea or 'truth' other than the force of better public argument: put your idea on the table, await critical scrutiny, argue your case when challenged, but be prepared to accede to new and better ideas.

However, while Mill's rationale for open and free communication seems convincing in theory, in practice it is a different matter because powers of communication are not equally distributed. In the real world, media-moguls have the power to persuade and to influence the views of others. As Karl Marx argued, the free exchange of ideas may be good in principle but, when tied to the market and the free exchange of commodities, the reality of freedom becomes illusory for the majority of ordinary people. Habermas (1972) similarly warned against *the fiction that Socratic dialogue is possible everywhere and at any time.* To put it simply, liberal democratic philosophy presupposes the existence of the very sense of community that dialogue is intended to develop and, in so doing, overlooks the reality that debate rarely takes place on a level playing field.

In the citizenship education curriculum, discussion is not problematised and the term 'communication' is preferred, portraying debate as if it were a content-free skill (see Cameron, 2000). It presents classroom discourse as if it should mimic the procedures of debates that go on outside – in Parliament, in town councils, between parties and the electorate, and so on. This failure to acknowledge the power structures that determine or distort free communication has two main consequences for citizenship and democracy.

- Political activity is 'mediated'. Political issues are most often communicated to us via television, radio or newspaper and so we need to understand how media discourses are constructed. Understanding the media is fundamental to an understanding of politics.
- Because teachers largely mediate what pupils can or cannot say in school, there needs to be more clarity regarding the power structures that determine, restrict or enable 'open' discussion. In other words, we need to be clear about where the boundaries lie if our aim is to democratise schools through school councils and pupil involvement.

These two points are addressed in turn. First, there is inadequate theory or critique of the link between the media and modern democracy. This link is crucial in understanding democracy:

*So-called 'spin' originates in a bottom-line desire to look good. So it's essential to assert you are right, providing explanations and then reasons for why it has to be as you've presented it. If all else fails ... everything becomes a question of opinion ... Most people find this process unedifying. It is certainly deeply damaging to democracy.*

(Brighouse, 2004, pp18–19)

A curriculum designed to prepare pupils for the realities of debate in a modern democracy might, therefore, include a variety of media themes.

- It could explain the links between media ownership and political discourses (e.g. between the newspaper and publishing magnate Rupert Murdoch and the Prime Minister's office).
- It might examine work that has helped our understanding of the way the rhetorical styles of politicians are constructed (e.g. Margaret Thatcher was taught to lower her voice to sound more authoritative).
- It might grapple with democratically complex issues concerning the control of information during periods of international conflict (e.g. the Falklands, Afghanistan or Gulf wars).
- It could attempt to account for the rise and effect of 'synthetic conversation' in the tabloid press in the presentation of public policy.
- It could provide an understanding of the symbiosis between politicians and the media and how each exploits the other.

In short, while the citizenship curriculum makes a passing reference to media education, there is little hint about how pupils might develop an awareness of the constructedness of political discourses. Debate is not problematised and the political structures within modern democracy that obfuscate or enable genuine encounter are not explained.

The second point is that, within the school environment, the issue of free communication remains unproblematised. Education for democracy says it wishes to establish *'a classroom climate in which all pupils are free from any fear of expressing reasonable points of view which contradict those held either by their class teacher or by their peers'* (QCA, 1998). But the notion that teachers are responsible for what is reasonable classroom discourse glosses over complex and questionable areas. To illustrate the effect of the embedded nature of communication within the socio-cultural practices of the school as an institution, consider the effect that market-funding mechanisms might have on open debate in schools like city academies which are owned by private corporations. If the governing body has welcomed sponsorship of the school's computer suite by, say, Nescafé, Burger King or Nike, it could be difficult to hold a critical discussion of the use of child labour, or the merchandising policies of the companies that help augment the excesses of western consumption.

## school councils

The Crick Report (QCA, 1998) recommended the formation of school councils, although it did not suggest making them compulsory. There seems to be a consensus regarding the value of their consultative nature insofar as they give pupils responsibility and enable them to experience democracy first hand in a way that mimics the parliamentary process (Print et al., 2002; Hannam, 2003). Others have their doubts. Control of the agenda or topic, for example, is a major way of limiting such debate. Rudduck and Flutter (2000) have suggested that school council discussions often revolve around *the charmed circle of lockers, dinners and uniform*. For Fielding (2001) debate and discussion is often tokenistic:

> How many school councils can we all think of that have flourished for a while but have subsequently declined from their former vibrancy and engagement with real issues into a mechanistic and largely tokenistic set of procedures for recycling the minimum and predictable minutiae of the status quo?
>
> *(p105)*

The suggestion here is that the liberal philosophy of discussion and debate always needs to be grounded in social, political and educational contexts where it then becomes a much more complex notion than the education for democracy curriculum seems to acknowledge. There is inadequate coverage about how pupils might become aware of the constructedness of media discourses, and debate. Discussion is presented in an unproblematic way that prevents understanding of how social and political power limits the ability of some groups to engage, both within and outside the school.

# The rule of law

The third element of education for democracy is that it should foster *respect for law, justice, democracy* (QCA, 1998). Because of the difficulty with words like 'justice' we need to approach this issue with care, just as we should the rather provocative suggestion that young citizens should be helped to *distinguish between law and justice*. This appears to suggest that democratic citizens could, under certain circumstances, move their political ambitions outside the law and is perhaps what Her Majesty's Chief Inspector of Schools had in mind when he insisted that citizenship education should lead to 'genuine action' (Bell, 2005).

Democratic theorists have often accepted the possibility of unlawful dissent. They distinguish between principled unlawful dissent and other unlawful practices, like theft, which do not aim to change the law. The examples the curriculum documents give of illegal acts, like theft and glue-sniffing, are thus not politically disobedient for they imply no desire to engage in issues of social justice. The second point theorists frequently make is that there has been a long history of unlawful dissent within liberal democracies which has not toppled them. Healthy democracies, some say, can and should absorb these challenges.

*Pause for thought* | law or justice?

What is 'law' and what is 'just' are not synonymous in democracies. Think of the illegal acts performed by the women's suffragette movement; of Gandhi's peaceful march to take salt from the Indian Ocean in defiance of the colonial law that raised tax by selling it; or the occupation of woods around airports and supermarkets in protest at environmental degradation. Consider also how a senior Vatican official insisted that good Catholics should oppose Spain's law permitting marriage between gay couples since *a law as profoundly iniquitous as this one is not an obligation, it cannot be an obligation. One cannot say that a law is right simply because it is a law* (cited in Gledhill, 2005). Where do you stand on the issue of law and justice?

It is possible to imagine a classroom scenario in which the disparity between law and justice could open and flourish. Reaction in schools to the 2003 Iraq war is an example, with UK pupils taking illegal action to join street protests against the threatened war – illegal in that it was school truancy. The issue is not whether their action was appropriate and just, or simply naïve and ineffective. The point is whether this type of action is an appropriate activity in an education for democracy curriculum. We need to be clear that the stated aim of education for democracy is not just to *know* about politics but to take action: pupils should be encouraged *to recognise, reflect upon and act upon these values and dispositions ... this is vital in developing pupils into* active *citizens* (QCA, 1998; see also Bell, 2005).

Over a period of study about the war in Iraq these pupils could be shown to have demonstrated many of the skills and qualities valued by the citizenship curriculum. They have shown:

- a sense of commitment to the issue;
- they are able to communicate well and counter alternative views in a reasonable and responsible manner;
- they have developed a caring attitude to both their local and global community;
- they understand how liberal democracies work, as well as some of their limitations, such as governments refusing to change direction despite huge opposition by the public; or that in the past some, particularly colonial, wars have been fought to secure natural resources and not for reasons of justice;
- they have learnt about the media and about 'camera consciousness' and how politicians and members of the public use it to gain mainstream attention and maximum publicity for their cause.

In short, these hypothetical pupils are far from apathetic, have a good understanding of the issues and, as responsible citizens and as the recipients of a lively curriculum, have come to the point of conviction about their moral duty to take political action.

There are different ways of managing pupil action. The first is containment, where the citizenship education and education for democracy curriculum is akin to dramatic role-play, possibly enjoyable and active, but consequence-free and devoid of 'genuine action' (Bell, 2005). This would quite possibly reinforce pupils' cynicism and increase their apathy.

A second scenario is that political action would be permitted but only if closely controlled and monitored by what the Crick Report (QCA, 1998) calls 'those in authority'. Action would be legitimated, but only when the topics under discussion involved recycling or fundraising for charities, or where it addressed problems such as street litter. In this scenario, the school would permit action to raise money for new playground equipment for the local primary school, but forbid a demonstration against insufficient public funding in state schools.

A third scenario would be the fragmentation of views into what the curriculum calls 'personal opinions' (DfEE/QCA, 2000). Here a pupil would be permitted to write to a councillor or to the Prime Minister with an argument about the war, but only in a personal capacity and not as the representative of the class or school. This is to 'personalise' the opinion – to diminish it as simply the view of an individual – and to remove its public legitimacy. The tag (merely) 'personal' can be applied to those who are recalcitrant, intractable or intolerable, and serves to de-activate them. If teachers are 'in authority' to decide who is or is not a responsible student, or what or is not a responsible personal opinion, the rules for deciding whether pupils' views and actions should remain personal or become public rests squarely with them.

## Summary and conclusions

It has been suggested that defining a citizen involves understanding democracy and it has been shown that the problematic nature of what a modern democracy might be is not evident in the curriculum for citizenship. There needs to be a debate about what it is and what it could become in the light of the threats to the nation state today. Pupils should be part of this. The power structures underlying debate and discussion need to be far more clear and media studies should become a much more important and integral aspect of citizenship education and education for democracy. Teachers are a relatively powerless group required to teach citizenship. They need to see beyond a curriculum that bores pupils with the facts of government and to raise the stakes by looking very carefully at where their energised and enlightened pupils may roam. Responsibility for the success or failure of democracy is likely to rest with teachers, rather than government. A final question is: whose responsibility would it be if pupils actually made the decision to take un-civil action?

## References

Anderson, J (2002) Questions of democracy, territoriality and globalisation, in Anderson, J (ed) *Transnational democracy: political spaces and border crossings*. London: Routledge.

Bell, D (2005) *Education for democratic citizenship*. Roscoe Lecture by Her Majesty's Chief Inspector of Schools, Liverpool, 2 November. Available at **www.ofsted.gov.uk/publications/** (accessed 18 April 2009).

Bottery, M (2003) The end of citizenship? The nation state, threats to its legitimacy, and citizenship education in the twenty-first century. *Cambridge Journal of Education*, 33(1): 101–22.

Brighouse, T (2004) Tough on the causes of Tony. *The Times Educational Supplement*, 29 October.

Cameron, D (2000) *Good to talk? Living and working in a communication culture*. London: Sage.

Cleaver, E, Ireland, E, Kerr, D and Lopes, E (2005) *Citizenship education longitudinal study: second cross-sectional survey 2004. Listening to young people: citizenship education in England*. Slough: National Foundation for Education Research.

DfEE/QCA (2000) *National Curriculum – Citizenship*. London: Department for Education and Employment/Qualifications and Curriculum Authority.

Fielding, M (2001) Beyond the rhetoric of student voice: new departures and new constraints in the transformation of twenty-first century schooling? *Forum*, 43(2): 100–10.

Furedi, F (2004) *Where have all the intellectuals gone? Confronting 21st century philistinism*. London: Continuum.

Gledhill, R (2005) Vatican attack on Spain's gay marriage law. Available at **www.timesonline. co.uk/article/0,, 20709-1580888,00.html** (accessed 18 April 2009).

Goldenberg, S (1999) Coup to 'save Pakistan from ruin'. *Guardian*, 18 October.

Habermas, J (1972) *Knowledge and human interests*. London: Heinemann.

Hannam, D (2003) Participation and responsible action for all students: the critical ingredient for success. *Teaching Citizenship*, 5: 24–33.

Hertz, N (2001) *The Silent Takeover: global capitalism and the death of democracy*. London: Heinemann.

Hobsbawm, E (2001) Democracy can be bad for you. *New Statesman*, 5 March, pp25–7.

Mill, JS (1969) On the liberty of thought and discussion, in Warnock, M (ed) *Utilitarianism*. London: Fontana.

Parekh, B (2002) Reconstituting the modern state, in Anderson, J (ed), *Transnational democracy: political spaces and border crossings*. London: Routledge.

Print, M, Ornstrom, S and Skovgaard, N (2002) Education for democratic processes in schools and classrooms. *European Journal of Education*, 37(2): 193–210.

QCA (1998) *Education for Citizenship and the Teaching of Democracy in Schools: final report of the Advisory Group on Citizenship* (the Crick Report). London: Qualifications and Curriculum Authority.

Rudduck, J and Flutter, J (2000) Pupil participation and pupil perspective: carving a new order of experience. *Cambridge Journal of Education*, 30(1): 75–89.

Rushdie, S (1988) *The Satanic Verses*. London: Penguin.

Saward, M (2003) *Democracy*. Cambridge: Polity Press.

# Chapter 17

## Education and employability

### Jane Bates and Sue Lewis

**Introduction**

Globalisation and economic competition between nations have inevitably had an impact on educational policy in many countries. In the UK, this has led to an increasing domination of the more instrumental aims in education, with a relationship between education, individual employability and national economic growth often being assumed. The focus of this chapter, therefore, is the impact of the resulting 'employability agenda' on higher education now and in the future.

## Education and the economy – the employability agenda

*Once we worried about a global arms race. The challenge for this century is a global skills race ... In a globally competitive national economy, there will be almost no limits to the aspirations for upward mobility. Globalisation dictates that the nations that succeed will be those that bring out the best in people and their potential.*

(Brown, 2008)

In recent years, the concept of the 'knowledge economy' has emerged in which global competitiveness is factored through creativity, innovation and technical expertise. The key to success in such a global economy is considered to be through the expansion of educational opportunity, promotion of lifelong learning and the development of a highly skilled workforce involved in wealth creation. For any government, the economic and social benefits that accrue as a consequence of investing in an educated workforce appear obvious and, as a consequence, a huge emphasis has been placed on the importance of education, not only with respect to the development of individual potential but also for developing economic prosperity. According to evidence from the OECD (2007), its member nations spend an estimated 6.2 per cent of their collective gross domestic product (GDP) on education and their economic wellbeing is increasingly reliant on the supply of well-educated individuals. The benefits from that investment in education include not only economic prosperity, but also greater social cohension as a result of the shared values that are perpetuated through the education system. There are also economic benefits for the individuals who participate in education. Graduates on average have an 8 per cent return on their investment in education, while there are even higher returns, particularly for males, from upper secondary-level credentials (OECD, 2006).

# A human capital interpretation

According to Tomlinson (2008), theories of human capital, which underpin much of the current policy agenda in higher education, suggest that the economic benefits that accrue from an investment in education include:

- a more skilled and flexible workforce;
- a greater earning capacity for individuals;
- more career opportunities.

These benefits are ultimately reflected in an increased economic output at a national level with the result of national prosperity. A direct relationship between the level of investment in education and economic growth is assumed:

*There is now robust evidence that human capital is a key determinant of economic growth and emerging evidence indicates that it is also associated with a wide range of non-economic benefits such as better health and well-being. Investment in human capital, and by implication in education, has thus moved centre stage in strategies to promote economic prosperity, fuller employment and social cohesion. As a result, education is increasingly considered an investment in the collective future of societies and nations, rather than simply in the future success of individuals.*

(UNESCO – UIS/OECD, 2003, p5)

The recent expansion of higher education, through widening participation initiatives, can therefore be viewed as a direct attempt to increase the number of individuals attaining graduate-level qualifications and thus bring about an increase in the level of economic development, providing benefits for both the state and the individual.

This focus on the relationship between education and the economy is not new. In the 1970s, in the first wave of globalisation, and prompted by recessions, rising unemployment and a world oil crisis, governments started to focus on the relationship between the two. Possibly the most seminal example of this refocusing of educational aims was the speech given by the then Labour Prime Minister, James Callaghan, at Ruskin College Oxford in 1976, which for the first time formally acknowledged the link between standards in education and economic prosperity. Knight and Yorke (2002) suggested that since the late 1970s, governments have continually linked economic success to the educational level of the workforce which has led, in turn, to the imposition of an 'employability' expectation on higher education establishments. Such notions of a link between education and economic prosperity were also inherent in the Dearing Report (1997), which proposed that elements of employability such as skills development and reflection on personal development should be part of the higher education curriculum (Hinchliffe, 2008).

Although many studies of national economic indicators do suggest a link between an investment in education and economic growth (see UNESCO – UIS/OECD, 2003) others, like those of Pritchett (1996) and later studies referred to by Tomlinson (2008), pointed to evidence which contradicts this conventional wisdom. Such studies suggest that the acknowledged growth in human capital that has occurred over recent years has not produced the expected economic growth. Consequently, the theoretical underpinning of the policy agenda is brought into question. Some writers also point out that such a focus on employability per se is possibly resulting in a reduction of the human capital agenda to a very narrow conception of skills and self-audits (Hinchliffe, 2008).

# A credentialist interpretation

An alternative interpretation of current educational policy is that provided by a Weberian credentialist model which, as Tomlinson (2008) pointed out, focuses on the way in which groups within society use academic credentials for both cultural and economic advantage. Some experts would suggest that the expansion of higher education and the consequent rise in the number of individuals with 'graduate credentials' has not simply translated directly into an anticipated increase in economic growth but has instead resulted in:

- a devaluation of academic qualifications;
- increased competition for graduate jobs;
- many individuals being overqualified for the jobs they attain.

As Tomlinson pointed out:

*... the rise in credentials in no way reflects a genuine economic demand for more highly qualified labour, so often presented in recent government policy ... the spread of educational credentials is adding little or no value to individuals' human capital ... [and] the expansion of higher education, and the concordant growth in credentials has corresponded with the expansion of the middle classes, generating growing pressures for individuals to acquire further credentials to access jobs. Instead of reflecting an increase in the skills and knowledge demands needed to do jobs, the upsurge in higher education credentials simply means that the stakes have been raised for what is needed to get jobs.*

(2008, p50)

Tomlinson further pointed to a number of research reports that highlight the fact that there is little evidence from the labour market to support the continued policy to expand higher education.

More recently, the Leitch Report (2006), commissioned by the government to look at the nation's skills base, has reiterated a link between a failing education system and economic prosperity suggesting that without further investment in education and skills there is potential for the UK to lag behind other countries in terms of productivity. The government's response to Leitch is evident in the package of welfare reforms that included 'Education for All'. This initiative sets out the government's goals to ensure that all individuals are provided with the opportunity to develop personal, social and economic wellbeing and their desire to develop a world-class skills base in the UK:

*... the government has adopted an eclectic blend of the human capital and the work-first models ... Government programmes therefore, are now aiming to prepare workers for international competition and have begun to focus on training people to achieve 'greater individual self sufficiency over job stability and career advancement'.*

(Moore, 2008, p11)

A consequence of this approach, of linking economic prosperity and education, has been a tendency by governments and others, as was evidenced in the Leitch Report, to continue to lay the blame for the UK's perceived lack of international competitiveness at the door of what is still, despite continued reform, considered a 'failing' education system. As Moore (2008) suggested, there is now a tendency for discourses surrounding *employment and job creation* to be replaced by the notion of the *employable individual*:

*The ambiguity of the emerging debate seems to require a marriage of the productive individual (what Lefebvre calls 'productive man') with a contemporary form of idealised citizenship (or Lefebvre's 'political man') that in practice requires people to become entrepreneurs of their own fates in unprecedented campaigns triggered by unregimented globalisation.*

(pp2–3)

Thus, just as education has continually been blamed for failures in the economy, the 'new ethic of employability' is putting the onus on the individual, rather than society, if they fail to gain employment.

---

***Pause for thought*** | the employability agenda

Since the 1990s the UK government has based its education policy on what Tomlinson terms a *'micro-economic'* ideology and a rather simplistic view that:

> *... economic success depended on tight central control of education, meeting education and training targets, and persuading people to obtain more qualifications and skills ... [and] that the more people invested in themselves as human capital and the more schools overcame their shortcomings in preparing pupils for economic success, the more competitive the economy would become.*

(2005, p202)

Reflecting on Tomlinson's statement about the government's view of the relationship between education and economic success, do you consider 'employability' to be a valid aim of education and, in particular, of higher education? What do you think education should be for?

---

# So what is employability?

There is no consensus definition of employability and the variety of meanings that are generally attributed to the term are largely dependent upon the context in which the term is used. Both Yorke (2006) and Lees (2002) highlighted a number of ways in which employability can be conceptualised. From the government's perspective, employability is often viewed in terms of an individual's ability to gain appropriate employment, or more often, to get a job. From an educational perspective, however, employability is more likely to relate to the equipping of an individual, through both curricular and extracurricular processes, with the relevant skills and attributes that will enable them to gain employment.

## An employer's perspective

From an employer's perspective, employability is usually concerned with:

- an individual possessing the requisite attributes and skills to match the current employment needs;
- the individual's flexibility to respond to future demands in the workplace.

However, as Lees (2002) pointed out, notions of skills and the language used in describing employability are not always shared between higher education institutions and employers. The situation is further complicated by the way in which employability initiatives in higher education translate into graduate employability and, ultimately, employment.

In terms of what employers require of graduates then, Lees (2002) pointed to the fact that employers are not generally interested in the actual degree subject that has been studied and, as Yorke (2006) noted, have generally accepted levels of disciplinary knowledge. Employers, in the main, tend to be more interested in the skills and personal attributes that individuals possess, and tend to be more critical of the education system's ability to develop such attributes (see Lees, 2002; Hinchliffe, 2008). The range of attributes that are considered compatible with a general concept of 'graduateness' include:

- good communication skills, both oral and written;
- flexibility;
- the ability to work as part of a team;
- self-management;
- problem-solving;
- self-motivation and drive;
- reliability;
- creativity;
- an ability to be entrepreneurial.

Despite the increasing focus on skills development within education, employers continue to be critical of education for failing to produce individuals with the 'right' kinds of skills and, in particular, for continuing to produce graduates who cannot communicate effectively. However, as Tomlinson (2007) pointed out, employers have always been reluctant to invest in the development of work-related skills and to predict effectively the kinds of skills that workers will need in the future.

## An individual's perspective

According to Hillage and Pollard (1998), from an individual's perspective, employability is concerned with having the capability to:

- gain employment;
- maintain employment;
- obtain new employment if required.

They also suggested that for an individual, employability is mediated by a number of factors such as their skills and personal attributes and the ways in which they can demonstrate and use their assets in the context of their employer's, or potential employer's, workplace. Commenting on Hillage and Pollard's analysis of employability, Lees suggested that:

*Being in possession of employer-relevant knowledge, skills and attitudes is not enough for an individual to move within the labour market and to realise their potential. People need to be capable of exploiting their assets, of marketing them and selling them.*

(2002, p2)

For many individuals, education is solely aimed at employability and enabling them to get a good job. Young people, in particular, often hold a purely instrumental view of education. Tomlinson (2005) pointed to a study by Killeen *et al*. (1997) which demonstrated that many young people view the paper qualifications that they obtain as a form of 'currency' which they are able to exchange for employment, the content of the course or degree being almost irrelevant. Many, therefore, appear to adhere to a view that the longer the educational experience and the higher the level of qualification, the greater the job prospects and the rewards. A recent review of research in this area suggested that even young children in primary schooling conceived their education in instrumental terms, viewing the main purpose of education at this stage to be to equip them with the necessary skills for their future schooling and employment (Robinson and Fielding, 2008). This echoes the findings of earlier studies which similarly suggested that:

*The vast majority [of children] believed that schools should help them to do as well as possible in their exams and teach them things that would be useful when they entered jobs.*

(National Commission on Education, 1993, p151)

According to Tomlinson, students view a degree as a considerable asset within the jobs market and that *education credentials are vital commodities in the pursuit of relatively well paid, high status and rewarding forms of graduate employment* (2008). However, as Tomlinson also pointed out, students are well aware of the fact that the possession of a degree is not always a simple passport to a job, pointing out their understanding of a number of factors that affect their employability, which include:

- 'hard credentials' – grades and classifications;
- 'soft credentials' – the experiences and achievements gained outside of their studies;
- competition from other graduates – the relative currency of degrees from different institutions;
- personal 'distinctiveness' – personal attributes.

Students' views about employment also appear to be changing with time. While earlier studies in the 1990s highlighted students as holding very stereotypical views of 'the bureaucratic career', more contemporary studies demonstrate that students' views are now 'less ideal', perceiving the labour market as more high risk and flexible than in previous generations (Tomlinson, 2007).

Individual students also have different aspirations than in the past when it comes to their future employment, and one of the problems with the government's approach to employability is that it treats all students as if they were the same. However, '*in many cases, students do not in fact operate in rational and utilitarian ways, looking to optimise their potential for a return on their investment in education* (Tomlinson, 2007). Tomlinson went on to suggest that students' orientation towards their future employment is dependent on what *they perceive to be appropriate and meaningful courses of future action*. Based on his research findings, Tomlinson put forward an *ideal model of student orientations to work, careers and employability*, in which four individual orientations towards future employment emerge. These are:

- careerist – individuals who are proactive, instrumental, credentialist, flexible and conform to market rules;
- ritualistic – individuals who are passive, prefer more secure jobs, are less competitive and view work a means to an end;
- rebellious – individuals who are proactive in rejecting labour market goals;
- retreatist – individuals who are indifferent to labour market goals, disaffected/hedonistic youths and pursue other goals outside employability.

> **Pause for thought** | employability and you
>
> Carefully study Tomlinson's ideal model of student orientation to work and consider your own attitudes and aspirations and orientation with respect to work, career and employability. Next, draw up a list of the kinds of skills and attributes that you think a graduate should possess and that you feel you will need to succeed in the future. Now, consider your own degree programme and try to identify any modules or learning outcomes that are specifically concerned with developing 'employability' skills and attributes. How useful do you think your degree course is/has been in helping you to develop the skills and attributes that you will need in the future?

## Towards an acceptable definition

According to Yorke (2006), there are alternative perspectives on the notion of employability that are critical of more 'ideologically laden' views, such as those expressed by Hillage and Pollard (1998). Brown *et al.* (2002), for example, proposed that employability has two dimensions:

- the absolute – the skills and attributes that make an individual employable;
- the relative – the state of the labour market that affects the individual's ability to gain employment.

Possession of the relevant skills and attributes is no guarantee of employment, and evidence suggests that a degree may not actually confer any advantage on an individual within the labour market – it may only enable them 'to stay in the race'. Brown *et al.* therefore conceived employability as *the relative chances of (an individual) finding and maintaining different kinds of employment*. Yorke also highlighted evidence of a number of factors that can impact on an individual's employability that include:

- the condition of local, regional, national and international labour markets;
- the 'positional' value of the institution(s) that the individual has attended;
- the match between the individual's attributes and the employer's needs;
- selection criteria coming into play that are more representative of the employer's organisation as a consequence of the increasing proportion of graduates within the workforce (as a consequence of efforts to widen participation in higher education).

The view expressed by Brown *et al.* (2002) is, however, criticised by Yorke (2006) because it conflates two distinct terms: 'employability', which refers to graduate achievements and attributes and therefore the possession of the ability to gain employment; and 'employment', which refers to the actual gaining of a job. According to Knight and Yorke (2004), what is also often missing from the generally accepted views of employability are the personal qualities that individuals possess. By personal qualities they mean the 'self-belief and self-theories' students hold. Possibly, these aspects have been overlooked because they are very difficult to assess. Without them, however, Knight and Yorke suggested that employability is reduced to a narrow concept of key skills, which can become 'ghettoised' within areas of degree programmes, or is addressed very superficially so that the institution can improve its status in the league tables. The USEM model developed by Knight and Yorke (2002) provides a means of conceptualising employability within higher education and provides a useful platform for the development and design of curricular pathways aimed at addressing aspects of employability. The model conceives employability in terms of four areas of graduate attributes:

- understanding;
- skills (both subject specific and generic);
- efficacy and beliefs;
- metacognition.

The model is dependent on the principles of *malleable self belief* and capability and draws upon the definition proposed by Stephenson (1998), which suggested that a capable person is someone who has confidence in their ability to:

- take effective action;
- explain what they are trying to achieve;
- live and work effectively with others;
- continue to learn from their experiences in a diverse and changing society.

A commonly accepted definition of employability that avoids all the pitfalls mentioned above, is that provided by Yorke (2006):

*A set of achievements – skills, understanding and personal attributes – that makes graduates more likely to gain employment and be successful in their chosen occupation, which benefits themselves, the workforce, the community and the economy.*

(p8)

Harvey (2003) suggested, however, that there is an inherently flawed presumption underlying all of the definitions of employability, in that they appear to assume that there is a kind of 'magic bullet' of employability:

*The notion is that the institution provides employability development opportunities; the graduate engages with them and gets 'employability' which is a gateway to employment. This model presumes that employability is something that can be acquired. It also presumes that what is acquired is a set of skills.*

(pp1–2)

# Employability and higher education

Although there has generally been an acceptance that universities have been relatively successful in producing graduates with relevant levels of disciplinary knowledge or subject-based understanding, employers have been *less happy with graduates generic attainments* (Knight and Yorke, 2002). According to Watton *et al*. (2006), the employable graduate needs to be able to demonstrate and apply attributes and skills that relate to not only career and organisational management but also lifelong learning and an international outlook. Yorke (2006) pointed to the work of Reich (1991, 2002), who suggested that if higher education is to make a positive contribution to the development of economic prosperity then it needs to ensure that curricular developments and initiatives are designed to produce the type of graduates that the economy needs. He described such graduates as 'symbolic analysts' who are *imaginative, creative, have at their fingertips relevant disciplinary understanding and skills* and the *soft or generic skills that enable the disciplinary base to be deployed to optimal effect* (Yorke, 2006). Consequently, according to Yorke, higher education programmes should focus on:

- abstraction – theorising, modelling, and so on;
- systems thinking – contextualisation;
- experimentation;
- collaboration.

In 2001, the Higher Education Funding Council for England (HEFCE) went so far as to introduce an 'employment' performance indicator into the accountability mechanisms for higher education in the UK. The indicator measures the proportion of graduates in employment six months after they have graduated but does not distinguish between types of employment and, therefore, could be said to be a flawed form of measurement. Similarly, the Quality Assurance Agency (QAA) has emphasised employability skills, albeit in the form of broad and general statements of programme outcomes. It is questionable how far universities can exercise control over their graduates' ability to find immediate employment, particularly at a time of global financial crisis. However, it has become important for universities and colleges to be seen to be developing 'employability' at a graduate level while students are in their care.

The ways in which universities approach employability is very varied (see Hinchliffe, 2008). However, some of the initiatives may be little more than marketing strategies to attract prospective students. Most institutions use a combination of initiatives to enhance the employability of their graduates that can include:

- enhanced central careers provision;
- curriculum development to make programmes more relevant to particular careers either by emphasising the competences that the subject already offers or by developing new versions of degree programmes with particular destinations in mind;
- work experience or placement – with or without accreditation;
- mentoring programmes;
- personal development plans (PDPs).

A fundamental problem with all these initiatives is that they are, in the main, concerned with skills development outside of the employment context itself and that they take for granted that such skills, learnt in isolation, will transfer to the workplace.

Although the UK has actively sought to promote employability within higher education provision, many other nations have not (Bowers-Brown and Harvey, 2004/5). There is a general consensus among nations as to the kinds of skills and attributes that a graduate should possess although there are widely varying methods of delivering and assessing such qualities. For example, in some countries the possession of a degree is a guarantee of graduate employability, while in others, students are assessed against generic criteria or the production of work-based learning portfolios. However, as Little *et al.* (2003) concluded:

*While there is international concern that higher education should enhance graduate employability, there is little evidence of systematic thinking about how best to do it, let alone any model that can be badged as 'best practice' and adopted wholesale.*

(2003)

## Is employability a legitimate aim of higher education?

Education is often conceived as a 'preparation for life' – an intentional and purposeful activity in which the knowledge, skills, attributes and behaviours that individuals gain as a consequence of being educated are valuable both in an intrinsic and in an extrinsic sense. According to Winch (2002), such a 'preparation for life' includes not only 'individual fulfilment' but also preparation for roles in society and within the world of work. While many scholars object to the notion that education should have such a vocational focus, Winch defended this idea, and suggests that education should be aimed at providing *individual fulfilment through employment and social wellbeing through economic prosperity* (2002). Such aims, as we can see, are in full concordance with the aims of the government's employability agenda.

However, as Lees pointed out, the employability agenda and the focus on vocational aims *challenges traditional concepts of higher education and raises the question of what the point of Higher Education is: 'subject knowledge and understanding or learning to learn* (2002). Many academics are, therefore, resistant to notions of employability, feeling that it is something that is being imposed upon them and which could consititute an attack on their academic freedom to determine what is taught and how.

In defence of the employability agenda, however, Harvey (2003) pointed out that the main role of higher education is the exchange, not only of disciplinary knowledge, but also of the skills and attributes that will ultimately empower students to become lifelong, critical and reflective learners, thus:

*At root, employability is about learning, not least learning how to learn. Employability is not a product but a process of learning for life. It is not about training for a job; rather it is about empowering learners as critical reflective citizens.*

(p2)

---

### Research box

## the earnings return or value of education

Evidence of the 'value' or 'earnings returns' of different levels of education and types of qualifications is useful in informing policy and also provides a means of identifying those individuals who are most likely to be excluded from the labour market. Most research points to the fact that participation in education to degree level produces the greatest 'earnings return'. However, there is also evidence that other factors such as an individual's academic ability and social status are also important. Gasteen and Houston (2007) sought to address two perceived gaps in the data: the likelihood of gaining employment as a result of possessing a particular level of qualification and the need for more regionally focused policy-making. Comparisons of earnings and employability based on five levels of qualifications were made using data from the Labour Force Surveys carried out between 1999 and 2003. The research findings confirm earlier studies in indicating that wage returns increase in line with levels of qualification. However, the study also highlighted that there are actually extra earning premiums for those individuals who follow a 'standard route' through to higher educational qualifications. The study also pointed to a number of regional and gender differences in wage returns to education. Although some were minor, others were considered to be more significant.

---

# What of the future?

The UK government has placed its faith in a knowledge-driven economy to produce economic growth fuelled by the expansion of higher education, increased credentialism and the promotion of lifelong learning. However, the rise of competing economies (e.g. China and India), the global credit crisis and the new ways in which companies are engaging globally with their workforce are all raising concerns. Such concerns, according to Brown *et al.* (2008), together with the growth of a global knowledge economy and the global expansion of mass higher education, have led to the emergence of challenges to the traditional policy view that continuing to invest in human capital (knowledge, skills and attributes) will produce a high-skilled workforce, high-wage economy and economic prosperity.

The possible spectre of a high-skilled, low-wage economy brings with it the prospect that fewer students will go directly to university, with the focus being on alternative types of programmes that develop more applied technical knowledge and skills (e.g. Winch, 2002). Similarly, the alternative prospect of a low-skill, low-wage economy also suggests a decline in university education, with only a few, highly skilled graduates with the ability to deal with change, to be innovative and entrepreneurial. Despite such predictions, some, like Hinchliffe, still insist that *the demands on universities to produce employable graduates will increase ... it is therefore wise for universities to do what they can to shape and determine employability* (2008). Others too suggest that there is a need for a new *great debate about the future of education and skills and their relationship to career, prosperity and social justice in a global economy* (Brown et al., 2008, p1). Thus, rather than just responding to government demands, universities have a role in initiating and leading the employability debate.

## Summary and conclusions

The social and economic benefits of educational policy, for both the individual and the state, are of obvious importance when decisions relating to investment in education are made. Over the past few years the focus on such benefits has intensified as countries' economies have become increasingly interlinked yet remain competitive. Universities have responded to government pressure by emphasising the critical importance of gaining qualifications in order to enable individuals to market themselves successfully. However, the role of universities should not be to simply follow a government agenda but should be to develop thinking in new directions in anticipation of the demands of a changing world.

## References

Bowers-Brown, T and Harvey, L (2004/2005) *Employability cross country comparisons.* Prospects Net. Winter. Available at **www.prospects.ac.uk/cms/ShowPageHome_page/p!eLaXi** (accessed 21 April 2009)

Brennan, J and Williams, R with Blasko, Z (2003) *The English degree and graduate careers.* Report to the Learning and Teaching Support Network (LTSN), English Subject Centre, Number 2, January 2003.

Brown, G (2008) We'll use our schools to break down class barriers. The *Observer*, 10 February. Available at **www.guardian.co.uk/commentisfree/2008feb/10/gordonbrown/education** (accessed 6 December 2008).

Brown, P, Hesketh, A and Williams, S (2002) Employability in a knowledge-driven economy. In Knight, P (compiler) Notes from the 13 June 2002 'Skills plus' conference, *Innovation in education for employability* held at Manchester Metropolitan University. Available at **www.cardiff.ac.uk/schoolsanddivisions/academics/socsi/publications/worksingpapers/numeric21-30html**

Brown, P, Lauder, H and Ashton, D on behalf of TLRP (2008) *Education, globalisation and the Knowledge Economy.* Available at **www.tlrp.org/pub/documents/globalisationcomm.pdf** (accessed 10 November 2008).

Dearing, R (1997) *Report of the National Committee of Inquiry into Higher Education.* Available at **www.leeds.acuk/educol/ncihe** (accessed 20 April 2009).

Gasteen, A and Houston, J (2007) Employability and earnings returns to qualifications in Scotland. *Regional Studies*, 41(4) 443–51.

Harvey, L (2003) *On employability.* The Higher Education Academy. Available at **www.heacademy.ac.uk**. (accessed 28 October 2008).

Hillage, J and Pollard, E (1998) Employability: developing a framework for policy analysis. *Research Brief* 85. Department for Education and Employment.

Hinchliffe, G (2008) Towards rethinking graduate employability. Paper presented at the British Educational Research Association Annual Conference, Herriot-Watt University, Edinburgh, 3–6 September 2008, pp 15. Available at **www.leeds.ac.uk/educol/documents/174236.doc** (accessed 18 November 2008).

Knight, P and Yorke, M (2002) Employability through the curriculum. *Tertiary Education and Management*, 8(4) December: 261–76.

Knight, P and Yorke, M (eds) (2004) *Learning, curriculum and employability in higher education*. London: RoutledgeFalmer.

Lees, D (2002) Graduate employability: literature review. LTSN Generic Centre. October. Available at **www.exeter.ac.uk/employability/staff/publications.shtml** (accessed 10 November 2008).

Leitch, S (2006) *Prosperity for all in the global economy – world class skills*. London: HM Treasury.

Little, B and contributors (2003) *International perspectives on employability*. A briefing paper for ESCET and LTSN Generic Centre. January. Available at **www.palatine.ac.uk/themes/ emp/1260.pdf** (accessed 10 November 2008).

Moore, P (2008) *UK education and everyday life: campaigns for 'employability' after the globalised turn*. Available at **www.lancs.ac.uk/fass/events/changingcultures/docs/sem3/Moore%20 Education%20and%20Everyday%20life.pdf** (accessed 19 November 2008).

National Commission on Education (1993) *Learning to succeed*. London: Heinemann.

Organisation for Economic Development and Co-Operation (OECD) (2006, 2007) *Education at a glance. Highlights*. Available at **www.sourceoecd.org/** (accessed 12 August 2008).

Pritchett, L (1996) *Where has all the education gone?* Policy Research Working Papers. World Bank.

Robinson, C and Fielding, M (2007) *Children and their primary schools: pupils' voices* (Primary Review Research Survey 5/3). Cambridge: University of Cambridge Faculty of Education.

Stephenson, J (1998) The concept of capability and its importance in higher education. In Stephenson, J and Yorke, M (eds.) *Capability and quality in higher education*. London: Kogan Page, pp.1–13.

Tomlinson, M (2007) Graduate employability and student attitudes and orientations to the labour market. *Journal of Education and Work*, 20(4): 285–304. Available at **www.informaworld.com/smpp/section?content=a782970662&fulltext=7132409** (accessed 20 April 2009).

Tomlinson, M (2008) 'The degree is not enough': student's perceptions of the role of higher education credentials for graduate work and employability. *British Journal of Sociology of Education*, 29(1): 49–61.

Tomlinson, S (2005) *Education in a post-welfare society* (2nd edition). Berkshire: Open University Press.

UNESCO – UIS/OECD (2003) *Financing education – investments and returns. Analysis of the World Education Indicators. 2002 Edition. Executive Summary*. Available at www.unesco.org (accessed 29 October 2008).

Watton, P, Lintern, M. and Bunyard, T. (2006). Some approaches to employability in the curriculum. Available at **www.gees.ac.uk/pastevents/esect/pwatton.ppt** (accessed 16 November 2008).

Winch, C (2002) The economic aims of education. *Journal of Philosophy of Education*, 36(1):101–16.

Winch, C (2003) Education and the economy: A response to David and Foray. *Policy Futures in Education*, 1(1): 50–61.

Yorke, M (2006) *Employability in higher education: what it is – what it is not. ESECT.* Learning and Employability Series One. The Higher Education Academy. Available at **www.heacademy.ac.uk** (accessed 28 October 2008).

# Chapter 18

# Sex and relationships education

## Richard Woolley and Sacha Mason

---

### Introduction

Sex and relationship education (SRE) is a subject that attracts a good deal of media attention. Over the past century it has developed in different directions according to changes in society and particular needs and attitudes among the population. It is an area that can prove controversial and can cause teachers and those that they teach to feel vulnerable or anxious. This chapter explores the role of SRE in schools, some of the issues faced by children and young people, and the importance of effective relationships and communication in its development and delivery.

---

# The concept of sex and relationships education

The government's *Sex and relationship guidance* for England (DfEE, 2000) states that the aim of SRE is *to help and support young people through their physical, emotional and moral development*. Its objectives are to enable children to move with confidence through adolescence into adulthood and to enable them to respect themselves and others:

*All children, including those who develop earlier than the average, need to know about puberty before they experience the onset of physical changes. In the early primary school years, education about relationships needs to focus on friendship, bullying and the building of self-esteem.*

(DfEE, 2000, p9)

Thus SRE involves a continuum of learning that starts in the Early Years (with a consideration of the self and social interaction) and progresses and develops throughout a child's education. This is seen as a part of *promoting the spiritual, moral, cultural, mental and physical development of pupils at school and of society*. One common misconception is that SRE will lead to greater sexual activity among young people. Research evidence suggests that this may not be the case and that sexual activity or pregnancy rates do not increase as a result (Sex Education Forum, 1992; Wellings et al., 1995; Teenage Pregnancy Independent Advisory Group, 2008). A further misconception is that SRE is solely concerned with sex education. According to DfEE (2000), the main elements of SRE are:

- attitudes and values;
- personal and social skills;
- knowledge and understanding.

Attitudes and values address moral considerations, including the acknowledgement of moral dilemmas, and learning the importance of individual conscience and decision-making. This includes the concepts of care, respect and love. Personal and social skills encompass learning to manage one's emotions, developing self-respect, managing conflict, learning to recognise abuse, avoiding exploitation and developing empathy for others. This involves understanding that actions and choices have consequences. Knowledge and understanding are concerned with comprehending physical development at appropriate stages and this includes:

- understanding human sexuality, reproduction, sexual health, emotions and relationships;
- learning about contraception and the range of local and national sexual health advice, contraception and support services;
- learning the reasons for delaying sexual activity, and the benefits to be gained from such delay;
- the avoidance of unplanned pregnancy.

It is notable that the guidance is not value free. It infers that there are benefits in the use of contraception (which is contentious for some religious groups) and that it is positive to delay sexual activity.

There is an implied political agenda behind the title of SRE. Despite the focus on relationships, the subject is not entitled 'Relationships and sex education'. It is important to consider how the component parts relate and interact and why some documents refer only to 'relationship' in the singular, implying life-long monogamy. Unlike in Wales, Northern Ireland and other countries around the world, the plural of 'relationships' includes a focus on friendships, anti-bullying strategies and an understanding of different sexualities. While these may be implicit to curriculum materials in England, the title of the subject appears to be more limited and limiting: the contrast in titles is interesting and important. Firstly, the use of the plural 'relationships' suggests overtly that wider relationships are addressed and it opens up the possibilities for talking about how relationships sometimes change or end, including through divorce, remarriage and other situations. Secondly, to consider 'sexuality' rather than 'sex' is significant: the former is a way of being, the latter an act of doing. This moves the focus more to matters of identity, self-esteem and self-confidence, which are themselves essential if positive and constructive relationships are to be formed.

> ## Research box
>
> ### recent developments
>
> In the past, the non-statutory nature of documents on SRE has meant that it was an additional layer added to an already crowded curriculum in an increasingly target- and market-driven education system. This brought the possibility of SRE being addressed in a tokenistic manner. The introduction of the *National healthy school standard* (DfEE, 1999a) led the way in which SRE could be developed and implemented. SRE received additional support, at least in theory, and could gain a greater profile. In addition, and from September 2005, OFSTED, the body responsible for inspecting education provision, has expected schools to demonstrate how they are contributing to the five national outcomes for children stipulated by *Every Child Matters* (DfES, 2004): being healthy; staying safe; enjoying and achieving; making a positive contribution; and economic wellbeing. To this end, the government issued a revised and more rigorous National Healthy Schools Programme and stated that it wanted every school to be working to achieve the standard by 2009 (DfES and DH, 2005). Its revised standards require the effective provision of PSHE (the first core strand of the programme), which includes sex and relationship education. This was a first move towards encouraging all schools to provide compulsory SRE. Requiring all primary schools to provide SRE is a significant development.

# Sex, relationships and the media

The access that children in twenty-first century Britain have to the media through varied technologies is fundamentally different from their parents' generation (Buckingham, 2006). Many children are able to view digital television channels where music videos demonstrate a sexualised culture and reality television showing participants discussing and demonstrating their sexuality and sexual desires. On mainstream, prime-time television, a wide range of soap operas have addressed issues of divorce, homosexuality, incest, rape and, more recently, paedophilia. Children's worlds are flooded with examples of complex interpersonal relationships. However, does SRE address these diverse relationship issues in state schools and invite open and frank discussions about such sexual matters? A dichotomy exists. In one part of their world, young people are bombarded with sexually explicit messages with the implicit message that sexual activity and promiscuity are the norm. In another part, many parents and most public institutions are either embarrassed or silent on matters of a sexual nature (Corteen, 2006). The polarised worlds in which children find themselves allow for confusion in their expectations and understandings of relationships and sexual intimacy. The processing of information from the media images of sexual activity and sexual experimentation may pressurise some children into an early sexual debut with particular emphasis on performance and body image. These perceptions may take precedence over the desire for, or understanding of, an emotionally intimate relationship. Children may not have access to the information, or trusted adults to whom they may refer, to provide a different view of sexual relationships.

According to Corteen (2006), children's access to information regarding sexual matters outside of the media is *institutionally prescribed* with a *failure to equip children and young people ... with appropriate knowledge and understanding of sexuality that reflects their lives and the realities of the diverse society*. It is pertinent to consider the reasoning that results in restricted information regarding sex and relationships being available, particularly from parents/carers and teachers. The concept of childhood innocence has resonance in this discussion. Buckingham (2000) denotes childhood as a social and historical construction. He argues that childhood is *subject to a constant process of struggle and negotiation, both in public discourse ... and in interpersonal relationships, among peers and in the family*. The discussion arises from the perception that the various media have 'erased' the boundaries between childhood and adulthood and by doing so have undermined the authority of adults. Erriker (2003) develops this notion of adult control by suggesting that the protection of a *fantasy childhood innocence legitimates the fantasy of adult power*. The struggle that Buckingham refers to encapsulates the tensions between the media, adults and children, each with their own agenda. The idea of 'adult power' protecting childhood innocence is a strong concept. It may be argued that where adults address sensitive issues with children, the concern is not necessarily adult dominance, but rather adult uncertainty. In order to speak to children about relationships and sexual matters, adults need to feel comfortable in their knowledge and understanding of such issues. Sex and relationships are deeply personal and for parents and teachers to talk to children about them may be exposing and embarrassing. Perhaps the 'struggle' that Buckingham refers to is more that of adults recognising their responsibility to address concepts of sex and relationships with children, but not knowing how that may be successfully achieved. Erriker (2003) does, however, make clear that the protection of the innocence of childhood, for whatever motive, affects the development of *children's capacities to deal effectively with their experiences or reflect critically on their enculturation*, and as such, for children, sex and relationships may be shrouded with confusion. Lewis and Knijn (2002) comment that *where the concern among traditionalists is to preserve innocence among children [this] means that sex is much more likely to be viewed as [an] illicit (and therefore highly desirable) activity.*

Halstead and Reiss (2003) suggest that children are sexual beings who are deeply interested in sexual matters and it is, therefore, no surprise that they use the media to gain information on aspects of sexuality and relationships. Research suggests that boys are increasingly learning about sex and sexuality through pornography (Measor, 2004). Pornography provides information beyond the biological basics and vividly explores issues, among others, of sexual technique, sexual deviation, logistics and performance. The most concerning aspect of this source of information is the emphasis on sexual pleasure rather than sexual or emotional intimacy within the context of a loving, caring relationship. Likewise, the distortion of the role of the female in pornography, which communicates passivity and permanent receptiveness, may create expectations about how they and their partner ought to behave. If children and young people are having these direct experiences of pornography, as research suggests, it is perhaps increasingly critical that these sexual stereotypes are counterbalanced by informative sex and relationships education. Additionally, the discussion of sexual issues in the 'teenage' magazines accessed by girls of primary school age upwards (particularly on their 'problem pages') suggests an interest in performance, prowess, needs and expectations. As such, SRE is required to extend beyond the remit of the biological basics to address the wider issues of all sexual activity and sexuality within the context of relationships.

---

### Pause for thought | the influence of the media

Consider the implications of the different representations of sexual relationships that are transmitted to children and young people through popular soap operas.

- What images are being presented?
- Are they approached positively or negatively?
- What impact on children's moral values may they have, particularly in relation to family values?

Many children and young people have access to the internet and teenage magazines in their homes. These sources may introduce children to images or ideas about sex and relationships that conflict with those that are promoted by their families.

- Consider how easy it is for children to access pornographic and other sexually explicit material.
- Think about how these conflicting messages about sexual relationships may influence children and young people.

---

If children are to make responsible choices about sex and relationships, it is necessary for them to have access to information that will address their concerns and natural curiosities. Corteen (2006) proposes that SRE should be entitled 'Sexualities education' and comprise a *radical and inclusive agenda* which is informed by the increasing recognition of the rights of children in both national and international human rights law. Crumper (2004) makes clear that children have been accorded the right to *be consulted on matters that concern them*. This has traditionally not been the case and schools may be required to consider the impact of the Human Rights Act 1988, in particular pupils' right of access to information about SRE. The law, however, does stipulate caveats on children's rights to access information by restricting materials in SRE that are considered inappropriate for the age, maturity, religious and cultural backgrounds of the pupils concerned. Here a case for the necessity to listen to the needs of the pupils, who may themselves determine the developmentally appropriate content, is clear. Maxwell (2006) outlines the need for context and 'contextualisation' in sex and relationships education. The recognition of the varied needs of children, dependent on their personal context and understanding, is particularly relevant in SRE in order that content can be differentiated. This presents challenges for schools to be creative in their provision of SRE to ensure that differentiation is possible.

# Identity, challenge and professionalism

Education professionals need to be secure in their own identities, including sexual identities and to know a range of strategies to ensure that issues do not become personalised. Children and young people may ask a variety of challenging questions either to test a teacher's authority or out of genuine interest. It is essential that these are addressed in a professional, non-judgemental and inclusive manner. It is essential that schools can help children and young people develop confidence in talking, listening to and thinking about sex and relationships. Teachers and other staff may need to overcome their own anxieties and embarrassment to do this effectively. The DfEE (2000) states that there are a number of teaching strategies that can help this, including:

- establishing ground rules with pupils (e.g. whether personal questions are appropriate);
- using distancing techniques (e.g. role play or discussing literature);
- knowing how to deal with unexpected questions or comments from pupils;
- developing independent learning through project work;
- using discussion and encouraging reflection.

Teachers can model using appropriate language and can support children in its use. They have a key role in making issues accessible and ensuring that learning takes place in a safe, secure and supportive environment. They need to admit when they do not have an answer and offer to help children find out. If a child presents a difficult or personal question it may be most appropriate to agree to return to it later or in a more appropriate setting. Some teachers may feel vulnerable because they anticipate that young people will ask them personal questions. This may be particularly true for male teachers who feel a pressure to present traditional expressions of masculinity, power or potency. Setting ground rules that preclude the asking of personal questions can protect both pupils and teachers. In research conducted by Mason (2008), teachers commented that some Year 6 children challenge teachers through their questions, some of which are for genuine interest and others to test teacher authority, for example questions about different relationships or sexual activity such as homosexuality, lesbianism, anal and oral sex. It is essential that teachers are aware of a range of strategies, such as those outlined above, to cope appropriately with such situations.

It is important that educators do not project their own views or values about the nature and role of the family, relationships or sexuality onto their learners and children should not be stigmatised because of their personal identity or home circumstances. While marriage may provide one traditional form of family, other types of secure and committed relationships exist. Corteen (2006) records the comments of one teacher:

*The emphasis on the family [in SRE documentation] is good; it's useful as long as it's general. I take that to mean talking about relationships, bereavement and divorce but not so much marriage. The emphasis on marriage is unhelpful; it's not our place to promote marriage. A lot of pupils live with parents who are not married. You have to teach them in a way that reflects the pupils' own lives and it's up to them, they have to make their own decisions.*

Guidance provided by DfEE (2000) states that *there should be no direct promotion of sexual orientation*, which makes clear that teachers should not seek to impose their views on learners or show preferences for particular lifestyles or relationship patterns. This requires a professional approach, which will cause personal tension for some educators.

---

***Pause for thought*** | how do schools include families?

Anna is in Year 6. She lives with her mother and, since her parents' divorce, her grandmother. Her father moved from the family home four years ago to live with his new partner and they have a two-year-old son. He lives in the neighbouring village and she stays with him each weekend. Her parents take turns to attend special events at school and both are involved in her education. Anna's parents attend open evenings at school but request separate appointments. Her mum attends with grandma and her dad brings his partner, Daniel.

Anna's class teacher had to consider what issues about relationship and relationships education might arise from Anna's situation. He reflected on how to make sure that different kinds of family were represented and included in his classroom. Knowing about children's family backgrounds influenced the way in which he established the ethos and atmosphere in that educational setting.

- Do you think that all classrooms should be equally inclusive, acknowledging that there are many different ways of being family, or should they reflect the experiences of the children in the class?

---

# Respect, communication and negotiation

## The importance of respect in relationships

The notion of sexual ethics, a culturally acceptable way to behave sexually, is one that is intrinsically linked with SRE. The transmission of sexual values and behaviours through education is underpinned by a particular philosophical stance. It could be argued that the moral framework that underpins much of the current government SRE policy and guidance is in danger of not presenting an accurate interpretation of sex, sexuality and sexual orientation in the world beyond school.

---

### Research box

### developing a normalised approach

The Netherlands, whose high rate of teenage pregnancy triggered a radical change in SRE, has now adopted a different approach to sexual values. Lewis and Knijn (2002) suggest that by allowing a greater freedom to the professionals delivering SRE, a more confident message is communicated. The removal of a political agenda to reduce teenage pregnancy, the addressing of issues relating to homosexuality, teenage sex and sexuality, alongside a consideration of the responsibilities of parenthood, allow the exploration of the wider sexual context and realities of society. The disassociation from specific social sexual values enables a different approach. The Dutch approach is to promote and develop *self-reliance, respect for self and respect for others*. With the emphasis on self-respect, the approach to sex is positive; it is a part of everyday life. The child is perceived as an active participant in the process of understanding all aspects of sexuality, the biological and sexual pleasure, with emphasis on the *need to respect boundaries and the rights of others*. In England, respect for self and others is more frequently addressed through personal, social and health education (PSHE) from Key Stage 1 to Key Stage 4 (DfEE, 1999b, 1999c), and the personal, social and emotional (PSE) strand in the Early Years Foundation Stage (DCSF, 2008a). These aspects of personal, social and emotional education have the potential to provide opportunities to develop a more normalised approach to sex and relationships. An example of this is in the naming of body parts in Key Stage 1, where the biological names of genitals may be used alongside others. The normalisation of these terms assists children in seeing all of their body as important and to be respected. It may, in turn, avoid future confusion when children are required to reassess the familial childhood names for their genitals, particularly for females, whose adoption of terms such as 'front bottom' is perhaps misleading.

Alongside self-respect is the importance of developing a culture of mutual respect within the classroom. The establishment of ground rules to promote respectful behaviour specifically before, during and after SRE sessions is essential to develop empathy and respect for others. An explicit and honest dialogue about feelings of embarrassment in the sessions can encourage pupils to have a respectful understanding of their own and others' emotions. This may assist in developing essential skills for uninhibited dialogue in their future relationships. The role of the teacher is critical in modelling an honest, open approach that emulates respectful dialogue.

## The need for effective communication between individuals

The optional nature of SRE effectively gives parents and carers the right to determine their child's education in such matters (Walker, 2004). Parents have the right to withdraw their children from any or all SRE lessons. This stands in contrast to the requirements of Articles 12 and 13 of the United Nations Convention on the Rights of the Child (UN, 1989). These require that children be enabled to express their own views, that these should be given due weight according to their age and maturity, and that children shall have the right to seek and receive information of all kinds. It is important here that the right to be heard is coupled with the right to seek and to receive information. The guidance on SRE in England encourages schools to ensure that pupils' views are listened to. However, there is a significant difference between listening to and acting upon the views of children and young people. It is conceivable that the concerns of parents/carers will override those of children (Corteen, 2006). It is essential that effective communication take place between pupils, parents/carers and teachers on the nature and content of SRE and on how the needs of a child may be met through the curriculum.

Schools should work in partnership with parents in the provision of SRE and consult them regularly on the content of education programmes. Parents are key in teaching their children about growing up, relationships and sex. However, this is an area that many parents find difficult to address. Mullinar (2006) records comments made by children that indicate that even they are aware of the difficulties that may face parents or carers:

*If you didn't learn about sex and relationships in school, it might be hard for your family to explain these things.*

(Year 4)

If parents are confident and discuss sexual matters openly, there is evidence that this can have a positive impact on the health of children and young people (Walker, 2004). Schools are encouraged to support parents in such provision of SRE. Mullinar suggests that *in an ideal world all parents and carers would cover SRE with their children*. However, Mullinar also notes that in a survey of 800 parents of secondary age children nearly half *had not talked in depth about sex to their son or daughter*. This suggests that the role of the school in SRE has particular importance.

Research by the UK Youth Parliament (2007) with over 20,000 respondents under the age of 18 suggests that children and young people have specific views on the ways in which SRE should be delivered. Some 73 per cent felt that SRE should be delivered under the age of 13, with 56 per cent of boys under 11 wanting SRE in primary schools. Communication with boys can be particularly difficult for both schools and parents (DfEE, 2000). Hilton (2007) found that boys in secondary schools were aware of ways that SRE could be made more relevant for and useful to them. These included:

- the need to help boys to discuss, acknowledge and cope with feelings, emotions and love;
- the importance of using active teaching methods;
- teaching in groups small enough to allow discussion;
- covering materials from a male point of view, including masturbation, sexually transmitted infections and pornography.

On the basis of its survey, the UK Youth Parliament (2007) made recommendations which included that:

- SRE should be an entitlement for all children;
- no school should be able to opt out of delivering SRE;
- SRE needs to be taught throughout a child's time in education;
- relationships should be taught as a part of SRE.

Educators need to consider how they will take learners' views into account, and how they will identify and respond to their needs as they arise.

---

***Pause for thought*** | addressing children's questions

A nine-year-old boy once commented:

> We learned about things properly in class, things we might otherwise talk about in the playground and get wrong.

(Mullinar, 2006, p76)

While parents in England have the right to withdraw their child from some or all SRE provision, they do not have the ability to withdraw them from all contact with other children. There is a risk that those children withdrawn from SRE will be fascinated by what they have missed, and may gain inaccurate knowledge from other children on the schoolyard.

- Do you agree that parents and carers should have the right to withdraw their child from SRE?
- What impact may this have on the child socially, emotionally, and in terms of their learning?
- Consider how you might address this issue with a parent, guardian or carer who expresses concerns about their child participating in SRE. What role do you feel a child should have in this decision?

A girl in a Year 6 class asked her teacher how intercourse took place if the man had a large penis and questioned whether sex might hurt the woman. The teacher praised the girl for such a thoughtful question and explained that in a loving relationship this would be discussed by the couple and they would adjust sexual intercourse so that it was comfortable for both partners.

- Think about how this honest response from the teacher, delivered without embarrassment, offers the concept of negotiation between two adults in a caring and loving relationship.

# The importance of negotiation

In most positive human relationships, the concept of negotiation has relevance. Children and young people need to be equipped with the skills of negotiation in all aspects of their lives so that they can develop fulfilling relationships with others. This extends into the realm of sexual relationships where they are able to ensure that their needs and those of others are appreciated. Children usually develop a sense of themselves and their self-worth through their relationships with their parents and family. Where children are exposed to respect, trust, loyalty, honesty, mutual understanding and support, through their familial relationships, they are more likely to develop *successful sexual relationships in adulthood* (Halstead and Reiss, 2003). The influence of open and emotionally intelligent adults assists children in developing awareness of their emotions and needs. However, Gordon and Ellingson (2006) cite research conducted with teenagers who state the inadequacies of SRE in terms of addressing *real information about pleasures, intimacy, logistics and emotions related to sex*. In this context, the remit of parents and teachers may be to embrace a culture which addresses the gambit of human emotions positively and which empowers children to be autonomous in their relationships. Through autonomy in relationships, children may be equipped with the skills to remain safe, feel comfortable and maintain a sense of self worth.

## Summary and conclusions

The changing concept of childhood alongside the influences of the media on children and young people suggests a need for a radical review of SRE. The normalisation of sex and relationships may only be achievable by addressing sex and relationships in an increasingly open, honest and realistic way in schools, the home and in the media. In order to do this, teachers are required to address their reticence in broadening the curriculum to cover aspects of sexuality, sexual pleasure and a range of sexual relationships and for whole-school teams to be 'brave' in their pedagogical approach in SRE, specifically regarding content:

> Teachers and others with responsibility for education will not be able to help children reflect critically on their developing sexual values if they have not engaged in the same process.

(Halstead and Reiss, 2003, p52)

Pupils in the twenty-first century require a comprehensive SRE delivered through a flexible pedagogy, which is dialogic rather than didactic, and which enables children to understand the changes they face concerning their bodies, relationships and sexualities. This process might start by consulting the pupils to identify what they consider to be a relevant and purposeful SRE curriculum. However, there are certain aspects of SRE that children do not know that they need to know. In the decisions that teachers make concerning what they feel children need to know about aspects of SRE, there might also be a necessity to be 'brave'. Being 'brave' entails the development of a creative culture that has relevance (Casserley, 2004) to all those it engages with. The notion of relevance in SRE may be specific to the pupils' setting and, indeed, the historical and social context, and in turn be determined by the children engaged in the SRE provision.

The greater involvement of parents/carers at all stages of SRE is likely to increase parental confidence in a school's approach to this sensitive area of the curriculum. This, in turn, will empower teachers to be 'brave' when dealing with SRE. Parents might also, from their involvement with the school, have increased assurance in their responsibilities regarding discussions with their own children. This is particularly pertinent regarding issues of sexuality.

The policy change to make PSHE and SRE statutory from Key Stage 1 is one indication of its importance. The DCSF (2008b) claims:

> It's vital that this information doesn't come from playground rumour or the mixed messages from the media about sex. We need structured classroom teaching, set within a clear understanding of right and wrong that emphasises the importance of family relationships.

However, the emphasis on state-enforced moral values may not permit discussion of issues beyond that remit to fully embrace the needs that children might have for information. SRE may continue to be institutionally prescribed. In this context, teachers may feel less inclined to 'be brave' and the necessity for 'bravery' is critical for children and young people to develop understanding about what is an essential dimension of human adult life.

## References

Buckingham, D (2000) *After the death of childhood: growing up in the age of electronic media.* Oxford: Blackwell.

Buckingham, D (2006) Is there a digital generation? In Buckingham, D and Willett, R (eds) *Digital generations: children, young people and the new media.* London: Lawrence Erlbaum.

Casserley, M (2004) *Developing a creative culture.* Available at **www.standards.dfes.gov.uk/ntrp/lib/pdf/Casserley.pdf** (accessed 2 November 2008).

Corteen, KM (2006) School's fulfilment of sex and relationship education documentation: three school-based case studies. *Sex Education,* 6 (1): 77–99.

Crumper, P (2004) Sex education and human rights – a lawyer's perspective. *Sex Education,* 4 (2): 125–136.

DCSF (2008a) *Statutory framework for the early years foundation stage.* London: Department for Children, Schools and Families.

DCSF (2008b) *All pupils to get healthy lifestyle lessons.* Available at **www.dcsf.gov.uk/pns/DisplayPN.cgi?pn_id=2008_0235** (accessed 2 November 2008).

DfEE (1999a) *National healthy schools standard.* London: Department for Education and Employment.

DfEE (1999b) *National curriculum handbook for primary teachers in England.* London: Department for Education and Employment.

DfEE (1999c) *National curriculum handbook for secondary teachers in England.* London: Department for Education and Employment.

DfEE (2000) *Sex and relationship education guidance.* London: Department for Education and Employment.

DfES (2004) *Every child matters: change for children in schools.* London: Department for Education and Skills.

DfES and DH (2005) *National healthy schools status; a guide for schools.* London: Department of Health.

Erriker, C (2003) Against the protection of childhood innocence. *International Journal of Children's Spirituality,* 8 (1): 3–7.

Gordon, L and Ellingson, L (2006) In the eyes of the beholder: student interpretations of sexuality lessons. *Sex Education,* 6 (3): 251–64.

Halstead, JM and Reiss, M (2003) *Values in sex education: from principles to practice.* London: RoutledgeFalmer.

Hilton, G (2007) Listening to the boys again: an exploration of what boys want to learn in sex education classes and how they want to be taught. *Sex Education,* 7 (2): 161–74.

Lewis, J and Knijn, T (2002) The politics of sex education in England and Wales and the Netherlands since the 1980s. *Journal of Social Politics,* 31 (4): 669–94.

Mason, S (2008) *Braving it out! An illuminative evaluation of the provision of sex and relationships education in two primary schools in England.* Lincoln: Bishop Grosseteste University College Lincoln.

Maxwell, C (2006) Context and 'contextualisation' in sex and relationships education. *Sex and Relationships Education,* 106 (6): 437–49.

Measor, L (2004) Young people's views of sex education: gender, information and knowledge. *Sex Education,* 4 (2): 153–66.

Mullinar, G (2006) Sex and relationships education – we'll tell you what we want, what we really, really want. *Education Review,* 20 (1): 74–81.

Sex Education Forum (1992) *A framework for school sex education.* London: National Children's Bureau.

Teenage Pregnancy Independent Advisory Group (2008) *Fifth annual report.* London: Department for Children, Schools and Families and TPIAG.

UK Youth Parliament (2007) *Sex and relationships education: are you getting it? A report by the UK Youth Parliament.* London: UK Youth Parliament.

United Nations (1989) *Convention on the Rights of the Child.* Available at **www2.ohchr.org/english/law/crc.htm** (accessed 1 November 2008).

Walker, J (2004) Parents and sex education – looking beyond 'the birds and the bees'. *Sex Education,* 4 (3): 239–54.

Wellings, K, Wadsworth, J, Johnson, AM, Field, J, and Whitaker, LB (1995) Provision of sex education and early sexual experience: the relation examined. *British Medical Journal,* 311: 417–20.

# Chapter *19*

# The impact of new media technologies

## Elizabeth Hopkins

### Introduction

Today's children are surrounded by new media such as television, video, computer games and the internet. It would seem to be important, therefore, for those interested in children and their wellbeing to consider the impact such new technologies may have on children's learning. This chapter considers examples of where new media technology can have both a positive and negative impact.

## Educational technology *vs* entertainment technology

Traditionally, young people's relationship with digital new media has been characterised as either as seeing children as the victims of such technology, encouraged to indulge in violent computer games and helpless to the hypnotic power of the screen, or as canny 'cyber citizens' of the digital generation. Prensky (2001) refers to all such young people as 'digital natives', empowered by technology to discover and even create new worlds of communication and learning.

Historically for adults, there has been a fundamental distinction between what has been perceived as 'education' and what has been characterised as 'entertainment'. The 'educational' promise of new media technology is seen by some as beneficial, but the 'entertainment' such technologies can provide is condemned by others as both culturally worthless and even morally damaging (Sigman, 2007). Young people today, however, do not appear to differentiate between these two positions and the distinction is not as clear cut as historically it has seemed to be. 'Education' taught well can indeed be entertaining and likewise much quality 'entertainment' can inform and educate. Furthermore, what young people perceive to be educational or even entertaining may be different to adults' ideas.

What is certain is that new media technology is here to stay. With that comes the need for those involved in children's learning and wellbeing to embrace the potential benefits of such technology and to create new opportunities for using it for learning. It is also important to reflect on some of the negative impacts new media technology may have, in order to prepare those caring for and teaching children to become critically reflective of what new media technology can offer.

# The positive impact of new media technology

## Learning the e-way and a virtual school for children in care

Many young people are now part of online communities, downloading the latest instalments from websites of their favourite authors and belonging to a virtual community of 'flash' animators who post their efforts onto community websites. They critique their work and rate the contributions of others, offering advice and sharing with authors they have never met. In this aspect of life they are independent learners demonstrating many of the skills that formal education tries to cultivate. Many young people are now armed with the know-how that makes better learning possible. The *Learners and Technology: 7–11* report (Cranmer *et al.*, 2007) on primary children's use of ICT found that:

*The most engaging and most desirable use of ICT was reported by pupils to be 'games'. Conversely the least exciting and most objectionable uses of ICT were reported to be related to school 'work'. As such there was little sense of ICT leading children to be more engaged with school-related learning as is often claimed by education technology commentators.*

(p1)

However, the gap between new media technology used outside and inside school is closing in some schools. The government's e-strategy (DCSF, 2005), which stated that by *spring 2008 every pupil should have access to a personalised online learning space with the potential to support an e-portfolio* is some way away from being realised. There appears to be a drive to keep the curriculum moving, to take advantage of new methods in all subject areas, and to keep demanding a better response from the technology in order to engage all learners, even the 'hard to reach', with more motivating ways of learning, and more choice about how and where to learn.

The updated National Curriculum guidance allows for greater flexibility and schools are exploring new ways of organising learning using technology – often blurring the boundaries between formal and informal learning. Some schools are e-twinned with schools across Europe to exchange ideas, solve mathematical puzzles and learn about each others' culture. Other schools use technology to work with businesses so that the application of the curriculum has a real purpose and application. Online learning communities for pupils, parents and teachers are being developed. These tools are often referred to as virtual learning environments (VLEs) or learning platforms (LPs).

The *Care Matters* White Paper (DCSF, 2007) outlined the government's strategy for supporting children in care. As a result of the publication, eleven virtual schools were opened in England. By 2010 under the Children and Young Person's Bill (2008) every local authority will be required to have a virtual school to make sure that education is kept to the forefront of any decisions made about children in care. In 2006, only 12 per cent of children in care achieved five A* to C, GCSE's compared with 59 per cent of their age group nationally (DCSF, 2007). Children in care attend school but are also registered at a virtual school. They have access to technology such as laptops to use at home as well as access to online examination revision tools to use anywhere they can log on. As well as hardware, pupils in care also have access to a 'virtual' tutor to teach and mentor them as well as providing support and encouragement. The Global Education Trust (DfES, 2006) piloted a two-year study of new media technology virtual support which showed that the examination success of children in care is being raised.

---

**Pause for thought** | potential benefits of a virtual learning environment

Virtual learning environments open the doors to personalised 24/7 learning. Construct two lists of the potential benefits of a virtual learning environment, one for educators and one for learners.

---

## Potential benefits of children's television and language development

For many, the idea of children watching television as a positive occupation is unconvincing. However, Davies (1989) states that *there is no evidence … that watching television is a mindless activity – for children or for anybody else.* When under the control of the viewer, television may therefore have the potential to be an entertaining, informative educator.

Children view television primarily as a source of entertainment while their parents and carers see it as a useful educational tool for intellectual development (Rideout *et al.*, 2003). In order to be able to consider the impact of television on learning it is useful to understand how children acquire skills that help them to make sense of television. Children develop their understanding of television alongside their own cognitive development. They do not see television in the same way as an adult until about the age of 12. Research undertaken by the Literacy Trust (Close, 2004) found that parents and carers who share the experience of television viewing with their children can assist both cognitive and language development:

*Attention and comprehension, receptive vocabulary, some expressive language, letter-sound knowledge, and knowledge of storytelling all benefit from high quality and age-appropriate educational programming … co-viewing with parents aids oral ability and comprehension.*

(p15)

---

**Pause for thought** | television and language development

Early language acquisition seems to be related to age-appropriate programmes with specific educational purposes (Lemish, 2007). According to Marsh et al's (2005) research into the positive benefits of high-quality children's television, the overwhelming majority of parents and carers believed that their children's language development was assisted. Children were *'actively engaged with television content for some of their viewing time, with singing, dancing and copying characters'*. Marsh et al's research indicates that, when used in a measured way, New Media technology can be an extremely useful tool.

When considering the positive links between television, language development and the curriculum for the Foundation Stage in England, Marsh et al. identified that television viewing, in the right circumstances, can help pre-school children to be able to:

- use words, gestures, simple questions statements;
- listen to nursery rhymes, stories and songs, joining in with repeated refrains;
- enjoy listening to and using spoken language;
- sustain attentive listening;
- respond to extended vocabulary;

---

- explore the meaning and sounds of new words;

- use language to recreate experiences;

- use talk to clarify thinking, ideas, feelings and events;

- link sounds to letters;

- begin to be aware of the way stories are structured.

What do you think are the best circumstances in which television viewing can offer positive opportunities to help pre-school children to develop the above skills?

Research undertaken by Bazalgette (2003) for the British Film Institute found that children who watched television understood image sequences as well as combinations of images and sounds. This understanding of media could be transferred to the written word. Bazalgette suggests that children in their first year of school are *in a sense, bilingual, because they are already readers of television and film*. Earlier, Kremer *et al.* (2002) looked at six-year-old children's comprehension of non-written texts (the television cartoon *Rugrats* and the audio tape of *The Cat's Purr*). Children's recall of plot, character motivation and causal connectives were tested. The research found that these skills were a more significant indicator of reading ability at the age of eight than were the basic reading assessments of six-year-olds. This research suggests that there may be 'text level' concepts, for example genre and narrative structure, which are not restricted to print literacy, which can be developed through the engagement with quality screen viewing; these skills being transferable to print literacy.

Having looked at reading and the moving image, what about writing? Can media literacy help? Parker (1999) looked at the relationship between creative work with moving images and children's writing in two primary classes. The children looked at Roald Dahl's story *Fantastic Mr. Fox*. One class created simple animations of the story the other class read the story. The writing produced by the children demonstrated that the children who had worked with animations produced written work which contained more detail and depth. The children who used animation produced written work which showed character empathy, they understood that by *repositioning, the reader could get inside the character*. Having to select a camera position appeared to be the key for the children to be able to develop their writing. From this research it appears that teachers can encourage children to be actively engaged in media content without fear.

There has been little research undertaken into older children's learning from television. This could be because educational television has less of an impact on children once they have started school and in the decline of children's late afternoon television programming from the terrestrial channels. Older children prefer drama, verbal humour and relationships.

## How gaming can develop cognitive thinking skills

The early work of Greenwood (1984) found that computer game playing required a range of cognitive skills, including problem-solving, memory, inductive thinking, parallel processing, spatial awareness as well as the more obvious hand–eye co-ordination. Much of the research into the cognitive benefits of computer gaming identifies short-term effects which are transferable. American researcher Flynn (1994) suggested that the development of representational skills acquired through gaming may be responsible for the rise in American children's IQ scores. According to Williamson and Facer (2005), computer games aid learning and promote motivation more than formal education does. Their research identified a growing interest in the potential application of computer and video game environments for formal educational objectives and focused on children's gaming habits rather than the software used, to provide an insight into the relevance of formal educational settings. The findings highlighted the importance of playing games in peer groups and the social contexts required for gaming online and concluded that the social practices to which games-play provides young people with access are equally, if not more, motivating than the actual games themselves.

This new media gaming culture appears to provide an innovative resource for the kinds of learning which are often not present in a traditional school setting. So as with learning to play games, children need to be introduced to systematic ways of solving problems, the social networking offered by online gaming, or as Gee (2004) describes *affinity spaces* can provide for this.

### Research box

### the educational value of new media technologies

There have been contrasting assessments of the educational value of the new media technologies. Pappert's (1996) research described children's 'love affair' with computers arguing that they provide a more creative and spontaneous form of learning that can improve family relationships. Sceptics like Healy (1998) argue that such learning is superficial and trivial and that claims about computers' educational potential are highly overstated. According to research carried out by Livingstone and Bovill (2002), children choose computer games when they want to *stop being bored*. Favourite computer games are those which focus on sports and adventure, boys preferring sports and fighting games, girls favouring adventure quest, although these are also enjoyed by boys. Gee (2004) found that harnessing video games as a teaching medium was a powerful tool but found that *most schools seek to avoid invoking feelings of both pleasure and frustration, blind to the fact that these emotions can be extremely useful when it comes to teaching kids.*

If we want our children to benefit from technological innovations and to avoid the harm that some games may pose, educators need to embrace the potential benefits and incorporate the technology into their delivery.

# The negative impact of new media technology

## Early Years language development and screen viewing

Recent studies show that time spent reading before and after the advent of the medium of television has remained relatively stable through the years. It seems that children spent little time reading before the invention of television and they spend little time reading now.

It is known that the four significant stages which need to be in place before reading can be mastered are:

- phonological awareness (sounds);
- memory;
- co-ordination of perception and smaller motor movement;
- operation of symbols (letters).

Most children today recognise the golden arches 'M' of McDonald's by the age of three, but this does not mean that they can decode complex symbols and intended meaning. Children have to learn how symbols work, that numbers for example, can be represented by their Arabic symbols or spelled alphabetically and above all that letters stand for sounds that can be combined. Metacognition is also involved in the early stages of reading. Most teachers would agree that children need to grasp that language itself must be thought about and considered from different perspectives. Playing games with sounds, rhyming and discovering onomatopoeia are all aspects of metacognition that help a child to begin to read. Critics of television viewing have long suspected that television viewing is negatively associated with reading. Singer and Singer (1990) point out the fallacy of assuming that television viewing has a negative effect on reading. When children's television is removed or decreased, reading increases, so it is tempting to conclude that television viewing detracts from reading. However, studies by Snow *et al.* (1998) appear to show that it is the amount of television viewed at critical developmental stages which is significant.

Television may influence the type of reading that children prefer, not merely the amount. Morgan (1980) found that teenagers who were heavy television viewers preferred to read material that resembled television content. Likewise, younger children enjoy written stories about television characters. Reading had positive effects on oral and written expression as well as creative imagination. Educators have long observed that the presentation of a story on television causes curiosity about and demand for the book. This curiosity applies to both children and adults alike – one only has to think of the TV adaptations of classic stories by Charles Dickens and Jane Austen.

According to some research, the potential of television to aid a young child's linguistic development is limited. Too much early television viewing may hinder 'self-identity', as this is developed through real people rather than the screen. Light viewers of television have a better developed language shown in their use of more adjectives, adverbs and linguistic complexity than heavy television viewers (Singer and Singer, 1990).

---

*Pause for thought* | visualisation and imagination

The development of the imagination appears to be supported through reading (Singer and Singer, 1990). Another aspect from which to assess the impact of TV is to ask what the effect might be of too many messages and the degree to which children have become saturated by communication including TV. Gardner (1982) found little evidence that TV had a stimulating effect on the imagination. Interestingly, people denied perceptual stimulation such as TV, music and radio – for example those taken hostage (Horowitz, 1976) – reported an increase in frequency and vividness of imagery. Could it be then that saturation with sights and sounds reduces the capacity to visualise, to generate mental images?

Together with a group of friends or colleagues explore how your own capacity to visualise and be imaginative is linked with perceptual stimulation. For example, what might a school look like in 2020? Where did the images which you brought to mind come from? To what extent were the sources of these images helpful or limiting? Is it possible to be imaginative without a bank of mental pictures?

It has been found that children who listened to an incomplete story produced more imaginative story endings than children who saw the same incomplete story on TV. In a follow-up experiment by Greenfield and Beagles (1988), two groups of 192 socially mixed children were asked to tell a story about what would happen next. One group watched an animated TV cartoon while the other group listened to an audio version. Those who had watched the story used more words and ideas from the story. The group that had listened to the story produced far more creative and imaginative endings. Belton (2001) found that reading and writing ability and creative writing ability in children correlated positively with the number of books read, the level of parental education and paramount interest (including restriction of quality and type of viewing, watching TV together and discussing it, reading aloud when the child was small) and negatively to the number of viewing hours. In fact, the amount of viewing emerged as the single most significant factor in predicting writing ability.

Watkins in 1988 asked children to write two stories – one for television and one for 'real life'. Children used different contexts for the two genres irrespective of how much TV they viewed but those who were low viewers wrote more complex stories for both genres where the high TV viewers' stories were less developed, the TV story being more complex than the real-life story.

So TV images are widely seen and can create a collective memory which may limit the possibilities for original thinking. TV may leave little room for the creation of original images. Books can allow the mind to paint its own pictures. Children's ability to create visual, fluid, dreamlike images could be hindered by over-exposure to hard-edged detailed finished pictures.

## New media, aggressive behaviour and 'edutainment'

Concern about children and popular media has a long history. Plato proposed to ban poets from his ideal republic, because he feared their stories about immoral behaviour would corrupt young minds. In modern times 'moral' pressure groups have tried to protect children from:

- popular literature;
- the music hall;
- the cinema;
- comics;
- television;
- 'video nasties'.

TV does portray violence but there are broader social, cultural and historical factors which also influence. What did children do before the invention of television? Studies show that when television sets are removed for a while, children find other things to do (Buckingham, 1996; Davies, 1997). The romantic nostalgic image of childhood 50 years ago which offered little in the way of TV viewing conveys images of children running freely in fields and kicking footballs about in the street outside their homes. Now only one in five of today's children play outside in the street or local parks (Farmer, 2007). A fear of traffic accidents, paedophiles or bullies and the growth of home electronic entertainment have meant a whole generation are growing up without the joys of playing freely in their own neighbourhood. Research into the 'effects' of TV violence on children has focused on single cause and direct effect, putting the research into the behaviourist tradition.

## Research box

### television viewing and aggressive behaviour

Liebert and Baron (1972) looked at how willing children were to hurt other children. They found that children who had watched violent programmes were more prepared to do this than others. Boys appeared to be able to inflict pain more than the girls studied. These findings may appear shocking, but the research did not take into account that the programmes used in the research were not typical of these children's usual viewing and that most children do not usually watch television alone. The children also watched the violent programmes in an artificial situation which could have affected their responses. However, Rosenkoetter (2006) demonstrated that children understood moral lessons contained in situation comedy shows.

Berkowitz (1983) suggests that people are naturally aggressive but that normally this is repressed. Heavy violent television viewing, it seems, may weaken these inhibitions and leads them to feel that aggression is acceptable. The conditions of ordinary television viewing may encourage viewers to relax, accept and possibly enjoy violent images. Drabman and Thomas (1984) found that children between the ages of eight and ten who were shown a video of aggressive behaviour took longer to intervene in apparently real-life violence between two younger children they were left in charge of than children who had not seen the video.

Television programmes perceived by children as realistic are watched with more involvement, more emotion and less detachment than those programmes which seem fantastic (e.g. cartoons). Adults clearly have a role to play in monitoring children's access to violent television programmes. As violence sells, violent television programmes will inevitably continue to be made. This makes the monitoring and censoring role of the parent or other adult critical.

### *Pause for thought* | television viewing and academic performance

Research into the effects of television and other screen viewing on academic performance shows that children who view heavily experience difficulties with impulse control, task performance and delay of gratification. Smith (1986), researching in America, Anderson and Collins (1988) in Canada and later the American McIlwraith (1990) also found that children who watched a lot of television had significantly more trouble with mind wandering, distractibility, boredom and unfocused daydreaming. Based on your own experience, what factors might account for a link between television viewing and poor academic performance?

# The effects of new media technology on children's physical development and health

The apparent increase in the number of obese people not only in the United Kingdom but in the developed world is of growing concern. Much research into the causes of obesity has identified excessive screen viewing as one of the contributing factors. A study by Robinson (1999) for the Kaiser Family Foundation found that the average American child between the ages of eight and 18 spent over six hours a day with new media technology. This is more time than is spent in school, with parents or involved in any other activity other than sleep. In their research Cooper *et al.* (2006) identified that as viewing time increased, the resting metabolic rate of television viewers decreased. A number of studies have identified a correlation between weight gain and screen media usage, including television, video and electronic games.

Watching screen media frequently displaces other activities such as sports and playing outside and also appears to lead to a greater consumption of calories. Both children and adults eat more, even when they are not actually hungry. Early childhood is a time of rapid physical growth, and research on pre-school children by Janz (2001) found that girls who watched a lot of screen media had bone density which was lower than that of those who watched less. In 2007, Sigman reported that three-quarters of all meals are eaten in front of a screen.

The Office of Communications (Ofcom, 2008) implemented TV advertising restrictions on 'junk food' during programmes of particular appeal to children. The earlier Which Report, *Cartoon Heroes and Villains* (2005), had identified that nearly one in three children in England were overweight or obese, a trend reflected across the UK, and stressed the need for the government to restrict the advertising of foods high in fat, sugar and salt before 9pm. The National Opinion Poll by The Children's Society (2008) found that 66 per cent of children felt that computer and television viewing prevented active pursuits, 88 per cent of them wanted more educational advice about healthy eating and 95 per cent stated that physical health promoted mental health.

There appears to be a growing body of evidence which suggests that excessive viewing can lead to poor health and changes in cognitive development. While there are many factors which contribute to poor health, these studies indicate that children's engagement with new technology media is an important piece of the puzzle. It may well be worth considering the reduction of young children's exposure to screen viewing – particularly to advertising – and to increase the number of media messages which can promote fitness and sound nutrition.

### Summary and conclusions

This chapter has considered positive and negative aspects of new media technology. Technologies such as television, computer games and the internet are permanent resources for education, entertainment and play. They are part of children's everyday lives and children's relationship with them is undoubtedly complex. It may be shocking that children spend many hours engaged in screen viewing but is this necessarily a bad thing? While the ability to read and write has become essential to the processes of mental development, there appears to be every possibility that young children's access to new media technology may also develop children's minds. What is far from clear is how educators can prevent children from being exposed to harmful aspects, while simultaneously encouraging them to make the most of the educational and cultural potential which new media technology has to offer.

# References

Anderson, RE, Crespo, CJ, Bartett, SJ, Cheskin, LJ and Pratt, M (1998) Relationships of physical activity and television watching with body weight and level of fatness among young children. *Journal of the American Medical Association,* 279: 938–42.

Bazalgette, C (2003) *The children are watching.* London: British Film Institute.

Belton, T (2001) Television and Imagination: An investigation of the medium's influence on children's story making. *Media, Culture and Society,* 23(6): 799–820.

Berkowitz, L (1983) *Aggression: its causes and consequences and control.* New York: McGraw-Hill.

Buckingham, D (1996) *Moving images: understanding children's emotional responses to television.* Manchester: Manchester University Press.

Children's Society (2008) *UK failing to meet children's mental health and well-being needs.* GfK, National Opinion Poll.

Close, R (2004) *Television and language development in the early years: a review of the literature.* London: National Literacy Trust.

Cranmer, S, Potter, J and Selwyn N (2008) *Learners and technology 7–11.* London: Becta.

Davies, Marie Messenger (1989) *Television is good for your kids.* London: Hilary Shipman.

DCSF (2005) *Harnessing technology: transforming learning in children's services.* London: HMSO.

DCSF (2007) *Care matters: time for change.* London: HMSO.

DCSF (2008) *Children and Young Person's Bill.* London: HMSO.

Desmond, RJ (1997) Media literacy in the home: Acquisition vs. deficit models. Kubey, R. (ed) *Media literacy in the information age (pp.323–45).* New Brunswick, NJ: Transaction Publishing.

DfES (2006) *Making Progress Project.* HSBC Global Education Trust.

Drabman, PS and Thomas, MH (1984) Does media violence increase children's toleration of real-life aggression? *Developmental Psychology,* 10: 418–21.

Farmer, TW (2007) The developmental dynamics of aggression and the prevention of school violence. *Journal of Emotional and Behavioural Disorders,* 15(4): 197–208.

Flynn, JR (1994) IQ gains over time. In Sternberg, RJ (ed) *Encyclopaedia of human intelligence* (pp.617-623). New York: Macmillan.

Gardner, H (1982) *Art mind and brain, a cognitive approach to creativity.* New York: Basic Books.

Gee, J (2004) *Situated language and learning: a critique of traditional schooling.* New York: Routledge.

Greenfield, PM and Beagles, J (1988) Radio and television: their cognitive impact on children of different socio economic and ethnic groups. *Journal of Communication,* 38(2): 71–92.

Greenwood, PM (1984) *Mind and media: the effects of television, computers and video games.* London: Fontan.

Hart, R (2006) *Kids go mobile.* Bakewell: Intuitive Media Research Services.

Healy, JM (1998) *Failure to connect: how computers affect our children's minds – for better or worse.* New York: Simon and Schuster.

Horowitz, MJ (1976) *Stress response syndromes.* New York: J. Aronso.

Janz, KF (2001) Physical Activity and Bone measures in young children: The Iowa bone development study. *Pediatrics,* 107: 1387–93.

Kremer, KE, Lynch, JS, Kendeou, P, Butler, J and Van Der Broek, P (2002) 'Role of narrative understanding in predicting future reading comprehension. Universities of Minnesota and Kentucky paper presented at AERA conference (online) **www.clera.org** (accessed 20 October 2008).

Liebert, R and Baron, R (1972) 'Some immediate effects of televisual violence on children's behaviour. *Developmental Psychology.* 6: pp 469–75.

Livingstone, S and Bovill, M (2002) *Young people and new media.* London: Sage.

Marsh, J, Brookes, G, Hughes, J, Ritchie, L, Roberts, S and Wright, K (2005) *Digital beginnings: Young children's use of popular culture, media and new technologies*. Literacy Research Centre: University of Sheffield.

McIlwraith, RD (1990) *Theories of television addiction*. Boston, MA: American Psychological Association.

Morgan, M (1980) Television and reading: Does more equal better? *Journal of Communication,* 30(3): 159–65.

Pappert, S (1996) *The connected family: bridging the digital generation gap.* Atlanta, CA: Longstreet Press.

Prensky, M (2001) *Digital natives, digital immigrants*. On the Horizon. MCB University Press. Vol. 9, No.5.

QCA (2008) National Curriculum. London: QCA.

Rideout, V, Vandewater, E and Wartella, E (2003) *Zero to Six*. In Kaiser Family Foundation Report. California: The Henry J Kaiser Family Foundation.

Robinson, TN (1999) *Lids and media in the new millennium: a comprehensive national analysis of children's media use*. Washington: Kaiser Family Foundation.

Rosenkoetter, L (2006) The television situation comedy and children's prosocial behavior. *Journal of Applied Social Psychology*. Vol. 29. Issue 5: 979–93.

Sigman, A (2007) *Remotely controlled: how television is damaging our lives*. London: Vermilion.

Signorielli, N (2001) Television and the family: the cultivation perspective. In Bryant, J and Bryant, A (eds) *Television and the American family* (2nd edition). London: Lawrence Erlbaum Associates.

Silverne, SB and Williamson, PA (1987) The effects of video game play on young children's aggression, fantasy and pro-social behaviour. *Journal of Applied Developmental Psychology*, 8: 453–62.

Singer, DG and Singer, JL (1990) *The house of make-believe: children's play and the developing imagination*. Cambridge, MA: Harvard University Press.

Smith, R (1986) Television addiction. In Bryant, J and Zillman, D (eds) *Perspective on media effects*, pp 109–28. Hillsdale, HJ: Lawrence Erlbaum.

Snow, C, Burns, M and Griffin, P (eds) (1998) *Preventing reading difficulties in young children*. Washington, DC: National Research Council.

Watkins, B (1988) Children's representations of television and real life stories. *Communication Research*, 15: 159–84.

Williamson, B and Facer, K (2005) More than 'just a game': the implications for schools of children's computer games communities. *Education, Communication and Information*, 4(2 and 3): 255–70.

# Chapter 20

# Global citizenship and comparative education

# Les Hankin

## Introduction

*'We are all citizens of the world now.'*

Barack Obama, US President

The ideal that we should respect all humanity as equal and work together for a better world is gaining ground, particularly as our world becomes one community with shared concerns. Chaos threatens us all as we try to make sense of the challenges of the twenty-first century; from climate change to war, terrorism and financial mayhem. Only through education and understanding can a new world civilisation emerge, and new ways to live in relative harmony be found in order to survive.

The world is growing ever-more immediate, interdependent, intercultural and information-driven, ever more deeply interconnected. Yet it grows less sustainable: an extra Planet Earth will be needed soon as we run through our natural resources much faster than the world can replenish them. All these tensions are contained within the term 'globalisation'. Is globalisation a force of nature that cannot be checked, or a creation of humanity that can be tamed? As the phenomenon has taken hold, an allied concept has arisen, that of global education: the need to prepare the world's citizens for their roles and responsibilities. Unlike national and local belonging, however, 'global citizenship' does not come by legal birthright. Each individual must be persuaded and educated towards it. This chapter considers the part education might play in influencing the course of globalisation for the benefit of all individuals wherever they live.

# The globalisation debate

The world is changing so fast that the survival of individual nations may depend on the quality of their education systems. This is one view in a debate as intensive as the forces it seeks to explain (Held *et al.*, 2008). Among these forces is the vision of the globalists, who claim we are entering an era when the fusion of history, ecology and economics is creating a new world order in which states must converge economically and politically or be made irrelevant by the unfettered activity of transnational business. This parallels the belief of environmentalists that we are fatally confused as we stumble towards world changes more elemental than at any point since the dawn of civilisation. The *long slow accretion of epochs – the Jurassic, the Cretaceous, the Pleistocene – lulls us into imagining that the physical world offers us a stable background against which we can run our race* (McKibben, 2003). By contrast, the sceptics deny that we are in a period of irreversible transformation because governments, nationalism and geopolitics still dominate and will determine the course of history. Transformationalists take an intermediate line, more concerned with the shift of power across the world's major regions and continents. All interpretations acknowledge that the rich world is losing influence to the newer economies of China and India, who together account for nearly half of all humanity (Starke, 2006).

Undeniably the world is merging irresistibly and with a momentum that may be a force for good as technological change breaks down barriers between peoples of different nations. Paradoxically, however, just as connectivity and mobility of culture and labour are dissolving traditional national boundaries and widening horizons, our world seems to be turning into a place of greater individualism rather than community (Allan, 2005). Whatever people gain in longer lifespan and greater material wealth, they pay a human price in losing the narrative thread about who they themselves might be and their place in the world. As corporations alter working conditions to favour short-term jobs over careers, their employees lose the relationships that anchored them to other workers and their employers, around which communities once coalesced. Women become marginalised when they cannot match family and childcare commitments to less socially responsive work patterns and longer shift hours. Communities are eroded as workers are driven out of districts made too expensive by market forces.

Reassurances from governments that the *rising tide of growth will lift all boats* have been compared with the harsh reality that freeing global market competition from government regulation brings the opposite of rising standards of living and new freedoms. By most indicators of social and ecological life, from healthcare to literacy levels, from vocational opportunity to bio-security, *the restructuring of societies for corporate globalisation has been increasingly life-destructive* (McMurtry, 2006).

As the world's horizons shrink so fast that unremitting poverty coexists with extreme wealth, how is it that, despite global economic growth, the gap between rich and poor countries, regions and peoples is increasing dramatically (ILO, 2008)? How can it be that the experience of childhood remains so unequal across the world (Penn, 2005)? This highly partial world revolution challenges us to nurture global responsibility through education. This term signifies that human rights is an issue for each one of us now, wherever we live and however prosperous or secure we may feel ourselves to be.

# The narrative of globalisation

Globalisation is usually depicted as a relentless economic imperative concentrating wealth in multinational corporations, aided by advances in education in the knowledge economy and in technology. The term describes the trend by which all corners of the world have been edging together since the Middle Ages, when territoriality and the divine right of monarchs became the organising logic of nation states. Since the sixteenth-century voyages of discovery, societies have been converging towards one world economy in their search for the most efficient use of capital and labour. This has been driven by exponential increases in trade, cultural exchange and breakthroughs in travel and communications. Interrupted by two world wars and the cold war, globalisation gained unstoppable momentum from the early 1970s, barely checked by waves of devastating recessions. While the economic system has been more protective of national economies, with rules preventing people from following work freely around the world, the force of immigration has itself broken all bounds, with a quarter of a billion people now living as migrants (UN, 2007). At the same time the advent of true world electronic communications has brought about the *death of distance* and with it the birth of one world, one true *global village* (Cairncross, 2001).

The satellite news revolution has also meant the death of ignorance, for no longer can we not know what is happening elsewhere in our world. Economies and societies are becoming increasingly enmeshed: events in one country impacting directly on others as constraints of space and time dissolve, and socio-economic activity is less and less constrained as borders and geographical barriers erode. An alternative view suggests, however, that there has never been a true global economy, since the world's eight most economically powerful nations together direct world activity now just exactly as eight great self-interested powers held sway before the First World War (Hirst and Thompson, 2000). Richer countries can exert so much control that the poorer nations seem mired in a fatalistic belief that they can do little to change the world order to take control of their own destinies.

# The global citizen

Convergence around global markets has led to common international standards on fundamental human rights, including the status of women and of refugees, health and safety, employment and other measures of progress. Emerging from this new world order is a yearning for the 'global citizen': a responsible and responsive person owing allegiance to the world as much as to the nation state into which they were born. These citizens demonstrate this cosmopolitan loyalty by being actively concerned for all humanity, and they uphold the ideals of peace, justice, respect and sustainability as ways to achieve a better future for everyone. You may consider yourself to be such a mortal, *bound to other human beings by ties of recognition and concern* (Nussbaum, 1998).

With this level of concern comes a sense of complicity, culpability and responsibility for the state of the world. One view is that schoolchildren should not be burdened with such depressing truths, particularly as education for global citizenship is made to carry a range of ideas that are not necessarily connected. Yet there is a growing international consensus that education must encourage a global ethic among young people. This would require us all to respect the fundamental and inalienable rights of all other human beings by understanding the new realities of unprecedented global change early on.

Certain essential citizen characteristics associated with this ethic are common to nations' education policies: co-operation, tolerance, a belief in non-violent conflict resolution, a readiness to defend human rights and to rein in lifestyles to safeguard the environment, together with an appetite for action at local, national and international levels. Oxfam (2006) goes further, requiring the global citizen to be *outraged by social injustice*, galvanised with the *belief that we can make a difference* and be *willing to act to make the world a more equitable and sustainable place*.

As developed nations struggle to uphold democracy, combat terrorism and find economic harmony, their peoples are taking on this mantle of global citizenship, working for world peace, sustenance and sustainability in a multi-ethnic, multicultural world where national boundaries no longer define their total reality. However, many of these advances are luxuries denied to *majority world countries*, as Oxfam characterises those countries usually described as 'developing' (Young and Commins, 2002). Dogged by poverty, injustice and disease, these nations have little real influence over superpowers ready to act against the wishes of the United Nations, the one organisation that approximates to a world government upon which the concept of a world citizenry must in some way depend.

# The dimensions of global citizenship

Global citizenship involves the dualities of equality and inequality, justice and injustice, peace and conflict, and environmental diversity and damage. For children to gain the knowledge, skills and attitudes to respond to these tensions, a whole-school approach becomes essential. Resolving their contradictions is taken by many commentators to be the fundamental purpose of all schooling. This view is radical because the production of global citizens depends on co-operation and a dynamic regard for social justice more than on the competition that usually characterises young people's taught experience (Young and Commins, 2002).

Osler and Starkey (2005) propose three forms of citizenship: status, feeling and practice. Feeling, or belonging to a community, expands as the concept of community grows wider and more inclusive. Practice ties in with an emerging phenomenon, the active citizen (Nelson and Carr, 2005). Visible climate change inspired popular movements working around and beyond governments to unite in concern about where the planet was heading at the end of the twentieth century. Vast movements galvanised by rock stars, together with the dawning recognition of global warming and energy shortages, laid fertile ground for global citizenship to force its way onto the curriculum. The countries of the UK have adopted a global dimension in the syllabus. Parallel but distinctive developments can be seen in nearly every state (Council of Europe, 2008).

---

***Pause for thought*** | the characteristics of the global citizen

A survey of any group of students will show that many locate their origins in other countries. This difference is a source of pride. We live and work alongside people from all over the world more than ever before. Indeed the added value that students and academics from all over bring to learning communities is recognised in the recruitment policies of most universities (Khamis, 2005).

We can plot the significance of every decision we each make as consumers. We travel where we wish as of right. Our culture is shaped by global influences. Whenever we go online to find similarities or differences with our counterparts abroad, or the moment we step on other soil, we become global citizens. Citizenship education is now a recognised curriculum thread in most education systems (Sears and Hughes, 2006). Each is concerned that young people learn about their position and role in relation to their world and develop the skills and insights that will dispose them to participate in society at local, national and international levels.

Ask your colleagues where they feel they come from, to confirm this impression of global (rather than narrowly national) belonging and citizenship. What do you consider to be the assets of a global citizen?

---

# Globalisation and a global dimension in the school curriculum

In England, all National Curriculum subjects at all phases are required to contribute to the global dimension, to enrich learning and secure pupils' commitment in graduated stages. Eight key concepts cover the enduring values and essential learning about global issues (DfID, 2005). These are:

- citizenship;
- sustainable development;
- social justice;
- values and perceptions;
- diversity;
- interdependence;
- conflict resolution;
- human rights.

National strategies to encourage excellence in teaching and enjoyment of learning are allowing schools to be more innovative and creative in how children are educated (DCSF, 2008). Such a concession has been seized upon by global educators (Hicks and Holden, 2007; Development Education Association, 2008). Official guidance on the teaching of controversial issues places globalisation at the heart of a range of concerns that have personal impact or deal with questions of value and belief (QCA, 2006).

Research has shown that children are able from their early years to form conceptions about issues of peace and conflict, human rights, racism, sexism, global development and the environment (Fountain, 1990). Long-term studies of the effect of citizenship education suggest that by Year 11 young people have a general interest in politics and that higher education (HE) students draw upon significant life histories in becoming global citizens (Benton *et al.*, 2008). HE has seen some of the most significant developments in the 'policy borrowing' that characterises globalisation, in encouraging the international outlook that is fundamental to global citizenship education. The Bologna Accords have harmonised standards and quality assurance so that students can move more freely between countries and international study is encouraged through networks such as ERASMUS. Universities are developing transnational initiatives, drawing in students from other countries through distance learning and setting up campuses overseas, so-called borderless education (OBHE, 2008). The Development Education Association argues for the concept of a global university, signifying that higher education should be concerned with preparing students ethically and intellectually for active global citizenship (Bourn *et al.*, 2006). Service learning opportunities are now offered by many universities, harnessing students' energy in work abroad, with their echo in the 'voluntourism' industry providing gap-year volunteers with often-controversial projects (Clarkson *et al.*, 2008).

# Where is globalisation going?

If many of the world's problems are not directly caused by the impacts of world integration, often they can only be resolved through international co-operation. For example, the weaker nations and their citizens need help to share in globalisation's benefits and beat the poverty exacerbated by global market inequalities. However, there are signs that globalisation has stalled and may be in retreat. There is evidence for this in the emergence of *ad hoc* alliances of China, India, Brazil, South Africa and others and the huge demonstrations against the effects of globalisation at every economic summit meeting of the great powers. Outrage has been expressed over, for example, the pricing policies of Western drug companies in the fight against disease.

Most world events can be read in terms of the progress of globalisation as a philosophy of prosperity, from asylum-seeking through to the state of Africa and all points between, including natural disasters which are popularly seen to be caused by wholesale economic abuse of the planet. The USA has been held to be the driving force behind globalisation. As its foreign policy has taken more nationalistic turns, its economic policies could turn inwards against the threat of the vast economic rise of China and India. The closing of American and European borders, as protectionism against the influx of cheap goods from the East, is one symptom of resistance to such economic dangers.

A vast and disparate international movement has massed in opposition to the impacts, rather than the underlying inexorable process of globalisation. It may be hypocritical to condemn globalisation without renouncing so much of modern life. This tension has led to the rise of alliances such as the Global Justice Movement, which uses popular education to mitigate the unequal effects of globalisation. Naomi Klein, whose seminal book *No Logo* (2001) railed against the damage inflicted by world marketing brands, has used this term to identify the growing lobby calling on decision-makers to stop commercial policies that hurt the world's poor.

---

## Research box

### the global dimension in the higher education curriculum

Several UK government initiatives have sought to stimulate a global dimension in universities' curricula. These include the international strategy for education *Putting the world into world class education* which integrates international considerations into study programmes (DfES, 2004). It sets three interrelated goals that will help the UK keep its 'unique position' as a confident, outward-looking society and leading-edge economy playing its full part in the world.

- Goal 1: equipping young people and adults for life in a global society and work in a global economy. This involves instilling the learning experience of all young people with a global dimension, raising the national capability to speak and use other languages and moving towards greater transparency and international mutual recognition of qualifications.

- Goal 2: engaging with international partners. This involves benchmarking UK performance against world-class standards, drawing on best practice everywhere and working with European partners to make the EU *the most competitive and dynamic knowledge-based economy*. It also demands that expertise and resources are shared in support of the improvement of education and children's services worldwide, particularly in Africa.

- Goal 3: maximising the contribution of the UK education and training sector and university research to overseas trade and inward investment. This calls for further expansion in the number of international HE students in the UK, making the UK an international leader in the creative and supportive use of ICT for education, promoting UK universities as international hubs for learning and research and encouraging education providers to work internationally in partnership with business.

Compare these major goals with the grassroots work of the Development Education Association (DEA), the umbrella body for a raft of organisations promoting awareness of global issues and the role people play within them. The higher education section of its website sets out projects (many student-led) illustrative of the role of HE in global responsibility.

---

# Comparative education

The goals of global education can be illuminated through understanding how education relates to wider social forces. Comparative education is a tradition of academic studies that investigate how education works in different cultures. Its many strands all explore the processes, structures and dynamics of different countries, regions or educational systems for meaningful similarities and contrasts between them. Comparativists unite in a belief that analysis of the practices and outcomes of any educational system or grouping is instructive, on the broad principle of learning from others. However, not all agree about whether comparisons actually enlighten educational practice.

## The dimensions of comparative education

The speed of global change has altered the integrity and identity of nations. The bonds of culture, tradition and territoriality that once clearly defined them and held them together have been loosened by the effects of trade, conflict and population movement. Where once they found clear answers from within to the complex questions taxing their educational systems, now they must look further afield to emulate success. Comparative studies have a range of purposes whose consequences tend towards copying or 'borrowing' successful practice (Phillips and Schweisfurth, 2008). By examining alternatives they set yardsticks to judge how well an education system is working. They can anticipate how policy reform may succeed by looking to other countries' experience. They can form a bridge of understanding among nations by accounting for cultural differences and similarities. In providing objective data they can also test official accounts of how a country's education provision is performing by comparison with other nations.

Paradoxically, the absence of external threat after half a century of relative world peace has undermined the solidarity that once united countries around their national distinctiveness. Social bonds, networks and identity have become threatened by the dissolution of communities and the fragmentation of the family. The pressures of a global economy have led governments to undervalue their own distinctive and precious cultural heritage. In response many states have adopted uniform school curricula that they have seen introduced elsewhere to drive the vast educational improvements needed to keep their place in the world. What may have been most eroded in this process is motivation. Education has lost some of its power to attract populations to learning for its own sake rather than as a pressing economic necessity.

# Cross-national trends in education

Common imperatives can be seen emerging as countries strive to shape their educational policy initiatives and strategies to ensure equity and economic survival in the punishing global climate. A set of trends can be drawn from sources including the OECD. While these are not exhaustive, they give some sense of how educational systems have to deal with similar convergent and insistent phenomena.

- A greater proportion of populations is engaged in education than ever.
- Take-up of post-compulsory education shows how life chances and educational success still depend on socio-economic background and inheritance.
- A link persists between the educational success of parents and that of their children.
- Principles of lifelong learning and widening access have led to the 'massification' of higher education.
- Female educational attainment outstrips male, swelling concerns about male underachievement and disaffection (subject choice and consequent career direction remain gender-influenced).
- Careers are ever harder to sustain without educational qualifications, as knowledge-based economies shed low-skill occupations,

- The educational success of ethnic communities falls into predictable patterns.
- Cost influences policies of fairness and widening participation helping students with special needs into mainstream education.
- The relentless growth of digital education is creating a 'digital divide' of excluded groups who will never catch up.
- The balance of power between governments and practitioners may be shifting, as education is increasingly expected to be an agent of social change.

Many of these trends follow the transformation of societies into economies where the production, refinement and transfer of knowledge must be fed by new armies of flexible 'knowledge workers'. Such economic necessity may need to give ground to educational values involving *the emotional, perhaps even the spiritual, lives of those who learn* (Newby, 2006). Put differently, they need the depth of global citizenship.

# Difficulties of comparison

Systems may share common educational concerns but meaningful comparison becomes problematic given global disorganisation, social fragmentation and the decline of clear-cut national systems. The essence of any educational system is its particular cultural map, so that concepts, variables and indicators of educational effectiveness can never be treated as directly comparable when setting evidence about one system against that of another. Every detail is open to question on these terms. Simply establishing age and stage equivalence between systems is problematic .The very word 'education' is itself loaded with associations within and between languages, so that in every country it has a different scope and range of meanings (Corner and Grant, 2008).

If there are great variations between countries educationally, then the power and relevance of comparative education might lie in the reasons behind such difference. No two countries possess quite the same educational contours, because these are formed by history and shaped by unique traditions. So questions arise about the social forces and factors in knowledge production that are considered so vital to each country's success. What economic, political, cultural and community influences have been at work?

---

**Pause for thought** | an example of international comparison

Despite reservations about comparing data, the propensity for government-sponsored, cross-national research is increasing with advances in communications. The International Adult Literacy Survey, for example, considered factors in the development of adult skills across the OECD countries, whose combined populations account for over half of the world's entire gross domestic product. It measured levels of advanced literacy, defined as the ability to cope with written material in the information age. A vast underclass was revealed with a quarter of 16- to 65-year-olds in the richest countries shown to be functionally illiterate. Significant differences in the level and distribution of literacy skills within and between countries were revealed, against such parameters as the changing demand for skills in a knowledge economy. The survey concluded that policies to develop skills should be directed at the workplace and family settings, as well as towards high-quality learning in schools (OECD and Statistics Canada, 2000).

In Britain, young people appeared less well qualified for the world of work than those in other industrialised countries and a connection was drawn between the British television addiction and their comparative weakness in advanced reading skills, with 22 per cent proving functionally illiterate. However, 35 per cent of young people surveyed gained a university degree in the UK, compared with fewer than 20 per cent a decade previously and against an average of 23 per cent for other countries.

The survey demonstrated more than a link between the possession of good literacy skills, better pay and a longer life. It showed that every country involved had a literacy problem, but that responses were very different: most funded proactive bodies equivalent to Britain's Basic Skills Agency because poor reading is considered the easiest of the poverty indicators to tackle. In contrast, some states, such as Germany, took few steps to counter functional illiteracy.

What do you think are the most important skills for the effective functioning of labour markets and for the economic success and social advancement of individuals and societies?

# Shared principles

What is the common ground among educational systems as they have developed over time? Certain fundamental principles have emerged. Take the ancient belief coming down to us from Plato, that education should be provided for the masses through the action of the state. This may now seem self-evident and only right and just, but was strikingly revolutionary once. It may have taken two millennia to become universally adopted, but it has not been seriously destabilised in any country by movements such as the 'deschoolers', whose critique of the corrupting effect of educational institutions reflects a wider scepticism about the competence of governments anywhere to make them work.

One of the earliest principles to emerge was the perception that children were not simply 'adults waiting to happen' and that childhood had a value in its own right. This can be traced to Rousseau, whose insight that children were naturally good but vulnerable, that they learned differently and needed the support of mentors to learn how to live, marked a paradigm shift in the understanding of the child. This made space for the child-centred thinking of subsequent influential educationists, including Pestalozzi, Steiner, Piaget and Froebel in Europe and Dewey in the USA. All such principles are, of course, modified by circumstance. Descriptions of the nature of childhood in a range of present-day societies show how market forces distort educational opportunities for children as their families seek simply to survive. At the other end of the spectrum (from concern for the child's interests) is the belief that education has the power to deliver the will of a country's political elites and that it is the key to that country's future economic prosperity.

Some principles owe less to tradition than to modern expediency and developing notions of equity, expressed forcefully in the OECD's watchword that *society's most important investment is in the education of its people*. Educational policy is formulated under intense pressures, ranging from the demographic to the social and economic, as education systems seek to be more sensitive to the needs of individual learners than to those of the systems themselves. Lifelong learning, Widening participation and extended schools, are all markers of a universalised recognition of the shifting purpose of education in the twenty-first century.

# Lessons from systems and social structures

Comparativists are also concerned with the function of education systems within societies as they mesh with other components of the social structure. Comparative education is thus forever looking backwards, always assessing inherited systems of education that will have been formulated around societies' shifting needs. This has echoes in Santayana's famous axiom that *those who do not remember the past are condemned to repeat it*. This statement confronts visitors to the Auschwitz concentration camp. Writ large in that dreadful place is the terrible lesson that an education system somehow bred a generation capable of the 'banality of evil' that made genocide so easy so recently and that such conditions must not be allowed to arise again anywhere.

The focus, concerns and intentions of comparativists have shifted over the last century as governments have coveted educational institutions and practices that appear to have succeeded in other countries (King, 2000). Often this process has been driven by military and economic rivalry and competition for international esteem and influence. This impulse to imitate contributes to the global convergence of educational systems, as the curious are said to look abroad to see into the future.

Studies of education systems, and their relative effectiveness, are often driven by statistical evidence, particularly when institutionalised through the work of inter-governmental agencies such as those of the United Nations or the European Union. The tensions around what constitutes unequivocal evidence are illustrated by the presence of independent indices of educational success, although the level of independence needs to be examined. An example of this is the *Human development report*, a composite of measures gauging the development of nations in terms of education, life expectancy and gross domestic product (UNDP, 2008). The programme is concerned to explore progress towards the Millennium Development Goals, eight targets for the eradication of poverty by 2015, as agreed by all UN member states and the world's leading development institutions. The second of these goals, after the eradication of extreme poverty and hunger, is the achievement of universal primary education (UN, 2005).

The Qualifications and Curriculum Authority for England projects its mission in comparative and competitive terms, in *helping the UK become the most dynamic knowledge-based economy in the world*. Its INCA programme provides system summaries of governments' policies on teaching from 3 to 19 and teacher training in a range of countries. It also offers thematic probes and summaries, comparing strands across countries such as learner motivation and skills and curriculum progression.

The impulse to compare and judge educational arrangements in other societies, from information that can never be complete, carries its own dangers, such as those of prejudice. Wainaina condemns the stereotyping of Western writing about Africa and the exploitative undertow of its supposedly comparative approach: *Broad brushstrokes throughout are good. Avoid having the African characters laugh, or struggle to educate their kids ... Have them illuminate Europe or America in Africa* (2005, p94).

Against such dangers, comparison and contrast may become more important to preserve variety, as globalisation draws systems into compliance with supposed ideals and norms of what is 'best' in education for every human being, regardless of the conditions in which they live. Could it be that there is a set of irreducible principles of education to which all systems should subscribe, by looking for the best in each other in pursuit of the best of all possible educational worlds?

*Pause for thought* | are there universal principles of education?

Should there be universal assumptions and goals of education by which every country can ensure they are serving the interests of their learners as well as the economic imperatives of the state? Consider this list of principles. Do you agree with them? Can you add to them?

- A country's education provision is best regulated nationally but provided locally.
- Education is most successful when parents, teachers and local and national government work together.
- Teachers need freedom to teach.
- Children must attain functional levels of literacy and numeracy close to the expectations of their age group.
- Personal and social education is important.
- There should be coherence and continuity between the different stages of a child's education.

# Explanations and perspectives on the development of nations

The relevance of comparative education rests on an understanding that decisions made by any nation are intimately tied to those of all other nations within the global society. As knowledge and information become among the most valued of commodities in world trade, yet are less and less restrained by any precise physical location, this fusion becomes more pronounced. As we have seen, there are also shifts in the balance of economic power: the rich 'North' is being challenged by the much higher growth rates of the newly industrialised countries (NICs) of Asia.

The learning paths of developing nations are diverging from those of developed states. Technology, for example, is being applied to overcome severe shortages of resources. India, needing 10,000 new schools a year to meet targets to erode its 35 per cent illiteracy rate, is bypassing the old constraints of landline provision over vast distances by launching the world's first dedicated education satellite linked to cheap mass computers and adopting the concept of virtual classrooms. In Africa, a pan-continental e-school programme seeks to provide all 600,000 of its schools with computers and internet access. Those cross-national forces of change that characterise globalisation are exerting pressures to make countries converge and grow alike in their education systems as much as in their other institutions.

## Summary and conclusions

This chapter has considered what globalisation entails, what its impact might be and how it might be better understood. Education's role in creating global citizens through comparative education has been emphasised. The chapter has reviewed recent developments in globalisation and considered where this phenomenon may go in the future. The enduring image of globalisation is of a vast watering place where the herds of nations converge to draw sustenance and ensure their survival in the one huge world market. It is responsive to none but the most competitive and has gained acceptance as the most efficient system for creating the wealth and prosperity that all nations must seek. The challenge must be to find ways to ensure that all members of all societies have their share, including the least favoured, who cannot fight so well for their place at the trough.

There is nothing new in the philosophy that we are more answerable to the global arena than to the narrow concerns of whatever country we call our own. Thomas Paine, founding father of the United States of America, famously said three centuries ago: *The World is my country, all humankind are my brethren. To do good is my religion.* While many resist the equation of global citizenship with the international doing of good, education for global citizenship must go beyond awareness-raising to instil an active concern for social justice. In a world growing ever smaller, we each have a big responsibility.

## References

Allan, C (2005) The global university: quality education for life in the 21st century. In Development Education Association (2005) *Conference report on graduates as global citizens: quality education for life in the 21st century.* London: DEA.

Benton, T, Cleaver, E, Featherstone, G, Kerr, D, Lopes, J and Whitby, K (2008) Citizenship Education Longitudinal Study (CELS): 6th Annual Report. *Young people's civic participation in and beyond school: attitudes, intentions and influences* (DCSF Research Report 052). London: DCSF.

Bourn, D, McKenzie, A and Shiel, C (2006) *The global university: the role of the curriculum.* London: Development Education Association.

Cairncross, F (2001) *The death of distance: how the communications revolution will change our lives.* Boston: Harvard Business School Press.

Clarkson, J, Bamber, P, and Bourke, L (eds) (2008) *In safe hands: guiding principles for international service-learning.* Stoke on Trent: Trentham.

Corner, T and Grant, N (2008) Comparing educational systems. In Matheson, D (ed) *An introduction to the study of education.* London: David Fulton.

Council of Europe (2008) Education: Country profiles. **www.coe.int** (accessed 20 December 2008).

Development Education Association (2008) *Global matters: case studies of education for a just and sustainable world.* London: DEA.

DCSF (Department for Children, Schools and Families) National Strategies. **http://nationalstrategies.standards.dcsf.gov.uk/** (accessed 20 December 2008).

DfID (Department for International Development) (2005) *Developing the global dimension in the school curriculum.* East Kilbride: DfID.

DfES (Department for Education and Skills) (2004) *Putting the world into world class education.* London: DfES.

Fountain, S (1990) *Learning together, global education 4–7.* Cheltenham: Stanley Thornes.

Held, D, McGrew, A, Goldblatt, D and Perraton, J (2008) The Global Transformations website. **www.polity.co.uk/global/default.asp** (accessed 20 December 2008).

Hicks, D and Holden, C (2007) *Teaching the global dimension: key principles and effective practice.* London: Routledge.

Hirst, P and Thompson, G (2000) *Globalization in question: The international economy and the possibilities of governance* (2nd edition) Cambridge: Polity.

ILO (International Labour Organisation; International Institute for Labour Studies) (2008) *World of Work Report: income inequalities in the age of financial globalisation.* Geneva: International Labour Office.

Khamis, A (2005) Global partnerships workshop report. In DEA (2005) *Graduates as global citizens: quality education for life in the 21st century.* Gloucester: DEA.

King, E (2000) A century of evolution in comparative studies. *Comparative Education,* 36 (3): 267–77.

Klein, N (2001) *No Logo.* London: HarperCollins.

McKibben, W (2003) Worried? Us? *Granta,* 83: 7–12.

McMurtry, J (2006) Foreword to Ellwood, W, *The no-nonsense guide to globalisation* (2nd edition). London: New Internationalist Publications.

Nelson, J and Carr, D (2005) *Active citizenship: definitions, goals and practice.* London: QCA/ INCA (International Review of Curriculum and Assessment Frameworks).

Newby, N (2006) Foreword to L Gearon, *Education in the United Kingdom: structures and organisation.* London: David Fulton.

Nussbaum, M (1998) Cultivating humanity. *Liberal Education,* 84 (2): 38–46.

Organisation for Economic Co-operation and Development and Statistics Canada (2000) *Literacy in the information age: final report of the International Adult Literacy Survey.* Paris: OECD.

OBHE (Observatory on Borderless Education) **www.obhe.ac.uk/home** (accessed 5 December 2008).

Osler, A and Starkey, H (2005) *Changing citizenship: democracy and inclusion in education.* London: Open University Press.

Oxfam (2006) A curriculum for global citizenship. Oxford: Oxfam.

Penn, H (2005) *Unequal childhoods: young children's lives in poor countries.* London: Routledge.

Phillips, D and Schweisfurth, M (2008) *Comparative and international education: an introduction to theory, method and practice.* London: Continuum.

QCA (2006) *Education for citizenship and the teaching of democracy in schools.* London: QCA/DfES.

Sears, A and Hughes, A (2006) Citizenship: education or indoctrination? *Citizenship Teaching and Learning,* 2 (1): 3–17.

Starke, L (ed) (2006) *State of the World 2006.* London: Worldwatch Institute.

United Nations (2005) *Report on the world social situation.* New York: UN General Assembly.

United Nations (2005) *UN Millennium Development Goals: keep the promise.* **www.un.org/millenniumgoals/** (accessed 5 December 2008)

United Nations (2007) *World population policies.* New York: Dept of Economic and Social Affairs, Population Division.

UNDP (United Nations Development Programme) (2008) *Human development report.* **hdr.undp.org/en/** (accessed 5 December 2008).

Wainaina, B (2005) How to write about Africa. *Granta,* 92: 91–5.

Young, M and Commins, E (2002) *Global citizenship: the handbook for primary teaching.* Cambridge: Oxfam/ Chris Kington Publishing.

# Index